D0929460

Shakespeare's
Promises

Shakespeare's Promises

Shakespeare's Promises

WILLIAM KERRIGAN

THE JOHNS HOPKINS UNIVERSITY PRESS
Baltimore & London

CARLYLE CAMPBELL LIBRARY
MEREDITH COLLEGE

822.33
A4454

© 1999 The Johns Hopkins University Press
All rights reserved. Published 1999
Printed in the United States of America on acid-free paper
2 4 6 8 9 7 5 3 1

The Johns Hopkins University Press
2715 North Charles Street
Baltimore, Maryland 21218-4363
www.press.jhu.edu

Frontispiece art by Marina Favila

Library of Congress Cataloging-in-Publication Data will be found
at the end of this book.
A catalog record for this book is available from the British Library.

ISBN 0-8018-6163-2

FOR TED TAYLER AND MARINA FAVILA

Contents

Preface

After *Hamlet's Perfection*, I did not want to write another book on a particular Shakespeare play or standard group of plays. I rather wanted to get hold of something *in* the plays that could let me give definition and point to Shakespeare's preoccupation with the creation, and the loss, of ideals. For a while the concept of honor appeared to be the right handle. But honor led me to promising, which at the time I thought of as one among several ethical behaviors of interest to the honorable. The opposite turned out to be true: honor now seems to me but one of the forms of conscience sprung from the seminal seed of promising. As the new topic began to open up, I wrote in my notebook: "When you look at Shakespeare with promising in mind, it seems to be everywhere in his work." A week or so later, a bit overwhelmed, I added, "When you look at any segment of human existence with promising in mind, it seems to be everywhere in the segment." Promising led to marriage, law, philosophy, religion, politics, and the history of conceptions of social order. Promising ramified. To the dismay of mortals trying to finish scholarly books, everything is connected to everything. I have been more than ordinarily aware of this truism while working on *Shakespeare's Promises*.

By *promises* I mean the many ways in which people, by using customary words ("I promise," "I swear," "I give you my word," "I do") or other conventional means of signification (nodding, clasping hands, receiving a token, signing), obligate themselves to do something: to tell the truth, to perform or not perform an action in the future, to incur a debt, to be the same or different "henceforth," from this moment on. Historically, the most important varieties are the oath, the vow, the contract, and the ordinary or "gratuitous" promise. Sworn between men, oaths are witnessed by a god; divine curses are either specified or implied should an oath be broken or falsely sworn. For centuries oaths have been divided into the assertory (the whole truth and nothing but) and the promissory (binding on future action). Vows were originally promises made to a god, though by Elizabethan times a "vow" could mean a particularly solemn promise given by one person to another. Contracts are promises, usually concerning exchanges of labor, property, and money, that were originally felt to be more binding in oral form, but gradually with the rise of capitalism came to be preferred in writing; an entire branch of law exists to define and regulate them. Ordinary promises are made between people without the presence of notaries or magistrates, and although the boundaries of legal enforcement sometimes impinge upon them, their keeping or breaking, forgetting or forgiving, is left by and large to our own scruples.[1]

My first chapter opens with a brief discussion of vows in Shakespearean comedy and closes with the nested perjuries of Sonnet 152. I am hardly the first to notice the decisive role of promising in Shakespeare's characterizations and dramatic structures generally. In particular, the labor of simply pointing out this ubiquity has been admirably carried through in Frances Shirley's *Swearing and Perjury in Shakespeare's Plays*.[2] If at times I duplicate her work in my opening chapters, it is in part because the footnotes of subsequent critics have led me to believe that her insights still await appropriate recognition. Unlike Shirley, I try to evoke the prevalence of promising in contemporary life, while also locating this subject in the history of ideas from, roughly, the Elizabethan assumption that social order is nothing less than a chain of promises predicated on the fear of God to the contention of the twentieth-century British philosopher J. L. Austin that promises are "performative utterances," felicitous or infelicitous but not true or false.

I am well aware that my account of changing ideas about promising is sketchy. To discuss Austin, Forster, Nietzsche, Kant, Godwin, Smith, Hume, Montesquieu, Locke, Hobbes, and some British thinkers from the sixteenth and seventeenth centuries, with occasional regard for the classical precedents behind them, is to hit the high points only, and only some of those. But sketches can have an excellence of their own. As with promising, so with other aspects of his drama, Shakespeare should be discussed more often in the company of such minds.

The sheer size of the topic invited exclusions. I have acquired some understanding of promising in the history of law, but not a deep understanding; I feared that my grasp of Shakespearean promising would dissipate in the proliferating details of case law. Nor have I, for similar reasons, gone very far into the history of legal philosophy; I feared getting lost in the ever nicer distinctions of casuistry's sister discipline. Although here and there my subject borders on "swearing" in the sense of casual blasphemy, the jesting or profane use of "the holy Name of God or of Christ Jesus, or of the Holy Ghoste or of the Trinity" forbidden the theater by the Act to Restrain Abuses of Players (1606), this is not the kind of oath-taking with which I am concerned.[3] Other angles of approach besides intellectual history seemed pertinent. By taking note of Shakespeare's *will* and *shall*, *would* and *should*, I at least initiate a philology of obligation; throughout I pay close attention to the mating habits of Shakespeare's words. The reader will also find a brief but not undetailed history of political and religious oath-taking during the Tudor reconstruction of the English church. I would count it a success if this first chapter seems coherent while also making plain the sprawl native to its subject.

Chapter 2 turns to the character and ultimate fate of Richard III in the first tetralogy. Richard's first signature irony is found in a speech instructing his father on how to break an oath yet salvage his honor. The doubleness of this first really Shakespearean character—the unconscionable, self-delighting ambition he shows to the audience and the supremely scrupulous, tender conscience he shows to the world—has been rightly understood as a fusion of the Vice figure from the old moralities with the more recent theatrical stereotype of the dissimulating Machiavel. I hope to deepen this understanding of Richard's two faces by connecting them to a doubleness in Elizabethan minds about the utility of oaths. Shakespeare was of an age, I maintain, in devising an art form from shades of duplicity rendered momentous by the history of his times. "In a discussion over any subject connected with Shakespeare," H. H. Furness once remarked, "who ever heard of resting content with what we know? It is what we do not know that fills our volumes."[4]

In *Richard III* itself, the character avoids swearing a formal oath on stage until the second wooing scene. Here the arch dissimulator must win the trust of a woman wholly without illusions about him. Shakespeare arranges the wonderful intellectual comedy of determined deceit paying court to an equally determined mistrust. Finally, in his attempt to win belief, Richard takes an oath stipulating self-destructive curses should he be swearing falsely. The career of ambitious deceit calls down its own failure on Bosworth Field: giving theatrical form to the presuppositions of serious promising, Shakespeare translates the structure of an oath into dramatic irony. I try to illuminate some of the mysteries of Richard's famous last soliloquy. Why, for example, should charges of "Perjury, perjury, in the highest degree" ring out as loudly as "Murder, murder, in the direst degree" in the interior courtroom of his conscience?

With respect to my own mood, writing about *The Merchant of Venice* in the third chapter was the high point of this book. Promises everywhere! The most powerful binary in the play pairs off the freely given with the obligatory. The major conflict in the drama stems from a competition for priority between the friendship tie and the marriage tie. Its many bonds range from the oaths of casket choice, with their aura of ancient nobility, to the notarized bond between Shylock and Antonio, backed with the legal force of mercantile Venice. There is even news about Shylock from this perspective: his sacred oath not be merciful has been insufficiently appreciated in the criticism of the play. Propelled by promises at every turn, the plot describes two circles. As the first closes in the trial scene, the second opens with the separation of the rings from the fingers of the two new husbands. This second circle closes at the return of the two rings, symbolic of the plot itself, during the mock trial for oath-breach in the final act, where the comedy's last word centers the whirling obligations of the play on a quibble. Perhaps literary critics have grown unnecessarily ashamed of their inherited word hoard. Whatever some may think, Shakespeare's dramas do have themes, and the theme of this one, in an old-fashioned sense I believe to have fully justified, is obligation.

In *Othello*, the play discussed in my last chapter, marriage vows are subjected to an unremitting dramatic irony. Desdemona's innocence seems in particular vulnerable to the misfortune of false interpretation. The later scenes between Othello and Desdemona generate the irony of a charge that cannot be denied by any vow Desdemona is able to frame, since her very denials have been preinterpreted as confirmations of perjury. As Othello strides toward the bed, addressing his soul about "the cause," he cannot name the embarrassing crime of adultery but can and does name the second, more honorable charge of betrayal: "Yet she must die, else she'll betray more men." He will hear no more oaths of denial. So Desdemona flatly, without support of oaths, denies the adultery, as Othello once again finds in her very denials further instances of perjury. It is perjury that makes her killing into "A murder, which I thought a sacrifice": if one assumes that someone who dies in falsehood goes to hell, there is no way to kill a woman who persists in perjuring herself without murdering her soul as well as her body. After Desdemona's death, which I understand in relation to the two meanings given the singer's death in her "Willow Song," Shakespeare plants the famous crux of Othello's partially recovered self-esteem. What can be said of his contention that he is "an honourable murderer, if you will," who acted out of honor, not hate? With Othello's last words, the relentless moral turbulence of the play gives way to pity.

The Epilogue discusses the plays in relation to issues raised in my first chapter and ends with a visit to the swearing scene in act 1 of *Hamlet*. I hope by then to have conveyed to my readers something of what I glimpsed when scribbling in my notebook about the ubiquity of promising in Shakespeare. "*Hic et ubique*? Then we'll shift our ground," says Hamlet, trying in vain to sidestep the voice from the floorboards yelling "Swear!" Hamlet himself has suggested the swearing. But the Ghost's inescapable enthusiasm for his own proposed oath-binding trips the prince's wild sense of humor. Here and everywhere, now as then, tomorrow as today, the voice of past generations urges us to swear. Promise-keeping is by no means the same thing as virtue. It may have driven us from nature, saddled us with immeasurable burdens, and snarled the ethics of action with all sorts of extraneous complexities. But try to stop. Shall we promise to stop? It may be best, like Hamlet, to laugh at the tremendous solemnity with which history teaches us to promise, as of course, generation after generation, we seem to want to go on doing anyway.

It might be thought a satisfying end for a study such as this to arrive at a taxonomy of the promises found in Shakespeare, then to sort them out, by genre for instance, determining the promises mainly featured in histories, comedies, and tragedies. Shirley's work moves in exactly this direction. But I have not aimed at closure of this kind, for as the history of Shakespeare Studies has repeatedly discovered, there are a lot of ways in which our author will not be brought to rule—and the complex matter of promising seems to me one of them. An especially memorable instance of this abiding wisdom occurs in Maurice Morgann's *An Essay on the Dramatic Character of Sir John Falstaff*, where, in a delightful piece of historical dramaturgy, Shakespeare is brought face to face with Aristotle, who falls on his knees and asks forgiveness for having itemized tragedy's features with no foresight of the definition-defying "magic" in Shakespeare's work.[5] This writer ramifies, wild above rule of nature or art. What Morgann intended as a rebuke to the boxiness of eighteenth-century neoclassicism seems to me a timeless reminder of how consistently Shakespeare thwarts the ambitions of theory builders.

No doubt promising does have a marked generic aspect in the obvious case of marital vows and precontracts in comedy, with which my first chapter begins. But beyond that, promising and genre refuse to match up. One might suppose, with Hegelian precedent, that Shakespeare's tragic plots will devise conflicting obligations.[6] Evidence will not be far to seek. Coriolanus, for example, vows to burn Rome, but this promise comes up against his obligation to his family, and the conflict results in his destruction; Othello, too, suffers a lethal self-division in the conflict between his troth-plight to Desdemona and his reverent vow to take revenge on her. Yet conflicting promises also drive the comic plot of *The Merchant of Venice*. So I have tried to be precise but not definitive, rigorous but not exhaustive, and ultimately to be suggestive in the best sense rather than conclusive in the worst sense.

Certain scholars, as I have noted, have indeed written about the pervasiveness of promising in Shakespeare. It can be fairly said, however, that promising, everywhere evident once you are attuned to it, is a subject whose centrality pretty much eluded A. C. Bradley, G. Wilson Knight, and the New Critics, as it still pretty much eludes Stephen Greenblatt and the New Historicists. Few critics, and certainly not these, would be *surprised* to hear of the ubiquity of promising in Shakespeare; but none of them have really addressed its importance. I hope to discuss the topic in such a way as to give future interpreters of Shakespeare something fairly fresh to talk about, and the best way to do this, I have assumed, is to demonstrate that promising leads with some depth from Shakespeare to literary structure, history, politics, philosophy, and psychology.

Although it has historical, political, philosophical, psychological, and philological episodes, *Shakespeare's Promises* is for the most part a work of literary criticism. I have chosen my three plays in part because they exemplify three different genres, in part because they take us chronologically from the early Shakespeare to the mature tragic phase, in larger part because they illustrate a progression in Shakespeare's understanding of promising, and most of all because they seem to me among his profoundest explorations of this subject. Since I have no way of proving the last two assertions apart from the interpretations in this book, my results on those scores must speak for themselves.

The reader should be forewarned that issues arise in my explications of the three works, especially in my long chapters on *The Merchant of Venice* and *Othello*, that do not in an immediate way involve promising. But to have a chance of comprehending promising in a play, one must also comprehend the play. A distortion familiar in Shakespeare Studies (and elsewhere) might be termed the hermeneutic half-circle: discussions of a theme, motif, trope, gesture, or linguistic feature of a drama proceed without establishing an adequate sense of what the whole play might arguably mean. Such curtailment is defensible in the name of efficiency in an essay. But one advantage in writing a book—indeed, one good reason for writing a book at all—is that one can take the time to show how the pieces of a play being highlighted for analysis look in relation to the entirety (and vice versa). I therefore circle.

Acknowledgments

My friend and mentor Edward Tayler read draft versions of my chapters, and as always his comments, suggestions, and admirably clear reactions ("Ugh!" is among his favorite bits of marginalia) greatly improved the book. Marina Favila read a later state of the print-out, and I'm grateful for her encouragement during this work's darkest hours. Final revisions benefited from the sharp intelligence of Laura Vogel, my new partner in the study of poetry. Robert Creed advised me on some details; Philip White was always there with sound counsel. Irma Garlick, my copyeditor for the Johns Hopkins University Press, indulged the traditional habits of my prose while insisting that I rise to higher standards of clarity and accuracy. Bernice Soltysik prepared the index. To my wife, Amelia Burnham Kerrigan, fell the task of keeping the daily levels of my vanity high enough to write this book and low enough to write this book. In thanking her the articulate silence between her eyes and mine must still, and will still, suffice.

1

The Promising Animal

〜 〜

*A*ny drama, like any life, may be plotted through its promises, which is not to say that every promise indicates a playwright's deep interest in this form of human behavior. Some promises rest unthematized, *données* of art and life. But in his comedies and romances Shakespeare deliberately turned his attention to the dramatic potential and moral resonance of promising.

Love's Labour's Lost, for example, opens with four men swearing "deep oaths" (1.1.23) to give up for three years "The grosser manner of these world's delights" (1.1.29), including all dealings with women, for the sake of study and contemplation.[1] Their quasi-monastic vows do not survive for long when a delegation of courtly Frenchwomen arrives on the scene. The men betray their promises seriatim in the beautifully mechanical movements of act 4, scene 3, as first Berowne enters, discoursing on a love poem he has written and stepping aside as the king enters, reading his own love poem and stepping aside as Longaville enters, reading his own love poem and stepping aside as Dumain enters, reading his own love poem. The scene is wound up like a knob controlling the spring in a kitchen timer: one, two, three, four oath-breaches. Then, as the three hidden observers come forth, the spring unwinds. One, two, three, four ridiculed hypocrites. Ding! Shakespeare has taken his quartet of big promisers from the solemn ambitions of the opening scene to the knockabout moral comedy of exposure and humiliation. Although the death of the princess's father supplies an immediate reason for the postponement of comic closure at the end of the play, the immature vowing of the males provides a second explanation, one rooted in the substance of the drama itself, for the temporary loss of love's labor.

Another example will suggest how inventive Shakespeare remained in treating the love vows toward which his comedies move. In *As You Like It*, written on the brink of *Hamlet* and the problem plays, Rosalind secures promises from the lovers of Arden that they will meet her at a certain time. She makes a compact with Phebe: if Ganymede is ever to love a woman, Phebe will be the one, but if not, Phebe is to marry Sylvius. She secures her father's promise to support a marriage between Rosalind and Orlando. When couples assemble at the appointed hour, Rosalind and Celia leave the stage, then return with the god Hymen in tow. The ensuing transformation of gratuitous promises into wedding promises puts me in mind of one of those spectacular musical numbers by Busby Berkeley, where the guys and gals of the chorus, shot from an overhead camera, form and re-form in a kaleidoscopic sequence of designs. In Rosalind's

number, all of the subsidiary promises evolve into marriages. The celebration of Hymen makes it clear that he is
a god of vows; vowing is, so to speak, his genetic signature.
Couples have been led through lesser promises to The Promise: the life-centering, village-peopling, family-generating
promise, the promise that is comedy's soul. Such is the "magic" Rosalind works on the plot of *As You Like It*.

Comedy must be thought of as a kind of promise: the
audience expects the play to end as comedies convention-
ally do, by fulfilling the genre through the creation of nuptial couples whose love vows are given, received, and acknowledged by a community. The value of the comedies
rests in large measure on our sense of the worthiness of
these vows. Beyond the wordplays, humiliations, intrigues,
and incongruous vexations of circumstance, vows are the
genre's precious stuff. Shakespeare understood that if the
vows of his main lovers were not complete and enthusiastic, worthy of being celebrated with images of social and
cosmological harmony, the comedy, amusing as it might be,
would never move us.

In his early *The Taming of the Shrew* Shakespeare of
course emphasizes the marriage vow of the woman, with
Kate as the unlikely victor in a contest of wifely obedience.
Certainly he never lost a sense of the rightness of that obedience. Disguised as a male servant in the household of
Duke Orsino, Viola in *Twelfth Night* observes, contrary to
the duke's opinion, that men "may say more, swear more"
than women, yet prove "Much in [their] vows, but little in
[their] love" (2.4.117–19). During the revelation scene at
the end, Orsino reminds her that in the role of his page she
swore she would never love a wife as much as she loved him
(5.1.265–66, alluding to 5.1.132–35). Her answer rings

with considerable metaphysical force in this play about twins destined to conclude with a song whose last stanza remembers how "A great while ago the world began":

> And all those sayings will I over-swear,
> And all those swearings keep as true in soul
> As doth that orbed continent the fire
> That severs day from night.
>
> (5.1.267–70)

The world began when God, twinning time, separated light and day from dark and night in words that were at the same time promise, command, and enacted law. Viola, in one of Shakespeare's most beautiful promises, rests her love vow on that model of truth.

In the same play Olivia, having sworn to forsake society for seven years in mourning for her dead brother, is led by the intriguing matchmaking of the comic plot to, in the priest's words,

> A contract of eternal bond of love,
> Confirm'd by mutual joinder of your hands,
> Attested by the holy close of lips,
> Strengthen'd by the interchangement of your rings,
> And all the ceremony of this compact
> Seal'd in my function, by my testimony.
>
> (5.1.154–59)

Helena in *All's Well* rights her marriage by obediently fulfilling Bertram's seemingly impossible conditions. Thaisa is finally reunited with her husband in *Pericles*, having spent the years of their separation in a temple devoted to the goddess of chastity. Imogen eventually returns to the once faith-less Posthumous in the disguise of Fidele, the eponym of her unwavering virtue. Sixteen years after his lethal attack on her honor, a monumental Hermione waits for Leontes in the alcove of the chapel; her chastened husband need only, as Paulina says, awaken his faith. An honorable female love vow is perhaps the most precious thing in Shakespeare's universe. Ask Othello at the end of the play. Ask Hamlet at the beginning.

By and large, however, the concern manifest in *Love's La-bour's Lost* for the mature constancy of the male's love vow is decisive for the trials and tribulations of Shakespearean love. In *A Midsummer Night's Dream* Lysander, who has assured Hermia that they are "Two bosoms interchained with an oath" (2.2.48), awakens, juiced by Puck, to declare "I had no judgment when to her I swore" (3.2.134). The formerly unloved Helena perceives as mockery the sudden devotions of Lysander and Demetrius: "You would not use a gentle lady so:/To vow, and swear, and superpraise my parts,/When I am sure you hate me with your hearts" (3.2.152–54). They have insulted her class, not to mention her womanly savvy. No one coming to *A Midsummer Night's Dream* in the full context of Shakespeare's work will be sur-prised that Helena finds the love-vowing males unbeliev-able. Before entering the woods in pursuit of Demetrius, she herself noted ruefully that "As waggish boys, in game, them-selves forswear,/So the boy Love is perjur'd everywhere" (1.1.240–41).

There are two opposed masses of proverbial wisdom about male and female promises in Shakespeare's work. One is that women are innately fickle and inconstant: this was a truth assumed when men spoke man to man, as Orsino to Caesario, or bantered with fast-tongued women. But there was also a contrary gender cliché, to the effect that men make unreliable vows, especially when wooing. Hermia wittily swears to meet Lysander "By all the vows that ever men have broke/(In number more than ever women spoke)" (1.1.175–76). Men will promise anything to have their way with maids. As husbands, prone to wonder whether their horns have sprouted yet, they are often fatally vulnerable to undue suspicion of female vows.

The second of the two commonplaces is the more fully scrutinized on Shakespeare's stage.[2] Demetrius, whose love once shifted from Helena to Hermia, must be reattuned to his initial choice by the fairy potion. Deviating males, like Angelo in *Measure for Measure* and Bertram in *All's Well*, must be rerouted back to fidelity through the efficacy of bed-tricks. Rosalind/Ganymede, in her prolonged trial of the infatuated Orlando in *As You Like It*, seems in part to be expressing an intuitive female mistrust of male vows. The shame of slander must be transferred from Hero to Claudio before *Much Ado* can rearrange their marriage. Those who swallow commonplaces become commonplace: the proverbial suspiciousness of males stems in large part from their attachment to the cliché concerning female inconstancy. Good vowing and good faith in a female vow are tests that Shakespearean men seldom pass, if they pass at all, without a hitch. We will encounter some of the suppositions behind this male waywardness, this tendency to swerve from promised love, in our chapters on *The Merchant of Venice* and *Othello*.

Although promises of various kinds drive Shakespearean plots and test the mettle of his characters, promising could not always have been steered by the deliberate authorial attention endemic to comedy and romance. For promises crisscross every life in every society in every historical period—even to the depths of unrecorded time. Promising is too close to us to be in every instance a full-fledged theme. It is impossible to imagine any kind of moral life without obligations, and impossible to imagine obligations without types of promises. We are always up against them. Before we ever reflect on what a promise is, we have made them and are expected to make more of them. We are born into nations that enter into treaties and agreements. Promises are with us like gravity. Man is a promising animal.

It may be true, as theorists of the social contract maintain, that the ability to make and keep promises is the key difference between nature and culture, animality and civilization. The obvious, as Heidegger liked to say, is always partially hidden. So I begin this study of Shakespeare's promises with a general discussion of the matter, hoping to remind us of how many members there are in the family of promises and how much of the human landscape they have settled.

The individual moral agent surrounded by friends and family seems a bit of a fiction to many commentators these days, but let's begin with him anyway. I can make a promise to someone, perhaps in exchange for his promise. I can make a legal contract, with stipulations intended to clarify and make public the exact terms of the deal. I can make a promise to myself and call to witness a deity, saint, or beloved relative. I can swear on a whole host of touchstones: on my mother's grave, on the heads of my unborn children, in the name of God, in the name of all that is holy. Some of these vows and promises are forgotten almost as soon as they are made. Some, because unkept, produce a general atmosphere of guiltiness and unworthiness. Some change us decisively. "As God is my witness, as God is my witness," Scarlett O'Hara vowed with raised fist in the pivotal moment of her life, silhouetted against an orange sky, "They're not going to lick me. I'm going to live through this, and when it is all over, I'll never be hungry again. No, nor any of my folk. If I have to lie, steal, cheat, or kill, as God is my witness, I'll never be hungry again."

Keeping a promise is one of the simplest empirical tests for virtue. But there are, to be sure, good reasons for not keeping certain promises. A few of the ones mentioned in the philosophical tradition include the fact that it is impossible (I can't give you the moon, though I promised to), that it is a small matter superseded by unforeseen considerations (I promised to meet you for dinner today, but my son took ill), that it is unlawful or blasphemous (I promised that I would do whatever you want this month, but now you want me to poison the neighbor's dog). Still, the general presupposition down through the ages is that a promise ought to be kept.

Boasting is akin to promising. In warrior cultures, boasting can become a contest with elaborate rules, a *flyting*, as in the encounter between Beowulf and Unferth.[3] A boasting soldier, making vehement promises about the dire fates he will inflict on his enemy in a forthcoming battle, may simply be heightening his courage, supplying himself with a load of battlefield spirit; his promises sharpen his motivation, in that they will increase his shame should his courage fail. Boasting is a brand of promising full of lying and indulged grandiosity.[4] A professional athlete asserts, if nothing else, the absolute centrality of his own performance when he "guarantees" a victory.

Boasting borders on threatening. When threatening, we

make all sorts of conditional promises, ranging from the believable, and meant to be believable ("If you don't stop that, I'll call the police"), to the grotesquely surreal ("If you do that again, I'll cut off your head and piss down your throat"), which is intended to stun someone into compliance at the very thought of such a bloodcurdling fate having actually been *promised*. The formulas of solemn oaths tend to return, varied, in threats: "God help you, because I sure won't, if you ever . . . " Such threats, intended to impress, are indeed impressive. They even possess an aesthetic quality. Today's so-called action films cannot fully satisfy their audience without inventing memorable threats ("Go ahead, make my day"). Shakespeare also devised great cursers and threateners. It was a kind of speech at which he excelled; to think of the *Henry VI* plays, *Richard III*, and *King Lear* is to recall only the obvious successes. In solemn vows we attempt to change our own future behavior—to make ourselves loyal to a current allegiance or resolution; by means of threatening promises we seek to change the future behavior of others. A threat is a promise that we hope we will not have to keep. Of course there is a kind of threat that we *do* intend to make good on, and Shakespearean histories and tragedies are deeply involved with this variety of promise: the vow of revenge.

Most promises are aimed at the future. They address the future, attempting to determine it in line with current accords and resolves. Promises generate obligations; without an accompanying sense of obligation, promising would be an empty formality. By sending out, through promises, ties of obligation, we try to bind the future and reduce its uncertainty by rendering ourselves or others constant, trustworthy, reliable, predictable. Henceforth, *from this mo-*

ment on, a promiser asserts, he will be different, will be a person under an obligation, until his promise is performed—or in the case of certain oaths, bound unto his death. When promising we treat ourselves almost as physical objects. Put in a certain place, we will stay there; bent in a certain configuration, we will stay bent.

It is worth noting here that the realm of the future is recurrently an object of suspicion in proverbs. Proverbial wisdom tells us that the present, the bird in the hand, is what really counts. Some of the proverbs about promising current in Shakespeare's day included "One acre of possession is worth a whole land of promise," "All is not paid that is promised," "Great promise, small performance," "He promises like a merchant and pays like a man of war," "He promises mountains and performs molehills," "He that promises too much means nothing," "He that will swear will lie," and "Promises, like piecrusts, are made to be broken."[5] Proverbs belong to a general fund of shrewdness in a society; they are rules for how to get along—what to expect, what to beware. Promises, these sayings remind us, are often used to deceive and manipulate. The promising animal being also a lying animal, the medium of the promise is the birthplace of the scam, the con, the trick, and only a fool, a gull, enters into promises with an attitude of blind trust. Herman Melville's great monument to the wisdom of mistrust, *The Confidence-Man*, dilates proverbial shrewdness to a brilliantly skeptical extreme. All religions, belief systems, and organized ideals are baited with false promises to swindle the unwary.

People love to be promised things. There must be a stage in childhood when promises overlap with primal satisfactions. "But you *promised*," the child implores, your promise being equivalent to his cherished wish. Aging, we either discipline our credulity or become embittered. The everyday disappointments of politics and advertising (both of them ever pointing to an improved future, ever promising) ease the way to the more admired of these choices: disciplined credulity. In our day there is a species of promise, the so-called campaign promise, that almost everyone suspects, since it is so often broken after election day. These manipulative promises count against neither the right nor the left but instead fuel a healthy national cynicism akin to the promise-beware proverbs of Elizabethan England.

Promises are formulaic. The right words in the right order matter. I remember as a child imparting a secret to a playmate that I did not want him to tell to anyone else. "Do you promise?" I asked. If he just nodded, that was not good enough. "Then *say* it," I would insist. If he then replied, "I promise," I could proceed with some confidence to tell my secret. Of course, even in childhood the rules were elaborate. Crossed fingers behind the back might undo a promise. A particularly good promise could be achieved with the words "cross my heart and hope to die." This appears to be a relatively recent formula; the reference books I have consulted can trace it back no further than the early years of the twentieth century.[6] But again, promising is so formulaic that even new incantations will reach back to ancient predecessors. Crossing the heart seems to date back to the crusades, as a gesture promising that Christendom would indeed, in the end, win back the Holy Land.

"Hope to die" takes us to the history of oath-swearing and begins to pry us away from the individual moral agent. In ancient Greece and Rome, oaths always referred to a deity and always combined a promise with a threat. Should an oath not be kept, a deity was encouraged in the oath's very formula to take vengeance upon the wayward promiser. Animal sacrifice often accompanied an oath-taking in Greece, the idea being that, should the oath be broken, the oath-breaker would be to the deity as the slaughtered animal was to him; since the worst fate imaginable in the Greek world was the destruction of one's lineage, the testicles of the animal were oftentimes severed and stomped on to signify this Thyestean fate. Oaths have a tendency to mutate in the direction of terribleness; a variant on the formula of childhood swearing goes like this: "Cross my heart and hope to die, stick a needle in my eye." Even today, oath-takings often end with the formula "so help me God." So may God help, that is, if I am telling the truth, am true to this vow; but on the other side of the coin, if I am not telling the truth, and not true to this vow, God is encouraged *not* to help me—a polite way of implying that God is free to curse me as he sees fit.

God is the guarantor of truth. Thus it is that God swears to Abraham "by myself" in Gen. 22.16 (see also Heb. 6.13–19). In "A Hymne to God the Father" Donne for two stanzas has "more" sin than, to his mind, God will be able to forgive. Only one promise can satisfy his "sinne of feare":

> Sweare by thy self, that at my death thy Sunne
> Shall shine as it shines now, and heretofore;
> And, having done that, Thou hast done,
> I have no more.[7]

Donne, with his lawyer's training, associated credibility with being under oath, and God's oath upon himself was the most believable testimony conceivable.

We have looked back in history to the point where, as Walter Burkert writes, the oath "was the one place where religion, morality, and law definitely met."[8] Soon we must, in the face of these vistas, part company for a time with the individual moral agent, but before doing so we may pause to consider one of his last appearances in respected modern philosophy. He is a bit hard to recognize in this turn on the philosophical stage, for he no longer has any insides. But he can nonetheless be discerned in the famous "performative utterances" of J. L. Austin.[9] Austin proposed that a certain class of statements can best be treated, not as descriptions of states of affairs, but as actions. Promising was his most impressive example, and with regard to promising, his main point was to oppose a particular traditional picture of the matter, namely, that when I say "I promise to . . . ," my words are the outward sign of an inward mental state, an act of will by means of which I obligate myself. A promise is either made or not made, and that is solely a question of whether or not the correct formula has been invoked. The inward spiritual state, the mysterious self-obligating act of will, falls into irrelevance. For if I say I promise, have I not really promised so long as I harbor inward reservations, so long as I refrain, deep in my private being, from clenching my will? To argue so, Austin insists, is to provide "the bigamist with an excuse for his 'I do' and the welsher with a defence for his 'I bet.' Accuracy and morality alike are on the side of the plain saying that *our word is our bond*" (10).

Austin is writing out of the tradition of Wittgenstein, in which it is assumed that to have recourse to a language about private states of mind in talking about anything important to human affairs—and promising is clearly important—will lead to pernicious philosophical conundrums and ultimately to corrosive skepticism.[10] For example, if we are thinking about promising in terms of acts of the will, must not a sincere promiser in some sense have obliged himself to accept obligation, and then have obliged himself to oblige himself to accept obligation, and so on, into an infinite recess of mumbo jumbo? Saying "I promise" makes the promise, and we can deal appropriately with kept or unkept promises without lapsing into discussions of the will. One can see immediately that Shakespeare, above all else a dramatist, could only have entertained this argument in a mood of bemusement, for Austin would in effect cover over the theatrically exciting interplay between good faith and deliberate deception—the very stuff of Richard III, his first great character.

In the wake of Austin, philosophers maintained that there must be a practice of promising, or rules of promising, in place in any given society before statements like "I promise" can perform a comprehensible action. John Searle argued in a famous paper that Austin's account of "I promise" had in effect located the site of a long-sought philosophical transubstantiation: the movement from an *is* to an *ought*.[11] By simply saying something the ordinary human promiser jumps that famous gap. But subsequent commentators, by shifting interest from the individual moral agent's "I promise" to the background "practice of promising" that makes his performative comprehensible, in effect dissolved Searle's *is/ought* transformation into the details of history and sociology. For a time, that is, philosophers could talk about the rules that promising implies and perhaps distinguish them interestingly from other rules, but before long someone was bound to point to the past and declare, "*There's* your rules. They all evolved in idiosyncratic ways. We might begin with the mingling in England of Germanic law with a largely Roman canon law."[12] Whence arises obligation? If it does not arise from an individual act of will, it must derive from the "practice of promising," which is in turn derived from the particulars of history. The individual speaking magic words that conjure *ought* from mere *is* gets buried in the landslide of social time.

We may suspect that promises are not very reliable. We may not believe that oaths are especially credible. We may not take with much seriousness some of the promises we make to ourselves—witness the annual folly of New Year's resolutions. But if we think about the social order that surrounds us, it is clear that we are the inheritors of a tremendously serious ethic of oath-keeping. Early in the sixteenth century Thomas Elyot railed at length against the terrible spread of perjury in his day.[13] About a century later a great scholar, John Selden, whose life overlapped with that of Shakespeare, left the following anecdote in his *Table Talk* to represent the epitome of earthly contracts:

> My Lady of Kent articled with Sir Edward Herbert, that he should come to her when she sent for him and stay with her as long as she would have him; to which he set his hand. Then he articled with her, that he should go away when he pleased and stay away as long as he pleased, to which she set her hand. This is the epitome of all the contracts in the world betwixt man and man, between Prince and subject: they keep them as long as they like them and no longer.[14]

Elyot was full of outrage, Selden of worldly cynicism. But both were well aware that in the past this issue had been addressed with the full brunt of human seriousness. Cicero, for example: "Now the great foundation of justice is faithfulness, which consists in being constantly firm to your word, and a conscientious performance of all compacts and bargains."[15]

A reader of Livy finds numerous occasions to marvel at the overriding strength of the ethic of oath-keeping in Roman culture. Among their national heroes was Marcus Atilius Regulus, a general of the First Punic War celebrated by Cicero and Horace. When captured by Hannibal, he was released to bring back to Rome unfavorable peace terms (he himself had proposed them before capture) on his oath that, should the mission fail, he would come back to face a grueling death. Advising the Romans to fight on, he returned to Carthage and suffered his promised end.[16] In heroic literature, works such as *The Battle of Maldon* or *The Song of Roland* celebrate warriors whose gloomy oaths require self-sacrifice.[17] In the Bible, God covenants with man, and men swear oaths in the name of God; in Christian hermeneutics, the figural designs of time "promise" fulfilling futures. Christ, it is true, flatly declares "Swear not at all" in the Sermon on the Mount (Matt. 5.34). But at the end of the New Testament, Paul repeatedly swears oaths of his veracity in spreading the gospel (Rom. 1.9; 2 Cor. 1:23; 11.31; Gal. 1:20). The ethic of the solemn oath flows into Western civilization from all its major tributaries.

Look around us. Teenagers already make a joke of "scout's honor," but there can be no doubt that society seeks to instill the morality of promise-keeping. And why not? As a way to secure social order, to promote reliable human transactions, and to foment the trust without which government itself cannot proceed, there is nothing cheaper than morality; it is certainly cheaper than a criminal justice system, which is also required to adjudicate the liabilities, damages, and penalties stemming from business contracts, labor contracts, marriage vows, and a host of other serious human promises. When someone testifies in court or before a congressional committee he does so under oath; indeed, in the earliest sketch of a trial in Germanic law, an accused man who swore his innocence brought forward a number of "compurgators" to swear oaths that they believed his oath— and that was the end of the matter. At some schools, students take honor oaths or honor pledges that they will not cheat on tests and papers. Certain groups and societies require an oath of their members. The president, when sworn in, takes an oath of office—indeed, an oath much the same in spirit as the Coronation Oath taken in Shakespeare's time by English monarchs. Judges, doctors, lawyers, priests, soldiers, and policemen enter into their professions by taking a solemn oath. The first document printed in America was the "Oath of a Free-man."[18] The long and complex history of loyalty oaths in America, to which we will turn later in this chapter, is far from over.

Oaths and vows become progressively more serious as we mature in our sexual lives. Dating, while it may involve implicit understandings and mutual promises, does not bind. Becoming engaged requires a more serious vow, one that may in some circumstances be found legally binding, but most breakers of the engagement promise do so with impunity. The vows exchanged at a wedding ceremony are, however, quite serious, even sacred, and they certainly can have legal consequences when bent or broken. Words, as always, lead us into the invisible past every present has been built upon. *Fiancée* comes from the French word meaning "promised." In Old English the *wed* in *wedding* meant a stick or twig given to signify the transference of property; the *gage* in *engagement* has a similar history. The sacred democratic word *vote* comes from Latin *votum*, a "promise" or "pledge."

Those of us who like to think in terms of individual moral agents and acts of will may not be able to agree with Kant, who was in his way the supreme exponent of this picture of obligations: "the ground of obligation must be looked for, not in the nature of man nor in the circumstances of the world in which he is placed, but solely a priori in the concepts of pure reason"—concepts to which, in Kant's view, the will is self-bound.[19] But some of us may still be inclined to consider our obligations in the manner of E. M. Forster in his remarkable essay "What I Believe": "reliability is not a matter of contract—that is the main difference between the world of personal relationships and the world of business relationships. It is a matter for the heart, which signs no documents."[20] A matter for the heart: here again is that mysterious inward act of will that obliges one and is all the more to be treasured when it, and it alone, obliges one. We mint in solitude, in the heart, our *oughts* in a network of personal relationships. We have no greater loyalties, as we learn in the most famous sentence of this essay: "I hate the idea of causes, and if I had to choose between betraying my country and betraying my friend, I hope I should have the guts to betray my country" (78). However appealing this vision is, however thrilling its substitution of the guts of personal sacrifice for the guts of patriotic sacrifice, we must conclude, I think, that a sense of personal obligation this intense, this ready for supreme sacrifice, can be understood to some degree only as a back formation from obligations that have everything to do with society and its manifold varieties of force.

Whence arises obligation? Hobbes declared that human beings have only two reasons to keep their promises: honor or reputation on the one hand, and fear of consequences on the other.[21] The first is no doubt significant; historically, honor is the ethical principle that has always sanctioned promise-keeping. Remembering the solemn vows of honor binding thanes to their lord in heroic literature, we cannot underestimate its authority as a human motive. But honor, for Hobbes, is not in the end much of a binding force; it is no more, after all, than what Forster would call "a matter for the heart." Bonds could only derive their power, he concludes, since "nothing is more easily broken than a man's word," from "fear of some evil consequence upon the rupture" (86). The truth that for Donne was underwritten by God, is for Hobbes created and maintained by the state.

But in his account of the origins of civil order, Hobbes is also aware of what he terms "consideration" (86)—the idea that a right is only ever given away in return for some benefit. The concept derives from British common law.[22] We think of contracts as enforceable agreements, but this abstract idea of contract did not appear in British law until the middle of the eighteenth century. In the older common law tradition, promises were recognized by law only if they involved a "consideration." The goodness of the contract in legal terms arose, that is to say, from its original rationale. The promiser expects some benefit; the person to whom the promise is given may, if it is not performed, incur some penalty or suffer some detriment. These "considerations" make the contract binding.

Hobbes leaves open an argumentative path that will later

be traveled by David Hume in his *Treatise of Human Nature*.[23] In Hume's view, Hobbes was closer to the truth than Locke, for Locke had based his idea of the social contract on the "consent of the governed."[24] This seemed to Hume merely a fiction intended to make government seem more palatable. Hobbes was right. The obligations of the governed to the government rest on civil power, not on the fiction of some original consent. But the origins of society do involve benefits, or in the language of common law, "considerations," and this is especially evident in the case of promises. Let's say that I have received property from someone and in return promised to give him my labor at a specified time in the future. Keeping the promise, once I have already taken possession of the property, is not in my immediate self-interest. As another one of the Elizabethan proverbs spelled out, "Promise is debt."[25] But if not immediately to my benefit, the keeping of the promise is in a remote way self-interested. Should I break my agreement, no one thereafter will be likely to enter into promises with me, and I will be de facto excluded from the realm of transaction and exchange. What else is society? To keep a promise is to be as good as one's word; to break one is to risk forfeiting all trust in the goodness of one's word. Such a person has, as we still say, "lost his good name." In Hobbes we keep promises mostly because we fear legal consequences, only secondarily because we are honorable. Hume revises Hobbes by locating fear within the logic of honor: blackened reputation alone is enough to secure kept promises.

Nietzsche seems at first glance an even more ferocious opponent of the autonomous moral will than Hobbes or Hume. Brilliant and sardonic, he sought to destroy the myth of the social contract by exposing the unsavory prehistory of promising. In *The Genealogy of Morals* he notes, quite rightly, that Roman law acknowledged debt long before it acknowledged stipulated contracts.[26] The creditor was permitted to exercise lurid cruelties on the body of the debtor. Why could suffering substitute for the debt? Because it was enjoyed: the history of promising leads back to the first masters of society, quick to act, quick to demonstrate their power through sadistic impositions on the conquered and the subjected.

It is from these masters that the whole idea of an autonomous moral will comes into being, and for Nietzsche, this unimpeded will, the will to power, constitutes health. For will was originally designed to serve as action's trigger. Such men possessed an "enthusiastic impulsiveness in anger, love, reverence, gratitude, and revenge by which noble souls have at all times recognized one another."[27] Promising, and the moral mechanisms that sponsor it, such as conscience and guilt, represent a turning inward of the original sadism of these happily willful masters. In place of the will to master, morality offers the mastery of the will. Turned inward, the enthusiastic, sadistic impulsiveness becomes a bar against immediate action, an unhealthy blockage of the will that we term "conscience" and mistake for a precious inwardness. We no longer rid ourselves of willful impulses through immediate action. Instead we become promisers, savoring will's obstruction, "so that between the original 'I will,' 'I shall do this' and the actual discharge of the will, its *act*, a world of strange new things, circumstances, and even acts of the will may be interposed without breaking this long chain of will" (58). Through promising we in effect punish ourselves in blind imitation of the great happy punishers at the origins of social order.

Nietzsche's theory, with its much remarked similarity to Freud's account of superego formation, is in several respects the most Shakespearean of the major anatomies of promising; its lines of argument point toward *The Merchant of Venice* and *Hamlet*. It puts us back in touch with the will. Will, for Nietzsche, is the medium through which social history reaches the individual moral agent.

But we cannot remain with will alone. Our end lies in Shakespeare, and Shakespeare is a phenomenon of language. If Hobbes, Hume, and Nietzsche are on the right track, correct in tracing the morality of promising back to social history, then obligation in all its complex ubiquity should lie before us in the field of language. Language, preeminently, is the thing both social and individual. No one creates it; everyone creates it. How does the will announce itself?

The devil is in the details. Or as Wallace Stevens put it in a more positive light, "Imagination applied to the whole world is vapid in comparison to imagination applied to a detail."[28] To get a first grip on obligation in the English language, to gauge the weight of it, we might begin with *will* and *shall*, *would* and *should*.

In the fourth act of *Hamlet*, Claudius addresses a hotly vengeful Laertes. He cautions Laertes about what should not happen, he hopes, to this vehement state of mind:

> That we would do
> We should do when we would; for this 'would' changes
> And hath abatements and delays as many
> As there are tongues, are hands, are accidents,
> And then this 'should' is like a spendthrift sigh,
> That hurts by easing.

(4.7.117–22)

"The fundamental idea of the whole tragedy," a German editor remarked in 1869.[29] But what exactly does it mean? We correctly sense a proverb in the background here. The saying achieved its most familiar form in John Heywood's *Proverbs* (1546): "He that will not when he may,/When he would, shall have nay." The contrast between *will* and *shall,* or in Shakespeare's version *would* and *should,* gives the proverb its point and density. A fourteenth-century version perhaps displays the verbs most elegantly: "He that wyl not when he may,/He shal nat when he wyl."[30] The contrasting verbs have something to do with time's effect, delay's effect, on an act of will—and an action.

Would is an auxiliary form of *will,* and *should* an auxiliary form of *shall.* We have reason to suspect important irregularities. *Shall* is a peculiar verb; it has, for example, no infinitive, as if its force could not meaningfully be abstracted from particular occasions. Gert Ronberg notes that the use of *shall* and *should* was "wider and more variegated" in the English Renaissance than it is today.[31] Although some of the distinctions between *shall* and *will* now in use in England postdate Shakespeare, his verbs of willing must teem with precedence, since the long and complex entries in the *OED* on *shall* and *will,* covering, respectively, seven and eleven double-column pages, repeatedly cite him.

We have come upon one of the supreme problems in English lexicography. Perhaps I should say "British lexicography," because as Fowler maintains, a particular way of using *will* and *shall, would* and *should,* once marked national identity:

There is the English of the English, & there is the English of those who repudiate that national name; of the Eng-

lish of the English *shall* and *will* are the shibboleth. . . .
The mere Englishman, if he reflects upon the matter at
all, is convinced that his *shall* & *will* endows his speech
with a delicate precision that could not be attained without it, & serves more important purposes than that of a
race-label.[32]

I doubt that such nationalism is much invoked today, when
English lexicographers seem most eager to present their
language as a worldwide phenomenon. But that the distinction has indeed functioned as a "race-label," demarcat-
ing the English of the English, there can be no doubt. The
OED (*Shall,* sb., 2) quotes Macaulay: "Not one Londoner
in a million ever misplaces his *will* and *shall*." Austin called
shall the "primary performative" (157), the verb of commitment, the word that, when we utter it, really changes us.

The root sense of *will* is intention, that which is in our
control, what we can do and may do, while the root sense
of *shall* is "ordering, commanding, promising, showing determination, being dutiful, being obliged," that which per-
tains to obligation or necessity, what we must do and shall
do. Coriolanus smarts at the arrogant speech of a tribune:
"Mark you/His absolute 'shall'" (3.1.88–89)? Marlowe's
world-enslaving Tamburlaine lays claim to both verbs of vo-
lition: "For will and shall best fitteth Tamburlaine" (*1 Tam*
3.3.41). Ronberg observes of Renaissance English that "an
element of obligation of some kind, even if it is only a note
of pre-arrangement, is present in the most weakly modal
instances of *shall*" (70). Americans retain some feeling for
the obligatory force of *shall* from the King James Bible,
where it is the signifier of command (Thou shalt not), and
from its prominence in legalese. Americans sometimes do

invoke the binding necessity of *shall*. MacArthur did not say "I will return" to the Phillipines, but "I shall return." The civil rights movement voiced its determination in the refrain "We shall overcome." "How things should be" is a very different question from "how things would be." A poll-ster wanting to know "Who would you vote for?" is not asking quite the same question as one who wants to know "Who should you vote for?"

So Claudius instructs a nascent revenger in the verbs of his trade. "That we would do"—that we "will" do—"We should do when we would"—that is, *should* do it, with all the word's load of obligation and command, at the time we would do it. Will should command action. *Would* should rise to *should,* producing a deed. For when *would* does not intensify into *should,* "this 'would' changes/And hath abatements and delays as many/As there are tongues, are hands, are accidents." We hear others ("tongues"), greet others ("hands"), and submit to delaying "accidents." Part of the wit here is that an accident in Shakespeare's English is not merely something that befalls; it is also a grammati-cal case in a declension into which a word falls. "I will," when a person turns awry and loses the name of action, becomes "I would have done it, but . . . I listened to another voice, consulted another advisor, became distracted by other projects." So the original *will* (or in Claudius's conditional, the original *would*) slides into the past tense, as a prior state of the will.

Claudius proceeds to reveal the fate or accident of the *shall* that was not applied to the *will.* "And then this 'should' is like a spendthrift sigh, /That hurts by easing." A sigh was thought to draw a portion of the blood from the heart, and thus to be self-damaging; we might recall Hamlet's gigantic sigh, which almost seems to end his being, when he visits Ophelia in her closet. The *should* that was not applied to the *would* is eventually expelled in the spendthrift sigh of "I *should* have done it": the very word is pronounced with an expulsion of breath. Here again *should* has all of its customary weight: "I really and absolutely *should* have done it, I *should* have, I *should*." The sigh in *should* hurts as it eases because, as philosophers both ancient and modern have noted, the will is impotent when turned backward toward the past. Shillyshallying and dillydallying get one nowhere. Will can be efficacious only when turned toward action in the future. Past states of the will never got into the world, never made anything, and are as barren as the false-birth of a sigh. All that is left in the present of a past state of the will is the self-indicting remorse of an impotent *should*.

The passage wittily traces the effects of time on will, which is to say, the effects of time on the two great families of English words for willing, *will* and *would, shall* and *should*. Laertes has been taught a lesson about obligation in the language of obligation. For Claudius as for Nietzsche, the will, denied action, declines into pathological futility.

Why are we so mired in obligation? Why do we make oaths and promises? Godwin argued that if we ought to do something, then we ought to do it, and no promise should be necessary. Yet no society in Western history has done without promising. The binding formality of its formulas seems to provide us and others, our kings and ministers, with some degree of security.

In the Tower of London, as he spun out the history of the world, Ralegh produced some of the best proof texts for what would one day be known as the Elizabethan World

Picture. Order, degree, hierarchy, things in their places: that was how it should be:

> And certainly, if it be permitted by the help of a ridiculous distinction, or by a God-mocking equivocation, to swear one thing by the name of the living God, and to reserve in silence a contrary intent: the life of man, the estates of men, the faith of subjects to kings, of servants to their masters, of vassals to their lords, of wives to their husbands, and of children to their parents, and of all trials of right, will not only be made uncertain, but all the chains, whereby freemen are tied in the world, be torn asunder. It is by oath (when kings and armies cannot pass) that we enter into the cities of our enemies, and into their armies: it is by oath that wars take end, which weapons cannot end. And what is it or ought it to be that makes an oath thus powerful, but this; that he that sweareth by the name of God, doth assure others that his words are true, as the Lord of all the World is true whom he calleth for a witness, and in whose presence he that taketh the oath hath promised? I am not ignorant of their poor evasions, which play with the severity of God's Commandments in this kind: but this indeed is the best answer, that he that breaks no faith, that hath none to break. For whomsoever hath faith and the fear of God dares not do it.[33]

Oaths can be equivocated; Ralegh is thinking of the Gunpowder Plot and the infamous trial of Father Garnet. But oaths are the chains that hold individuals in the framework of social order; they are the mainstay against anarchy. The links in the great chain of being are forged of promises. In the Elizabethan homily against swearing and perjury, the social goods of "common tranquillity and peace," law-abidingness, justice, "mutuall society, amity, and good order" are all attributed to "lawful promise and covenants confirmed by oathes."[34] At the level of the state, this vast network of promises represents a retrieval in social terms of the early certainty Erik Erikson called "*a sense of basic trust.*"[35] The world is solid. It will endure. It will provide.

Of course not everyone shared this trust, or had reason to, and that knowledge is part of an anxiety threatening the certainty Ralegh invokes. He would like to believe that the full Christian sense of oath-taking, backed by a vigilant God, is sufficient to meet the needs of human society. But why should one have to defend in polemical tones an abiding presupposition of Christian faith? The submerged appeal of the passage is less to the fear of God than to the fear of disastrous social consequences should that first fear, in the matter of oath-taking, somehow prove weak. The history of loyalty oaths in the sixteenth century, to which I now turn, gives to Ralegh's exhortation its aura of threatened urgency.

Oaths had for centuries been a political instrument for concluding treaties, firming factions, securing allegiances. The Magna Carta known and studied through Elizabethan times, until scholars like Coke and Selden revived the King John Carta of 1215, was the third one ratified by Henry III and resubscribed almost a century later by Edward I. His "Confirmation Charter" was attached to the document, swearing on the honor of God that he and his heirs would obey the provisions of the Magna Carta in perpetuity.[36]

The breaking of this ancient oath was thought as late as Elizabeth's reign to threaten a British monarch with terrible curses. As reported by Izaak Walton, John Whitgift, Elizabeth's rather zealous Archbishop of Canterbury, once reminded her of the gravity of this prospect with reference to the seizure of church lands initiated by her father:

> I beseech you forget not, that to prevent these curses, the Church's land and power have been also endeavoured to be preserved (as far as human reason, and the law of this nation, have been able to preserve them) by an immediate and most sacred obligation on the consciences of the princes of this realm. For they that consult the Magna Charta shall find, that as all your predecessors were at their coronation, so you also were sworn before all the Nobility and Bishops then present, and in the presence of God, and in his stead to him that anointed you, "to maintain the church-lands, and the rights belonging to it"; and this you yourself have testified openly to God at the holy altar, by laying your hands on the Bible then lying upon it. And not only Magna Charta, but many modern statutes have denounced a curse upon those that break Magna Charta; a curse like the leprosy that was entailed on the Jews; for as that, so these curses have and will cleave to the very stones of those buildings that have been consecrated to God; and the father's sin of sacrilege hath and will prove to be entailed on his son and family. And now, madam, what account can be given for the breach of this oath at the last great day, either by your majesty, or by me, if it be wilfully, or but negligently violated, I know not.[37]

The ancient parchment, the foundation of constitutional government, was signed in the eclipse and rigged with curses dark! But where exactly are we in the history of oath-taking? On a credence scale from 1 (absolute) to 10 (fat chance), I guess we are, with Queen Elizabeth I, at just about 5. Certainly her father, who must have heard this and thousands of similar arguments, was not moved to halt his appropriation of church lands. I doubt that Elizabeth was much moved either. But then again, oaths at this time still possessed power and authority. If the chains linking the sectors of society were coming apart, oaths might forge them anew.

Their use in the reformation of the English church makes up a real piece of sixteenth-century political history. Nor was that history exhausted at the crowning of James I. In fact, to stay with the example of former church lands, the credence scale seems to have inched upward in the seventeenth century, when it became widely feared that any family purchasing such properties would suffer God's curse to the third generation.[38]

Henry VIII, guided by the legislative genius of Thomas Cromwell, brought the church, its courts, and its lands within the sphere of his *imperium* through the momentous parliamentary statutes of the early 1530s.[39] Most of these changes were announced and implemented by royal proclamations; royal circulars were distributed to selected groups of authorities and followed up by visitation parties charged with investigating and correcting newly illegal practices. It was by these means, for example, that the Tudor government prevented the ecclesiastical courts from sending appeals to Rome, which had been forbidden by the Act in Restraint of Appeals (1533), and enforced the new kinds of treason defined by the Act of Supremacy (1534). The Act of Succession (1534), declaring the legitimacy of the children of Anne Boleyn and naming the newly born Elizabeth as an heir to the throne, required the first oath to be sworn throughout the kingdom.

Several versions of the oath were circulated. One of the earliest contained a preamble accusing the Pope of interfering in the authority "given by God immediately to emperors, kings and princes," and went on to enjoin support for "all other acts and statutes made in the present Parliament," which would have included the revolutionary Act in Restraint of Appeals; both houses of Parliament swore to the oath in this form. This was also the version of the Oath of Succession refused by Thomas More and John Fisher. Though it has been traditionally assumed that More, while willing to accept the succession, objected to the preamble about papal authority, it is more likely that he could not endorse in his conscience the legislation preceding the Act of Succession. The phrase about previous pieces of legislation was removed from the oath administered to the general populace; nothing in the general oath, in other words, expressly acknowledged royal supremacy. More, perhaps, had in the end won his point. In any case, the oath was dutifully tendered and accepted throughout England with strikingly little opposition. Such a thing would never happen again in the sixteenth century.

In 1544 a second Act of Succession was made necessary by the replacement of Queen Anne by Queen Jane, whose children, if there were to be any, had to be declared legitimate heirs to the throne. This legislation provided another oath to be subscribed throughout the realm, but the most respected modern historian of the period, G. R. Elton, finds no evidence in the bureaucratic leavings that the oath was ever administered.[40]

A great many oaths were imposed upon the clergy during the initial stages of the Henrician reform and in the Tudor reigns to follow. The first was the so-called Submission of the Clergy, granting Henry headship over the Church of England, performed by the Convocation of 1530. Clergymen installed in new positions were asked to swear that they owed their livings solely to the king of England. New bishops also swore to a tighter, more drastic form of the Oath of Succession, renouncing all ties with papal authority. In the last decade of Henry's reign, the clergy were whipsawed between sworn commitment to relatively Protestant beliefs and practices (the Ten Articles of 1536) and relatively Catholic ones (the Six Articles of 1539). Despite doctrinal wavering at the top, the forced resignation of clergy, the hanging and beheading of insurrectionists, occasional burnings of overzealous Protestants, and treason trials for imprudent aristocrats must have assured the populace that Henry's Church of England meant business. A general Protestant drift under Edward VI was of course abruptly reversed by the Catholic purification in Queen Mary's reign, which drove many of the new Protestant clergymen into exile and burned for the crime of heresy, by the most trusted modern count, 273 of those who stayed.[41]

In 1559, early in the reign of Elizabeth, Parliament passed the Act of Supremacy and the Act of Uniformity. The second enjoined the use in all services of the second prayer book of Edward VI (fairly Protestant in viewpoint), outlawed the Catholic mass, and made nonattendance at the national church a crime punishable by a fine of 12d.; Shakespeare's father paid it twice in 1592.[42]

But the first piece of legislation, the Act of Supremacy, is crucial in the history of sixteenth-century oaths. It provided a new oath—a "corporal oath," to be ratified by touching a sacred object, usually the Bible—for all clergy, all office-holders, and all degree candidates of the age of sixteen years at the two universities (though Oxford was the more eager to comply). The precise language of the new oath is of interest to students of English Renaissance literature, for it stipulates precisely where, in inward space, swearing takes place:

> I, A.B., do utterly testify and declare in my conscience that the Queen's Highness is the only Supreme Governor of this realm and of all other her Highness's dominions and countries, as well in all spiritual or ecclesiastical things or causes as temporal, and that no foreign prince, person, prelate, state, or potentate hath or ought to have any jurisdiction, power, superiority, preeminence, or authority, ecclesiastical or spiritual, within this realm, and therefore I do utterly renounce and forsake all foreign jurisdictions, powers, superiorities, and authorities, and do promise that from henceforth I shall bear faith and true allegiance to the Queen's Highness, her heirs and lawful successors . . . : So help me God and by the contents of this Book.[43]

Renunciation is utter. The binding word, the most magical and powerful of all the willing words, Austin's primary performative, gives steel to "shall bear faith and true allegiance." So help me God and by the contents of this book: here is the curse coiled in the promise. As Calvin wrote in the *Institutes*, "We cannot call God to be the witness of our words without asking him to be the avenger of our perjury if we deceive." The great compendiums of Protestant doctrine written over the next century would all confirm this oath-structure: "He who swears subjects himself to God's vengeance and curse."[44]

Where is the renunciation done, the *shall* made binding, the faith borne, the curses feared? All of this transpires in the place within us known as conscience. It is to conscience, home of obligation, faith, and fear, that the oath is administered. Although the forced attestation of oaths had other functions beyond securing obedience, its simplest presupposition was a general desire in the populace to enjoy a clean conscience. Even the Jesuit doctrine of equivocation, meant to circumvent the force of unpalatable oaths, preserved this desire. Swearing allegiance to the official meaning of an oath, yet transforming that meaning through "mental reservations," the equivocator protected his conscience against the sin of perjury.[45] At the price of a division between the tongue and the heart, the doctrine combined the two appeals of avoiding persecution and safeguarding a stainless conscience. Opponents, some Catholics among them, charged that the doctrine was no more than a clever justification of lying. Given the idea that intentional meaning combines spoken or written speech with mental speech, how could anyone ever lie?

The assassination by a militant Catholic of William of Orange in 1584 raised the possibility of a serious Catholic threat against Elizabeth. Mary Tudor was alive, though in custody, in England, and despite oaths to the contrary, corresponded with conspirators. Throckmorton confessed under torture; in 1583 John Somerville boasted of his intention to shoot the queen. In this atmosphere the Privy Council drew up the Bond of Association, pledging its signatories, in the event of Elizabeth's assassination, to prevent a conspirator (Mary, no doubt, was the figure foremost in mind) from claiming the throne, and indeed to avenge the queen's death by taking the life of the claimant. The bond was signed with enthusiasm throughout the realm. Its provision for sworn vengeance, so close to the conventions of revenge tragedy, sat well with neither the queen herself nor some of the members of the Commons before whom the bond was introduced in late 1584. But the exposure of yet another assassination plot against Elizabeth, the Parry plot, led to the passing of a modified Bond of Association. The claimant would still be put to death, but only after a trial had judged her to have been privy to the assassination. The bond created, so to speak, a public conspiracy to break the resolve of secret plotters.[46]

From time to time during the century a High Commission had been formed to enquire into, and punish, irregularities among the clergy.[47] In the 1580's, under the administration of Archbishop Whitgift, the High Commission became an ongoing institution—in effect, a new ecclesiastical court. Dreaded by nonconformists, it was intellectually opposed by common lawyers, who believed that its inquisitorial procedures were illegal. Its "trials," launched on the grounds of mere suspicion, or according to its opponents, malicious curiosity, began with the infamous ex officio oath: "You shall swear to answer all such Interrogatories as shall be offered unto you and declare your whole knowledge therein, so God help you."[48] Sworn to answer truthfully before knowing the questions to be put to him, a defendant was often compelled to testify against himself. The ex officio oath, according to its opponents, substituted for indictment and trial by jury and broke with the ancient belief later enshrined in the Fifth Amendment to the American Constitution that no one should be forced to incriminate himself:

nemo tenetur seipsum accusare. If a defendant refused to take the initial oath of truthfulness, he was bound over to the Star Chamber for punishment. The High Commission continued to function under James I. His first Parliament presented him with a millenary petition, signed by a thousand clergymen, requesting a more sparing use of the oath ex officio. James defended it. When Edward Coke and a panel of judges ruled against the High Commission's power of imprisonment and its offensive oath in 1606, James refused the verdict.

By this time, however, James himself had introduced a new and controversial Oath of Allegiance (1605), the first one since the 1534 Oath of Succession to be sworn throughout the realm.[49] The Gunpowder Plot of that year inspired the new swearing. Whereas Whitgift's High Commission was aimed primarily at radical reformers, the new oath was directed toward hard-line Catholics. Englishmen had to acknowledge James as their sovereign and deny that the Pope had power to depose him, authorize foreign governments to invade, or free his subjects from allegiance. The doctrine of equivocation first came to public notice in England during the trial of Robert Southwell in 1595. In 1605–6, with the Gunpowder Plot and the conspiracy trials, this blip of notice ballooned into fascinated alarm. The new oath contained language intended to inoculate it against equivocation: "And all these things I doe plainely and sincerely acknowledge and sweare, according to these express words by me spoken, and according to the plaine and common sense and understanding of these same words, without any Equivocation, or mentall reservation whatsoever."[50]

Such a clause, though no doubt tightening the screws on Catholic consciences, could hardly disallow equivocation.

All a determined equivocator would have to do is recite the clause, then add the mental reservation, "Except in the case of this particular mental reservation, by which I deny my assent to this unlawful oath." Was the meaning of an oath determined by the giver's intention or the taker's intention? While authority of course upheld the first view, it is impossible to know how many silently, by means of mental reservations, adopted the second. As an old adage declared, thought is free—or in the prescient formulation of Shakespeare's *Measure for Measure*, written a couple of years before Father Garnet's trial, "Thoughts are no subjects" (5.1.451).[51] It would seem that equivocation must have eroded somewhat authority's confidence in the bindingness of oaths. If so, it was a slow erosion.

The questions arising from the anti-Catholic oath were hotly debated in England. This climate of oath awareness perhaps helps to explain the king's remarkable declaration to Parliament in 1607, when he appeared to urge the unification of England and Scotland: "For I will not say anything which I will not promise, nor promise anything which I will not swear; what I swear I will sign, and what I sign, I shall with God's grace ever perform."[52] This might be termed a hyperpromise, a promise to say, promise, swear, sign, and perform. Notice how the repeated word *will* stiffens in the last clause to *shall*. A more binding way of stating that one means what one says can hardly be imagined.

The ecclesiastical courts of England, along with the Star Chamber and the High Commission, were abolished in 1641. But the revolutionary parliament had not forsworn oath-taking. In 1643 a parliamentary delegation, working with the Scottish Convention, hammered out the Solemn League and Covenant, a document providing for "uniformity of religion" between the two kingdoms and securing Scottish support for the war against Charles I. After having been scanned and slightly amended by the Westminster Divines, the document was duly passed by both houses of Parliament and signed by the legislators. It was then either signed or sworn throughout England by friends of Parliament—which is to say, those whom Parliament considered true Englishmen. As Masson reports in his great biography of Milton, "From Sept. 1643, onwards for some years, the test of being a Parliamentarian in England was 'Have you signed the Covenant?' and the test of willingness to *become* a Parliamentarian, and of fitness to be forgiven for past malignancy or lukewarmness, was 'Will you *now* sign the Covenant?'"[53]

In 1649 the Commonwealth required all Englishmen over the age of eighteen, at home or abroad, to subscribe to the "Engagement" oath: "I do declare and promise that I will be true and faithful to the Commonwealth of England, as the same is established, without a King or a House of Lords."[54] Liberty of conscience was a great rallying cry of the Puritans, and it may be that the absence of the word *conscience* from the Engagement represents a desire to bypass an inner place tested so rigorously by prior regimes. But the hypocrisy of the "good old cause," breaking the old oaths only to impose new ones, was not lost on a skeptical observer like Samuel Butler.[55] Dr. Johnson was succinct: "To oblige people to take oaths as to the disputed right, is wrong."[56]

Looking back to the sixteenth century, we may wonder why oaths were used so sparingly with respect to the general populace. Perhaps they were not entirely trusted. The Oath of Succession was, after all, just a straw poll of conscience, an announcement of government determination.

Probably most people just went along with an oath, and if
ease of conscience was necessary, found some way or another to get that ease: equivocation was only the most
extreme way, one might say the most formalistic way, of
making a divorce between the tongue and heart somehow
satisfactory to threatened consciences. One thing an oath
really might do during this period was to identify the hard
cases, the consciences dead set against the meaning of the
oath, the Mores and Fishers, for they would be the ones
refusing to take it.

Apart from the martyrs great and small, most people
probably mouthed the words or made their mark. As Selden
observed, "there is no oath scarcely but we swear to things
we are ignorant of—for example, The Oath of Supremacy.
How many know how the King is King, what are his rights
& prerogatives?"[57] In *3 Hen6* a couple of gamekeepers come
upon a disguised King Henry. Recognizing him, they take
him into custody and declare that they are "sworn in all
allegiance" to King Edward. Henry reminds them that, once
upon a time at his own coronation, they had sworn an oath
of allegiance to him: "And tell me then, have you not broke
your oaths" (3.1.79)? "No," one of them replies, "we were
subjects but while you were king" (80). As is his style, Henry
forgoes the opportunity for moral tirade. The world just
works this way:

Ah, simple men, you know not what you sware.
Look, as I blow this feather from my face,
And as the air blows it to me again,
Obeying with my wind when I do blow,
And yielding to another when it blows,
Commanded always by the greater gust,

Such is the lightness of you common men.
But do not break your oaths; for of that sin
My mild entreaty shall not make you guilty.

(82–90)

People go along, get along. You don't need a weatherman to know which way the wind blows. Real change in the Church of England took place not through oaths but through new liturgies and prayer books, new vernacular Bibles, new words from the pulpit, a reduced set of newly defined and administered sacraments, new institutions, and new bureaucracies.

But a feeling that oaths above all else undergirded public security outlasted, at least for some, the upheavals of the middle seventeenth century. Isaac Barrow, Anglican divine and Cambridge professor of mathematics, seems to echo Ralegh. An awesome regard for deity resides in the faculty of conscience, "and conscience, without fear checking, or hope spurring it on, can be no more than a name: all societies, therefore, we may see, have been fain to call in the notion of a future judgment to the aid of justice, and support of fidelity; obliging men to bind their testimonies by oaths, and plight their troth by sacraments; implying a dread of that divine judgment to which they solemnly do then appeal and make themselves accountable."[58] However, this neatly Euclidean passage (as we say today) demystifies the Elizabethan World Picture. Whereas for Ralegh social order emanates from the fear of God, for Barrow the fear of God emanates from the necessity of "all societies."

It is not very far from this formulation to the idea that the fear of God is just one form of self-interest, and not always, not even usually, the most compelling one. Samuel

Butler, once again, seems to recognize as clearly as anyone in the period a transition from a Christian society that conceives its basic trust as a network of oaths to a Hobbesian society that conceives its basic trust as a network of self-interests. "Oaths and Obligations in the Affairs of the world," Butler wrote in one of his notebooks, "are like Ribbons and Knots in dressing, that seeme to ty something, but do not at all. For nothing but interest does really oblige."[59] But as we move from Ralegh to Hobbes, Hume, and Nietzsche, must we exchange without remainder fear of God for fear of police, judge, jailer, and cell?

After the "practice of promising" and the "climate of obligation" have had their say in the language of history and sociology, there does in the end appear to be something about honor that quickens the individual moral agent. Promises must have deep psychic benefits. One of the greatest of these, I think, is that promises supply a locale and a focus for general or free-floating anxiety. A teenager has to make a lot of promises before he is allowed to drive a car, the last of which, it may be, is swearing to be home by a certain hour. The parents exacting these promises no doubt hope to push their child's will to the height of vigilance. But with regard to their own emotions, they can exchange an open-ended anxiety about his first solo outing for the focused anxiety of whether or not the car will enter the driveway on time. There must also be a certain relief in being bound by a promise. Behavior gains a structure. The worry of self-invention lessens.

But anxiety will never be entirely pacified. Meant to quell anxiety, promises create a new anxiety of their own—the fear or suspicion that they will be broken. Rosalind in *As You Like It*, as I earlier suggested, reveals a general mistrust of the extravagant language of love, its grand vows especially. But when Orlando says that he will return "by two o'clock," she makes this one promise into a symbolic focus of the constancy she both desires and doubts in her beloved:

> If you break one jot of your promise, or come one minute behind your hour, I will think you the most pathetical break-promise, and the most hollow lover, and the most unworthy of her you call Rosalind, that may be chosen out of the gross band of the unfaithful: therefore beware my censure and keep your promise. (4.1.180–86)

Human beings are prone to elevate this anxiety to a moral idealism—a peculiar sort of hyperbole with respect to honor. Such idealism, as will be clear in the context of *Othello*, can be destructive to all concerned. But here I want to call attention to our extraordinary investment of moral energy in the institution of promising.

Locke must have been at least partially right in holding that promise-keeping belonged to human nature, "to men as men, and not as members of society."[60] People are full of articulate moral energy when it comes to the making and breaking of promises. Montesquieu thought it one of the three supreme rules of honor that "what honor forbids is more rigorously forbidden when the laws do not agree in proscribing it, and that what honor requires is more strongly required when the laws do not require it" (34). Whence arises this mysterious excess, more severe than law itself? Is it simply a matter of pride, of being better than the ordinary law-abiding citizen?

For centuries philosophers passed down to one another

an old piece of moral casuistry. A highwayman has robbed someone and threatens to kill him unless he promises to deliver, in another time and place, a sum of money. If the waylaid man makes this promise, and therefore walks away with his life, is he obliged to keep it?[61] Writing in the waning years of the twentieth century, I am sure there is no obligation here whatsoever. But a surprising number of moralists and philosophers, some of the best minds in the Western tradition, maintained that this promise, though exacted by force and by a person disobeying the law, should nonetheless be honored.

Throughout this chapter we have observed a tendency toward extremity, a competitive urge to outdo prior promisers in boasting, threatening, and oath-swearing. The complement to this extremity is an overmeasure of shame and regret attached to promise-breaking. Adam Smith, an acute observer of these questions, notes that

> treachery and falsehood are vices so dangerous, so dreadful, and, at the same time, such as may so easily, and, upon many occasions, so safely be indulged, that we are more jealous of them than of almost any other. Our imagination therefore attaches the idea of shame to all violations of faith [broken promises], in every circumstance and in every situation. They resemble, in this respect, the violations of chastity in the fair sex, a virtue of which, for the like reasons, we are excessively jealous. (332)

The excessive moral scrutiny, the sense of shame, that accompanies promising is like the excessive scrutiny of male sexual jealousy. One road leads from here to *Othello*, whose hero, as we will see in chapter 4, makes use of this similarity in transferring his injured emotions from jealousy to a more exalted sense of betrayal.

Another leads to the fact that once we have made a promise to someone, no matter how deep the contempt we harbor for him, we are likely to keep it. Again, quoting Smith: "Fidelity is so necessary a virtue, that we apprehend it in general to be due even to those to whom nothing else is due" (332). I do not see how a theory deriving obligation from the history of fearful social consequences can account for the fact that some people are more conscientious, more virtuous than law and order either require or envision. Society is not, in my view, the ultimate source of this moral hyperbole, this super degree of probity. The individual moral agent has welcomed promising with all the strange excess that is its hallmark.

We have some evidence that Shakespeare himself was among these conscientious human beings. His drama suggests as much. We need think only of Hamlet, Othello, Lear, and Timon to realize that he was a great specialist in portraying states of moral revulsion against falsehood. But the most personal material resides in his *Sonnets*.

After the Dark Lady is introduced in Sonnet 127, lying and forswearing gradually come to dominate the sequence. Shakespeare's mistress and the idealized young friend of the first 126 poems establish a sexual relationship behind his back (133, 134), but despite his shame and his fear of losing both his loves, Shakespeare remains in thrall to the woman (135, 136, 137). In 138 the word *lie* is stretched out from sexual lying ("Therefore I lie with her, and she with me") to the pretended acceptance as truthful swearing of the lies of him to her, her to him ("And in our faults by lies we flattered be"). In 142 he fends off her accusation of falsehood by evoking a charge that he might with equal justice hurl at her: she has "sealed false bonds of love as oft as mine,/Robb'd other beds' revenues of their rents." The lies between Shakespeare and his mistress have sprung from a bed of broken marriage vows.

A religious exhortation to choose immortal life over mortal sin (146) fails before our eyes in the next poem (147), where the certain knowledge of her falsehood ("Who art as black as hell, as dark as night") cannot cure his lethal desire. In a painful state of conflict, the poet gives allegiance to two self-canceling truths, her unworthiness and her fairness (actually in complexion, metaphorically in trustworthiness). A mind thus divided can only observe, in ever more intense and self-hating ironies, the corruption of its own judgment.

This fraught entanglement in falsehood produces the densely layered exposure of perjury and forswearing in Sonnet 152. Although two mythological poems follow, the dark story of multiple betrayal seems to end here:

In loving thee thou know'st I am forsworn,
But thou art twice forsworn, to me love swearing;
In act thy bed-vow broke, and new faith torn
In vowing new hate after new love bearing.
But why of two oaths' breach do I accuse thee,
When I break twenty? I am perjured most,
For all my vows are oaths but to misuse thee,
And all my honest faith in thee is lost;
For I have sworn deep oaths of thy deep kindness,
Oaths of thy love, thy truth, thy constancy,
And to enlighten thee gave eyes to blindness,

Or made them swear against the thing they see;
   For I have sworn thee fair: more perjured eye,
   To swear against the truth so foul a lie.

One normally expects the turn in a Shakespeare sonnet to come in line 9. Throughout the sequence, moreover, this swerve in the development of the conceit has almost always been toward some retrieved idealization of the relationship, however tortuous—some means of continuing both the love and the love poetry.[62] Here the turn comes earlier, at line 5, where Shakespeare breaks off his indictment of the Dark Lady for being twice as false as he to launch a self-indictment of his own more numerous perjuries. He is forsworn—I think because he has broken his bed-vow.[63] She has also done that, but broken as well her vow of "new faith" in her "new love" with Shakespeare.

But he is "perjured most," an offender against twenty oaths. "For all my vows are oaths but to misuse thee." We certainly have contextual warrant to take "misuse thee" to mean "commit sin with you." Yet *misuse* must also carry the sense implied in Helena's "You would not use a gentle lady so." To misuse: to slander, to tell lies knowingly. Yet the sense of *misuse* evolves in the course of the sonnet and by the concluding lines means something close to, in John Kerrigan's formulation, "favorably misrepresent," swear the foul to be fair.[64] For it is the "deep oaths" of misrepresentation Shakespeare proceeds to catalogue. These misuses are simultaneously interior lies, lies arranged and compelled within the mind of Shakespeare himself. He either gave eyes to blindness, swearing to see a fairness when he did not see anything, or still worse in the way of self-deception, forced his eyes to swear the fairness of a foulness they did in fact behold.

The couplet adopts the second explanation. Shakespeare may have had *Astrophil and Stella* 47 in mind:

> Unkind, I love you not: O me, that eye
> Doth make my heart give to my tongue the lie.[65]

The couplets of both sonnets play on *eye* and *I* while rhyming *eye* and *lie*. But Sidney, his heart at war with his tongue, commits perjury against his spoken declaration; he is a Petrarchist going about his business, salvaging love from the suspicion of its folly or harmfulness. The completely disillusioned speaker of the Shakespeare sonnet indicts his "perjur'd eye": as we move from Sidney to Shakespeare, lying migrates from the tongue to the eye, from wavering commitment to inward falsehoods visited upon oneself.

In its punning sense, "more perjured I" returns to the opening lines: "I am more perjured than you, my own confession having revealed more forswearings than I began the poem by observing in you." His long history of forswearing must be blamed on his "more perjured eye," the eye compelled by overwhelming desire to tell self-misusing lies against its own beheld truth. No gesture of idealization from the Petrarchan genre sweetens this indictment. We are left with the moral self-analysis of a confessed perjurer.

If we feel that Sonnet 152 provides, in any satisfying way, closure to the sequence; if we feel that its self-analysis is exacting enough, and backed by sufficient moral conviction; if we feel that the revulsion against both mistress and self declared here will eventually, in some future outside the framework of the poems, result in Shakespeare freeing himself from self-misusing bondage to this woman and his perjured desire for her, then this freedom comes from having found in himself some place, deeper than the site of his deepest false oaths, where he is honest and true, a man repelled by those foul lies. If anything sees him through, it is the love of truth.

2

The Truth of an Oath and the Bias of the World

In the third and last of Shakespeare's *Henry VI* plays, the Wars of the Roses approach that state of savagery where, according to Greville's version of a popular maxim, men relate to men as "*One Wolf unto another*": "For only this Antipathy of mind/Hath ever been the bellows of sedition."[1] The English aristocracy, as Shakespeare represented it in these early histories, seems well stocked with irritable and envious men, quick to take and return insult, given to imprudent threats, hasty vows, and dire curses, champions of family honor nourishing long, clotted memories of wrongs and injustices. It is not surprising to find them embroiled in a blood feud, since they appear almost to have been bred for such a purpose. Here Shakespeare offers up for mockery an old truism of English patriotism that will later be spoken, and apparently endorsed, at the end of *King John*. "Why, knows not Montague," asks Hastings after King Edward insists on honoring his marriage contract to Lady Grey, "that of itself/England is safe, if true within itself" (*3Hen6* 4.1.38–39; cf. *KJ* 5.7.117–18)? In this context, the grand-sounding idea of England being "true within itself" means that Edward should ignore the French alliance negotiated by Warwick and honor an unpopular marriage contract destined to divide his own faction. There is of course a cause, a matter of right, at stake in these civil wars: the questionable deposition of Richard II, resulting in rival claims for the throne. But the question of whose claim is just, the Yorkist or the Lancastrian, seems more of a pretext than a cause.

The moralizers who wrote the "tragedies" in *A Mirror for Magistrates*, where ghosts from these years of internal conflict return to tell the tales of their rise and fall, blamed the Wars of the Roses on reckless ambition and heedless pride.[2] No doubt these venerable culprits still play a role in Shakespeare's version. But as the young dramatist created the English history play, he pierced moralizing abstractions to locate, behind them and at the heart of blood feud, a particular psychological mechanism.[3] His most bellicose characters refuse to mourn. Faced with a dead father, a dead son, or a humiliated husband, they immediately transform grief into revenge, and revenge into a career of self-proclamation.

Young Clifford enters the stage at the Battle of St. Albans and dedicates himself to "war, thou son of hell" (*2Hen6* 5.2.33), which must be pursued at the expense of "self-love." He then discovers the corpse of his father, recently slain by the Duke of York. Viewed in the full context of Shakespeare's work, his is not an atypical response to loathsome fact. He first supposes that, in registering with due seriousness the fact of his father's death, the world should end:

> O! let the vile world end,
> And the premised flames of the last day
> Knit earth and heaven together;
> Now let the general trumpet blow his blast,
> Particularities and petty sounds
> To cease!
>
> (2*Hen6* 5.2.40–45)

This is Seneca with a Christian accent—a massive egotism for whom the objective correlative of its loss is nothing less than the end of the world.[4]

But almost immediately this egotism gets slung back into the world as focused retaliation. There are Yorks to be slaughtered:

> Henceforth I will not have to do with pity:
> Meet I an infant of the house of York,
> Into as many gobbets will I cut it
> As wild Medea young Absyrtus did:
> In cruelty will I seek out my fame.
>
> (56–60)

An ego incapable of enduring loss, incapable of imagining a world without Lord Clifford, will regain itself in the "fame" of vengeful cruelty. The severity of his revenge, fashioned from the severity of his loss, seeks out the formulaic "Henceforth," a vow of dedication that changes everything *from this moment on.* When the king checks on the current state of Clifford's "vowed revenge," the bereft son rehearses its psychological history: "The hope whereof makes Clifford mourn in steel" (*3Hen6* 1.1.58).

We find the same mechanism, shorn of its classical framework, when Clifford succeeds in killing the Duke of York and his youngest son, Edmund of Rutland. Now, however, the two responses, of sovereign loss and sovereign revenge, are divided between two brothers. Edward, looking ahead, sees nothing but grief and death:

> Now my soul's palace is become its prison:
> Ah, would she break from hence, that this my body
> Might in the ground be closed up in rest!
> For never henceforth shall I joy again;
> Never, O never, shall I see more joy.
>
> (2.1.74–78)

But Richard of Gloucester has no tears, no lamentations, no vision of a joyless future. Mourning dulls loss, which has a fitter job to do:

> To weep is to make less the depth of grief:
> Tears then for babes; blows and revenge for me!
> Richard, I bear thy name; I'll venge thy death,
> Or die renowned by attempting it.
>
> (85–88)

Presumably weeping might lessen the depth of the original outrage because it would initiate a process of mourning that "comes to terms with," "makes peace with," and "lays to rest" the loss of a loved one. Richard will instead remain loyal to that original outrage and expresses his loyalty in the form of a vow. Revenge then becomes both a matter of integrity and a path to ambitious renown.

Queen Margaret also excels at this conversion from passive suffering to active aggression. She showed her mettle in *2Hen6* when given the head of Suffolk, her favorite and perhaps her lover:

> Oft have I heard that grief softens the mind,
> And makes it fearful and degenerate;
> Think therefore on revenge, and cease to weep.
>
> (4.4.1–3)

She affects the same transformation in part 3, as the French king, insulted by Edward's refusal of his sister, vows to move against the pretender in the name of her husband and son: "Tell him my mourning weeds are laid aside, / And I am ready to put armour on" (3.3.229). She repeats this wisdom before the Battle of Tewkesbury: "Great lords, wise men n'er sit and wail their loss, / But cheerly seek how to redress their harms" (5.4.1–2).[5]

The kept promises of these avowed avengers will of course be gruesome. Therein the drama lies. Clifford and Queen Margaret devise an awful death for Richard of York. They place him on a molehill to mock his mountainous aspirations, coronate him with a toy paper replica of the diadem he has sought, present him a napkin spotted with the blood of his murdered son, then taunt him with his frustrated hopes until he cries into the napkin. True to his kind, old York tries to wrest a vengeful meaning from his falling tears:

Why, now thou hast thy will.
For raging wind blows up incessant showers,
And when the rage allays, the rain begins.
These tears are my sweet Rutland's obsequies,
And every drop cries vengeance for his death
'Gainst thee, fell Clifford, and thee, false French-
      woman.

(1.4.144–48)

It is apparently some comfort to be able to say that his weeping cries out for vengeance. Clifford stabs him with the formal satisfaction of a man fulfilling an obligation: "Here's
for my oath, here's for my father's death. [*Stabbing him.*]"
(175). His head is fixed on the gates of York, the better to
survey his dukedom.

An arrow through his neck, Clifford groans his last just
as he is discovered by Warwick and the three remaining
York brothers. They will replace their father's head with
Clifford's—"that fatal screech-owl to our house," as Edward
calls him, remembering his clamorous vows of revenge,
"That nothing sung but death to us and ours" (2.6.56–57).
Pretending that Clifford is still alive, they proceed to taunt
him. Richard knows he must be dead when the taunting fails
to elicit an oath:

What, not an oath? Nay, then the world goes hard
When Clifford cannot spare his friends an oath.
I know by that he's dead; and, by my soul,
If this right hand would buy but two hours' life,
That I in all despite might rail at him,
This hand should chop it off, and with the issuing
   blood

Stifle the villain whose unstaunched thirst
York and young Rutland could not satisfy.

(77–84)

After his ironic proof of Clifford's demise, Richard himself enters into a suggestively incoherent vow ("by my soul"). If Clifford could be given two hours of life so that Richard could humiliate him, driving home his defeat by the house of York, his left hand would cut off his right hand—the hand normally used, it may be significant to remember, in swearing an oath. But as soon as Richard has produced the image of blood flowing from his arm, his vindictive mind catches at it, forgetting the railing that was in the first place the benefit to be gained from lopping off his hand. The image has suggested a better idea: he could use the blood issuing from his right arm to choke Clifford to death, a fitting end for someone so boisterously thirsty for York blood. The loss of Richard's own life, which seems implied in any rational examination of this passage, has simply passed out of his consciousness. The extra metrical foot in line 82 betrays Richard's forgetful excess. Good revenge is such a blissful thought that it cancels all regard for the self-destructive consequences to the revenger himself.

King Henry VI, "bashful" Henry, "faint-hearted and degenerate" Henry (2Hen6 1.1.189), whose "cowardice" is deplored by the Yorkists (41), whose "church-like humour" would subject the bellicose British nobles to a "bookish rule" (248, 260), is the only main character temperamentally unable to transform grief into revenge. As he says, assessing his treatment of his subjects, "I have not been . . . forward of revenge, though they much err'd" (3Hen6 4.8.44–46). He certainly proves unable to mount an aggressive pol-

icy capable of holding at bay the rival factions. On the battlefield Henry cuts such an uninspiring figure that Clifford
and Queen Margaret tell him to stay away from it, swearing they do better in his absence (2.2.73–75; 2.5.16–18). In
Henry, griefs merely accumulate, as he steps back from
events to become the increasingly impotent spectator of the
utter failure of his reign: "For what is in this world but grief
and woe" (2.5.20)? Like Richard II, the more complex,
more poetically gifted figure into which he will evolve later
in the canon, Henry is a king of griefs: "You may my glo-
ries and my state depose,/But not my griefs; still am I king
of those" (*R2* 4.1.192–93).

In a famously emblematic scene, Henry stands on a molehill, wishing he were a simple shepherd, as first a son who
has unwittingly killed his father, then a father who has unwittingly killed his son, enter the stage on either side of him.
Their words laced together in ritual repetitions, the three
compete in grief. Did a son ever so rue his father's death?
Did a father ever so rue his son's death? Henry declares
himself the victor: "Was ever king so griev'd for subjects'
woe?/Much is your sorrow; mine, ten times so much"
(*3Hen6* 2.5.111–12). Perhaps this cherished mournfulness,
this depthless accumulation of grief, is part of the reason
why he drifts into the fantasy of being a shepherd. For pastoral in the sixteenth century was a genre full of complaint
and lamentation.[6] In England, the woeful shepherds of this
literary form never learned to convert their sorrows into
revenge until Marvell's "The Mower's Song," and until Milton's *Lycidas* never managed convincingly to wipe the tears
from their eyes.

What force on earth can prevent these honor-bound aristocrats from destroying one another? Early in the play, a compromise is attempted. Henry will rule during his lifetime; York and his heirs will inherit the crown. The king, for once, appears decisive. He demands an oath from York:

> I here entail
> The crown to thee and to thine heirs for ever;
> Conditionally that here thou take thine oath
> To cease this civil war and, whilst I live,
> To honour me as thy king and sovereign;
> And neither by treason nor hostility
> To seek to put me down and reign thyself.
>
> (1.1.200–206)

York complies: "This oath I willingly take and will perform." As I noted in the previous chapter, an oath normally contains both a promise and a threat—a curse that, if the promise should be broken, will fall on the head of its maker. Although curses are not stipulated here, I believe they are implied. At York's death, the queen reminds him of his "solemn oath," and wonders at a heedlessness that would steal Henry's crown, "Now in his life, against your holy oath" (1.4.100, 105). Of course, oaths have been tried before. The one York took in *1Hen6* 3.1.167–68, when merely Richard Plantagenet, went to no avail. As Andrew Cairncross, the Arden editor of the *Henry VI* dramas, remarks, "The breaking of oaths is a recurrent theme in this series of plays."[7]

The latest one is also doomed. Even as the Yorks debate how best to break it, Queen Margaret is in the field to regain the lost entailment of her son Edward. The conversation about oaths among the aspiring Yorks seems to me the single most illuminating passage in the play. I quote it in full:

> *York.* I took an oath that he should quietly reign.
> *Edw.* But for a kingdom any oath may be broken:
> I would break a thousand oaths to reign one year.
> *Rich.* No; God forbid your grace should be forsworn.
> *York.* I shall be, if I claim by open war.
> *Rich.* I'll prove the contrary, if you'll hear me speak.
> *York.* Thou canst not, son; it is impossible.
> *Rich.* An oath is of no moment, being not took
> Before a true and lawful magistrate
> That hath authority over him that swears.
> Henry had none, but did usurp the place;
> Then, seeing 'twas he that made you to depose,
> Your oath, my lord, is vain and frivolous.
> Therefore to arms! And, father, do but think
> How sweet a thing it is to wear a crown,
> Within whose circuit is Elysium
> And all that poets feign of bliss and joy.
> Why do we linger thus? I cannot rest
> Until the white rose that I wear be dy'd
> Even in the lukewarm blood of Henry's heart.
>
> (1.2.15–34)

Something irrevocable is happening here. Shakespeare's creative ambition has emerged, reaching for the stars. As Richard's remarks about feigning poets may suggest, there is another writer in the picture: Marlowe. Tamburlaine the Great, his most famous character, has several speeches on the incomparably sweet pleasure of wearing a crown. But

Shakespeare has added a dimension peculiarly his own to Marlowe's crown-loving conqueror. It is found, concentrated, in the line "No; God forbid your Grace should be forsworn." Cairncross notes the specialness: "a characteristic piece of irony from Richard."[8] But, it should be added, this is the *first* piece of characteristically Richardian irony and is only characteristic at all when looked back on from the rest of this play and the greater play to follow, *The Tragical History of King Richard III*.

The irony belonging to this character in particular lies in indicting the unworthiness of others, their failure to live up to noble and pious ideals, or their willingness to so fail, while all the time pursuing a course unspeakably more base and demonic than the one he criticizes. "God forbid your Grace should be forsworn" has all the pretended moral tenderness, ever alert to the shortcomings of others and filled with uncomprehending disbelief at the hint of shortcoming in himself, we will soon come to know, indeed to savor, in Richard's powerful theatrical presence. The public hide of moral rectitude, wrapped over a Tamburlaine's heart, is the novelty Shakespeare sets against Marlowe, whose self-delighted ambitious supermen make little effort to put forth an honorable face. Tamburlaine revels in his ambition. Richard revels in his ambition *and*, with every bit as much self-delight, in his show of superior moral probity. "I . . . seem a saint, when most I play the devil" (*R3* 1.6.338). Nashe was probably alluding to *Richard III* when he wrote, in *Pierce Penilesse*, of "cunning drifts over-gilded with outward holiness."[9]

Richard's two-sided character is born on the subject of oaths. It is a terrible thing to be forsworn. Oaths *are* of moment, he implies, when sworn before "a true and lawful magistrate." But since Henry's authority is illegitimate, York's oath was "vain and frivolous": let ambition's race begin! Here the doubleness of Richard's character makes a fit with the uncertainty over the efficacy of oath-taking that emerged from our brief history of sixteenth-century church politics in chapter 1.

Shakespeare registered this ambivalence in Brutus's cynical account of formal oath-taking in *Julius Caesar* 2.1.114–40, but the richest expression of the weakness of oaths, their utter failure to bind our intractably self-interested nature, occurs in *King John*, as Faulconbridge the Bastard watches the French and English kings make a deal that compromises causes to which both have sworn allegiance. They came to the parley armed with zeal and conscience. But in the end they were

> rounded in the ear
> With that same purpose-changer, that sly divel,
> That broker, that still breaks the pate of faith,
> That daily break-vow, he that wins of all,
> Of kings, of beggars, old men, young men, maids,
> Who, having no external thing to lose
> But the word "maid," cheats the poor maid of that,
> That smooth-fac'd gentleman, tickling commodity,
> Commodity, the bias of the world,
> The world, who of itself is peised well,
> Made to run even upon even ground,
> Till this advantage, this vile drawing bias,
> This sway of motion, this commodity,
> Makes it take head from all indifferency,
> From all direction, purpose, course, intent:
> And this same bias, this commodity,

This bawd, this broker, this all-changing word,

·   ·   ·   ·   ·   ·   ·   ·   ·   ·   ·   ·   ·   ·   ·   ·   ·   ·

Since kings break faith upon commodity,
Gain, be my lord, for I will worship thee!

(2.1.566–82, 597–98)

Commodity is usually glossed as "self-interest," which is
accurate enough, but in light of the Latin *commodum* might
be spread out into "convenience," "opportunity," "profit,"
"reward," "advantage," "policy." All these, the whole range
of immediate attractions, constitute "the bias of the world,"
where bias is the weight on one side that makes the bowl-
ing ball curve.[10]

The word *indifferency* may be somewhat misleading to
modern readers, for it might to be taken to suggest that the
straight-line direction, the course we stray from because of
the bias of commodity, is aimless. But in context "indifferency" must refer to an undisturbed and yet directed path—
a line we had set ourselves on, a line determined by the will,
by "direction, purpose, course, intent." This firm line takes
its initial direction, its straight path, from faith and unbro-
ken vows. Running through the metaphor of deflected purpose and "daily break-vow" is a second metaphor about
prostitution and seduction: the sale made by "That broker,"
"This bawd, this broker," the pimp, the whoremongerer, or
the tickling smooth-faced gentleman who cheats the maid
of her name ("this all-changing word").

The passage combines an almost abstract acceptance of
infidelity—the bias in the ball, the terms of the game all
players have to accept—with a deep moral revulsion against
"that sly divel," that pimp, that smooth-face gentleman
who turns us away from the straight path of our virtuous

promises. Here Shakespeare presents us with a mind split between two attitudes toward broken vows and infirm faith: that's the way it is; the way it is is degenerate.

I will round back toward the oath-breaching Yorks via the Thirty-nine Articles of the Church of England. This creed has enjoyed an extraordinary longevity; it is to this day the doctrinal basis of Anglicanism and American Presbyterianism. Cranmer had formulated the Forty-two Articles in 1553. A Latin version of the Thirty-nine Articles, substantially the same as the Forty-two Articles but reduced by three, was adopted by Parliament in 1562, and subscribed by oath among the clergy. Slightly amended, and translated into English, the Thirty-nine Articles were again passed by Parliament in 1571, and again subscribed by oath among the clergy.

The thirty-eighth of the Forty-two Articles and the last of the Thirty-nine Articles was entitled "Of a Christian man's oath." This brief statement owes its existence in part to the fact that Anabaptists, like the Lollards before them and the Quakers after, believed that all oath-taking had been forbidden by Christ in Matt. 5.34–37, and confirmed by James 5.12; they consequently refused to participate in any legal proceedings:[11]

> As we confess that vain and rash swearing is forbidden Christian men by our Lord Jesus Christ, and James his Apostle: So we judge that Christian religion does not prohibit, but that a man may swear when the Magistrate requireth, in a cause of faith and charity, so it be done according to the prophets' teaching, in justice, judgement, and truth.[12]

In *Henry VI, Part 3*, at the council of ambitious Yorks, Richard virtually quotes "Of a Christian man's oath" in maintaining, contrary to his impetuous brother, that a momentous oath can be sworn only "Before a true and lawful magistrate / That hath authority over him that swears."

Richard finds a way to break the oath while making a show—or perhaps better than that—of saving conscience. Surely there were quite a few break-vows in Shakespeare's audience. Some of them probably spent the Sabbath listening to break-vows preach. William Perkins spoke of "the general sin of this age, which is to speak deceitfully every one to his neighbor. It is a hard thing to find a man that will stand to his word and lawful promise."[13] Precocious young Macduff runs his mother through a little catechism about oath-breach. What is a traitor? One who swears and lies. What must happen to a traitor? He must be hanged. Who will hang him? The honest men. "Then the liars and swearers are fools; for there are liars and swearers enow to beat the honest men, and hang up them" (*MB* 4.2.46–57). Use every man after his desert, and who shall scape whipping?

It must have been the case that a lot of sixteenth-century Englishmen were not much cowed by the solemnity of an oath. Elyot, like Perkins over half a century later, thought the entire country was rife with perjury. If the Tudor government thought otherwise, it would have used oaths more often on the general populace. Richard reminds the audience of what they know in their heart of hearts: how easy it is to break an oath, to conceal bad faith.

The excuse he offers for breaking the oath is no mere quibble. Henry lacked the kingly authority to administer the oath. Whenever oaths were argued about then, or are argued about today, the legitimacy of the authority dispensing the oath stands as the ultimate debater's issue, and there is always an argument for oath-breach based on illegitimacy. But as Shakespeare's passage suggests, the legitimacy question may have more to do with policy than with sweet reason. The promises of rulers, Machiavelli advises the prince, should always be subordinate to the self-interest of getting and maintaining power:

> But by no means can the prudent ruler keep his word—and he does not—when to keep it works against himself and when the reasons that made him promise are annulled. If all men were good, this maxim would not be good, but because they are bad and do not keep their promises to you, you likewise do not have to keep yours to them. Never has a shrewd prince lacked justifying reasons to make his promise-breaking appear honorable.[14]

By keeping his promises a potentate loses maneuverability; he becomes predictable to his promise-breaking rivals.

Immediately after indicting promise-breaking as the "general sin of this age," Perkins turns with unusual accuracy to the subject of Machiavelli. "It is a rule of *Machiavelli* that a man may practise many things against his faith, against charity, and humanity, and religion: and that it is not necessary to have these virtues, but to counterfeit and dissemble them" (109). On the Elizabethan stage, some of Machiavelli's hard-edged precepts for political success became absorbed into the stereotype of the Machiavellian villain, a successor to the Vice of the old moralities. Shakespeare's Richard, his first contribution to this tradition, swells with immoral ambition, but not before remembering, in Machiavelli's words, "to make his promise-breaking appear honourable." Once you get beyond the legitimacy debate, his speech goes on to reveal, Sir Commodity, that tickling smooth-faced gentleman, shows the way to some crown or other.

But the religious controversies of the sixteenth century had also produced men of conscience and integrity, martyrs to the seriousness of an oath. In his best-selling *Actes and Monumentes* (first English edition in 1563, revised and enlarged in 1570, again revised in 1576 and 1583), John Foxe had burned their heroism into the minds of English readers. In the Thirty-nine Articles, the pastors of the Anglican church swore an oath on the seriousness and solemnity of oaths. Oaths were not to be flouted. Wound up in them was the curse of the Christian God. As Richard invited the audience to join him in a comic league of oath-breakers, great suspecters of the forthcomingness of the curses incurred in oath-breach, men who might even be driven to conclude, as Richard will say in his Nietzschean (but originally Platonic) comment before the Battle of Bosworth Field,[15] "Conscience is but a word that cowards use,/Devis'd at first to keep the strong in awe" (*R3* 5.3.310–11), he also makes them aware that God does indeed forbid forswearing.

So there must have been an edge of fear and uneasiness in the comic identification between Richard and the bias of the world in Shakespeare's audience. Even if broken daily, and a fit target for worldly wit, oaths were still dangerous, still solemn, and he who trifled with an oath might just be trifling with the power of an angry God. Most divines would have agreed with Calvin that "we should not rashly or perversely abuse his Holy Word and worshipped mysteries either for the sake of our own ambition, or greed, or amusement," lest the name of God be "little by little rendered contemptible."[16] Perkins switches from his account of Machiavellian dissimulation to a brief homily on the obligation that binds conscience to God: "But let all such as fear God, make conscience of their word, because they are bound so to do" (109). Here we might also weigh the testimony of Bishop Gilbert Burnet, expounding on the thirty-ninth article, "Of Christian man's oath," in 1759. A false oath

> is an Act of open Defiance, which must either suppose a Denial of his [God's] knowing all Things, or a Belief that he has forsaken the Earth, and has no regard to the Actions of Mortals; or finally, it is a bold venturing on the Justice and Wrath of God, for the serving of some present End, or the gaining of some present Advantage.[17]

Richard openly defies, boldly ventures, for the sake of worldly end and advantage.

He stands between worldviews. He has seen Christian piety and acquired an immunity to its terrors. His brazen disregard for the customs and institutions of Christian morality holds an appeal for the audience. They love their comic Vice. They can see him at the same time as amusingly truthful and deceitfully evil. Audiences at popular entertainments perform this feat all the time, as Bethell maintains; Christopher Ricks reminds us that, although we can see Wittgenstein's duck/rabbit only as a duck or rabbit, we can see it as one while simultaneously knowing it as the other.[18] Richard taps currents of suspicion flowing in Elizabethan souls, flowing in their historical moment.[19] Though he may quote Plato while doing it, he takes on the ruthless policy of Machiavelli and the scornful intelligence of Nietzsche.

Richard III is heavy with portent. The third *Henry VI* play ends with the prophecy of Henry (5.6.37–56) and the curse of Margaret (5.5.63–65, 80). In an earlier moment of prophetic sight, Henry laid his hand on the head of young Henry, Earl of Richmond, the future Henry VII, destined victor over Richard III at Bosworth, and with "divining thoughts" declared him "England's hope" (4.6.68–70); the favorite of the gods has been sent off to Brittany, safe from the imminent terrors of Richard's reign. The feeling of a noose about to tighten, a floor about to drop, passes over to the opening of *Richard III*. Already in the cross hairs of destiny, Richard steps forth in soliloquy: Shakespeare had never and would never again begin a play this way.[20]

Richard has already told us in the unforgettable soliloquy of *Henry VI, Part 3* that "Love forswore me in my mother's womb" (3.2.153), and he begins his own play elaborating with delicious self-mockery on that cancelled promise:

I, that am rudely stamp'd, and want love's majesty
To strut before a wanton ambling nymph:
I, that am curtail'd of this fair proportion,
Cheated of feature by dissembling Nature,
Deform'd, unfinish'd, sent before my time
Into this breathing world scarce half made up

. . . .

Why, I, in this weak piping time of peace,
Have no delight to pass away the time,
Unless to spy my shadow in the sun,
And descant on mine own deformity.

(1.1.16–27)

It is now a time of peace, and the joys of peace, of courtship and love, are not for him. We are no doubt being prepared for his much-savored triumph over Lady Anne in the wooing scene. But in the last speech of the play, where Richmond hails the arrival in England of "smooth-fac'd peace," we may remember that Richard himself, in his opening speech, announced his alienation from peaceful times: "Now civil wars are stopp'd; peace lives again./That she may long live here, God say Amen" (5.5.40–41). The final words of the play confirm with divine sanction the self-expulsion Richard announced in the first words. The end clasps the beginning. Patterns stand complete.

What does it mean when Richard dies on Bosworth field? Fates of every kind converge on that end: narrative structure (a moralizing tragedy of one who rose through murder and treachery must end with his fall), mythic structure (the hunchbacked scapegoat, forced, as he himself says, to "buckle fortune on my back/To bear her burden whe'er I will or no" [3.7.227–28]), blood-feud logic (when someone has committed murders on both sides, the two factions can unite in taking revenge on him), political ideology (the ousting of a demon king clears the skies for the glory of the Tudor dynasty), providential justice (again the Christian God, as he will in the end, punishes sin), authorial design (an entire tetralogy written with his end in mind), audience satisfaction (somewhere around the slaughter of the princes, we have had enough). There is also the matter of androcide by the female gender. Against the writ of history and the laws of probability, Shakespeare has old Queen Margaret, his tiger wrapped in a woman's hide, wander into the court of Edward IV to renew her great curse. When she, a Lancastrian queen, sits down in act 4, scene 4 with two royal

women of the House of York to supervise the verbal quilt-
ing of their cherished ill-wishes for Richard, the Wars of the
Roses are imaginatively over. The sight of three cursing
women simply cannot bode well, and to the impact of that
tableau we must add the fact that one of these Richard-curs-
ers is his very own mother, who seems to have begun her
rejection of him when she bore him in her womb.

In *Henry VI, Part 3*, on a weird day, three suns rose in
the sky, to the amazement of Edward and Richard. Though
they did not know it at the time, their father had just been
murdered: the three suns represent, Edward decided, the
three sons of old York (2.1.25–40). On Bosworth field the
sun does not rise at all on the one remaining son of York:

> I have no brother, I am like no brother;
> And this word 'love', which greybeards call divine,
> Be resident in men like one another,
> And not in me: I am myself alone.
>
> (5.6.80–83)

So he has told us, and so finally he is. When Buckingham
cries "God save Richard, England's royal King," the citi-
zens stand dumbstruck (*R3* 3.7.22–26). If we have any
sympathy left for the character, we might feel in Richard at
the end of the play a first touch of the frosty isolation later
in store for Lear, Macbeth, and Coriolanus.

Cursing surely belongs to the rhetorical design of the play.
I would not classify it as a variety of promising. It takes us
back to the transformation of grief into revenge and can be
viewed as a special case of that transformation. Cursing is
what happens when a griever who would become a revenger
wants the power to exact revenge: the hate-speech of the

powerless. But cursing is, it seems to me, more an omen than a cause of Richard's downfall. Even Margaret, the queen mother of cursing, is not sure whether such malediction breaks through to the ear of God: "Can curses pierce the clouds and enter heaven" (1.3.195)?

In his superb recent study, *Revenge Tragedy: Aeschylus to Armageddon*, John Kerrigan rightly notes that the traditions of reforming zeal absorbed by Milton permitted him to pray for the just deliverance of divine curses: "Avenge, O Lord, thy slaughter'd saints," as one of his sonnets opens.[21] But the author is reckless in shifting back from Milton to Shakespeare with the idea that "the Christian view" presumes that "just anger is defensible" and "it is right to seek divine punishment through prayer."[22] In fact, as Keith Thomas has argued, the general drift of Protestantism was to deny to the clergy the power of calling down the curses of God. Even in a time of genuine persecution, such prayers were "believed to be petitionary rather than automatically effective."[23] Although, as Thomas goes on to note, this distinction was often lost in the heat of anger and frustration, Protestant theology discouraged men from praying for the defeat of their enemies. Anglican priests no longer cursed offenders with divine authority; the old General Sentence of Excommunication was replaced by the "Commination service," in which the minister, naming no names, reads out divine sentences against classes of vice. Whatever aura of fear or plausibility that might surround a specific curse arose, not from theology or church sanction, but popular sentiment.[24]

In his classic article on "The Objectivity of the Ghosts in Shakespeare," E. E. Stoll proposed that in portraying the fulfillment of the curses in *Richard III*, Shakespeare was merely exemplifying the beliefs of his age:

Not only do the curses hold, but, as in the most benighted byways of folklore, they hold by the letter only and to the last jot and tittle. Queen Anne and Buckingham unwittingly curse themselves, the fiendish Queen Margaret, herself bowing under the curse of York, curses eight princes one after the other, and Richard is cursed by his mother; and of all these every particular syllable comes true as if the gods kept books. In such matters Shakespeare knew not reason or symbol, where we moderns know nothing else. . . . We have been dealing with his art, but his art was the frank, unconcerned utterance of his belief. And of that of his age, to be sure.[25]

But it is truly misleading to ignore the shadings of belief in the continuum stretching from theology and church doctrine to popular superstition.

Cursing, though woven deep into the play's fate patterns, still belongs to superstition. But oaths and vows have real weight in the play, full Christian weight. Margaret once again points the way. Unrecognized for a long while in act 1, scene 3, her many asides rephrase the speeches of the court, Richard's in particular, as sharp denunciations and vile curses. But one of her asides seems itself to stand aside, allowing God to specify both the punishment and its timing:

Rich. Poor Clarence did forsake his father Warwick,
Ay, and forswore himself—which Jesu pardon—
Marg. [*Aside*] Which God revenge.

(1.3.135–37)

At the head of this crowded parade of prophecies, portents, and patterns stand oaths and vows.

The centrality of oath-breach may be discerned in the long and remarkably theological scene of the murder of Clarence, which foreshadows Richard's troubled night before the final battle. Clarence, as later Richard, awakens from a dream of guilt and accusation. Richard and he are aboard a ship. Richard seems to slip, knocking Clarence into the water; the dream foretells not just his death in the butt of malmsey, but the last of several disillusionments awaiting him. The murderers must tell poor, simple Clarence repeatedly that "You are deceived: your brother Gloucester hates you" (1.4.221). Richard's dream slip was a push, a death thrust, and it will happen in truth when Richard's murdering agents shout for Clarence to "Look behind you, my Lord" (258)—and stab him in the back.

As the dream continues, the drowning Clarence will be welcomed by fiends into hell after he hears two accusing voices. His father-in-law, Warwick, cries out, "What scourge for perjury / Can this dark monarchy afford false Clarence" (50–51)? When reconverting to Edward's cause in *Henry VI, Part 3*, Clarence does release himself from a sacred oath by charging it with impiety, and his oath-breach does call forth a denunciation from Warwick (5.1.88–109). But it is a touch puzzling to find him so guilty about this infidelity. After all, his imprisonment stems ultimately from the fact that he broke his allegiance to Edward in the first place: this is the treachery that now makes him vulnerable to the king's suspicions. The second voice in the dream, that of Prince Edward, stabbed by all three York brothers at Tewkesbury, accuses Clarence of murder. No surprises there—except that Edward's angelic ghost repeats the charge of perjury: "Clarence is come: false, fleeting, per-jur'd Clarence" (*R3*

1.4.55). It would appear that the crimes of perjury and murder have almost equal billing in Clarence's conscience-stricken dream.

Now Richard's black agents enter the Tower. The two murderers, the first eager to pocket his fee and the second suffering from bouts of conscience, externalize the audience's double-sided identification with double-sided Richard. One obeys the bias of the world. The other fears his conscience, which reminds him of being "damned for killing him" (108). Ultimately the first murderer will do the stabbing and the drowning while the second stands by "like Pilate," wishing he could "wash my hands of this most grievous guilty murder" (262–63).

Before the crime is done, however, we are treated to a prolonged episode of pleading and accusation. The murderers suddenly seem like magistrates, charged with the legalities of indictment and punishment. When Edward insists that he is not "convict by course of law" (176) and goes on to note in a Biblical vein that vengeance in any case belongs to God, the murderers proceed to list his crimes and identify themselves as the agents of divine revenge:

> 2 *Mur.* And that same vengeance doth He hurl on thee,
> For false forswearing, and for murder too:
> Thou didst receive the sacrament to fight
> In quarrel of the House of Lancaster.
> 1 *Mur.* And like a traitor to the name of God
> Didst break that vow, and with thy treacherous blade
> Unrip'st the bowels of thy sovereign's son.
> 2 *Mur.* Whom thou wast sworn to cherish and defend.
>   (190–97)

"And for murder too": what we are prone to think the greater crime comes in almost incidentally, and when the first murderer finally gets to the stabbing of Edward, the terribleness of the deed is made to reside mostly in the fact that its doing broke a vow, arose from forswearing; even the knife he used was a "treacherous blade." The scene alerts us to the fact that moral energies deep in the play are advancing the knotty question of oath-breach, conscience, guilt, and divine vengeance.

The first of the two great oath scenes in the play, act 2 scene 1, occurs immediately after the murder of Clarence, with its emphatic concern over the crime of perjury. Ill and dying, Edward IV wants desperately to heal the enmity between his old allies and his new relatives by marriage. Heaven is on his mind. He asks the squabblers to "take each other's hand" and "swear your love" (7–8). One by one, they do exactly that. Their oaths are fully sworn, the curses fully specified. Hastings: "So thrive I, as I truly swear the like" (11). Hastings again, varying the formula: "So prosper I, as I swear perfect love" (16). Rivers, accepting the formula: "And I, as I love Hastings with my heart" (17). Queen Elizabeth: "There, Hastings: . . . so thrive I and mine" (23–24).

Edward lays out the presuppositions of these oaths:

Take heed you dally not before your King,
Lest he that is the supreme King of kings
Confound your hidden falsehood, and award
Either of you to be the other's end.

(12–15)

Confound—a word the play will use again at a crucial point—means "to mix and mingle, confuse," and in the context of cursing is often synonymous with "bring to perdition" (*OED* 2), where perdition is the cosmological site of confusion and base mixture. Edward warns that "hidden falsehood" in these oaths may lead by God's plotting to the defeat or ruin of the false party by the party he inwardly detests. He directs his charges to kiss and embrace. Edward is trying through the instrument of the oath to make of his court a peaceable kingdom, elevated by solemn vows above the ill will of this imperfect world.

But of course none of these people will thrive. Rivers and Hastings have a date with the axe. Buckingham is the most copious in specifying his curses, and the play is answerably meticulous in dropping every last one of them on his head. He asks for it—indeed, begs for it:

> Whenever Buckingham doth turn his hate
> Upon your Grace, but with all duteous love
> Doth cherish you and yours, God punish me
> With hate in those where I expect most love.
> When I have most need to employ a friend,
> And most assured that he is a friend,
> Deep, hollow, treacherous, and full of guile
> Be he unto me: this do I beg of God,
> When I am cold in love to you or yours.
>
> (32–40)

And so, when Buckingham turns his hate to the child of Elizabeth, God punishes him with the hatred of Richard, the apparent friend who fails to keep his promise of an earldom ("I claim the gift, my due by promise" [4.2.87]), and eventually, inevitably, the duke, captured and on his way to be executed, remembers the specifications of his oath

(5.1.12–24). Just as Edward IV warned he should not, Buckingham "dallied" with the "high All-seer" and has in the end been "given in earnest what I begged in jest." Case closed.

But for the time being the future is as hidden as the falsehood of these oath-takers. They smile, kiss, hug. Whereupon Richard enters, to tremendous effect. Into this outwardly peaceable kingdom steps the crooked man of saintly show and inward evil. He personifies hidden falsehood, and his sudden presence in the room demonstrates as no argument could the utter futility of Edward's little community of the oath. Richard pretends to take part in their rites of communal love, but he does not—and this has to matter— swear their oaths. When he quietly drops the news of Clarence's death, the peaceable kingdom comes crashing down to earth. "All-seeing heaven," Elizabeth exclaims, "what a world is this" (83)? The real kingdom, ruled by a dying monarch and now with one uncle fewer to protect its heir, foresees the renewal of civil war. The audience, having witnessed the creation by oath of an ideal community, is back with the disillusioned comedy of their villainous companion. The bias of the world has as usual changed the path of vowed intent.

The next great drama of oath-taking in the play is the so-called second wooing scene. Richard is now king. The princes are dead; James Tyrrel, the impoverished noble who hired the second set of two assassins, informs us that this time *both* murderers fell victim to "conscience and remorse" (4.3.20). Richard, remembering his success with Lady Anne, will now go forth "a jolly thriving wooer" (43) for the daughter of Queen Elizabeth, his very own niece, herself named Elizabeth, the destined bride of Richmond after his victory at Bosworth: the first Tudor Queen Elizabeth. I find this one of the two best scenes in the play, rivaled only by the first wooing scene, but I have promising on my mind.[26]

Up to this point, Richard in his own play has made no solemn vows—at least not onstage. The incredible success of the first wooing scene involves risking his life, opening his breast to a knife, and then offering, should it be Anne's wish, to plunge it in himself. But he manages the seduction without swearing a false oath. To be sure, he has the habit of idle swearing, making incidental and unnecessary oaths, oaths without conscience, oaths that make a show of saintliness, oaths that Calvin condemned by reference to "Paul's teaching that whatever is done apart from faith is sin."[27] He has a certain superstitiousness about cursing. At one point he interrupts a Margaret tirade, sure to end on the word "Richard," and interjects the word "Margaret" (1.3.233–34). Soon thereafter he makes a show of forgiving the enemies of the House of York but tells us in an aside that had he cursed them, he would have cursed himself (318–19). Given the way ill words come back to haunt their speakers in this tragedy, Richard's touch of superstition may be well founded.

But if he does harbor inside him some remnant of the fear of oaths and curses, he breaks all the rules of security in the second wooing scene. It is clear immediately that Elizabeth will do anything to keep her daughter from Richard, even to the loss of honor entailed by declaring her illegitimate (4.4.211). When her thoughts turn to the murdered princes, Richard appeals to astrology: "Lo, at their birth good stars were opposite" (216). Some other system of fate, not his purposed actions, led to their deaths: "All unavoided is the doom of destiny" (218). But Elizabeth knows too much, and is too good a Calvinist, to fall for this strained excuse: "True, when avoided grace makes destiny" (219). The scapegrace Richard made their bloody ends. Actions speak louder than words. His past actions strong against him, Richard has nothing but words to use in gaining the trust of Elizabeth.

How can he turn this angry and savvy woman? How can he salvage in this instance his great pride in his ability to cozen and command? How can this champion among manipulators, the man who would put the murderous Machiavel to school, triumph over these odds?

He turns to the strategy he has so far avoided, the false oath. His first formula is the same one used by the peaceable kingdom of Edward IV. Belatedly, Richard will join their community of love, and swear their vow:

> Madam, so thrive I in my enterprise
> And dangerous success of bloody wars,
> As I intend more good to you and yours
> Than ever you or yours by me were harm'd.
>
> (236–39)

The audience that has followed the great deceiver in his rise to the throne, the entire universe of the play, here cries out "Mistake! You yourself have just invited God to prepare his curse!" Consider a parallel moment in *Hamlet*'s play-within-the-play:

> *Player Queen. Nor earth to me give food, nor heaven light,*
> *Sport and repose lock from me day and night,*

To desperation turn my trust and hope,
And anchor's cheer in prison be my scope,
Each opposite, that blanks the face of joy,
Meet what I would have well and it destroy,
Both here and hence pursue me lasting strife,
If, once a widow, ever I be wife.
Ham. If she should break it now.
Player King. 'Tis deeply sworn.

(3.2.211–20)

One can imagine the audience at *Richard III*, Hamlet-like, crying out at the moment of his vow, "Should God let him go now!" Like Buckingham and Hastings before him, Richard has sworn a false oath inviting the wrath of God upon his head. The future licks its chops.

When Richard confesses (false) love for Elizabeth's daughter, offering the prize of a queenship and advancement for Dorset, she simply won't believe him. Besides, the alliance would be incestuous (4.4.337–42). In the face of such intransigence, Richard begins another round of vowing. None of the oaths will do. Everything he swears by he has already profaned. George, the Garter, the crown—all profaned. The world? Full of his wrongs. His father's death? Dishonored by his life. "Then by my self—" Surely nothing else in this world has been more sacred to Richard than "my self": that ought to do it! But no, "Thy self is self-misus'd" (376). Shakespeare is on a wonderful run of intellectual comedy here. The great deceiver, ever more desperate for trust and credibility, wanting to make a vow to another human being, and running through the chain of sacred touchstones available in their shared culture. Not even *his self*? If that is not good enough, just what might do?

What might this woman think is above the self? Richard, reckless now, plunges ahead. "Why then, by God—" How out of touch could he be? For of course, "God's wrong is most of all" (377). Richard has played what looks to be the highest card in his hand. Even Elizabeth cannot imagine another move: "What can'st thou swear by now" (387)?

But Richard is a master, a tactician of unparalleled brilliance. There is in fact one thing that he has not profaned, that indeed no living person has profaned. Richard is about to make a move in the great game of securing trust that saintly devils in time to come will study and ponder. Richard's audience, perhaps turned against him at this point, perhaps certain with Elizabeth that no other move can be made, will certainly ponder in time to come his next brilliant vow. "The time to come." The white, blank, innocent future! The time to which, as we saw in the last chapter, promises regularly refer—the time open to renovation and reform. Elizabeth, still unmoved, replies that his past crimes have poisoned with grief the time to come.

The scene goes on. But the play will remember this proffered vow. In its last speech, Richmond prays that God "Enrich the time to come" (5.5.32): Tudor time, a good time of peace and plenty, whose riches depend on Richard's absence from it.

Reaching for young Elizabeth, Richard is trying to stake out for his "self" a lot in "time to come." Earlier he lured her with the promise of grandchildren:

If I have kill'd the issue of your womb,
To quicken your increase, I will beget
Mine issue of your blood.

(4.4.296–98)

As a kind of epilogue to this memorable interview, he will repeat the same gesture of amends:

> *Eliz.* Yet thou didst kill my children.
> *K. Rich.* But in your daughter's womb I bury them,
> Where, in that nest of spicery, they will breed
> Selves of themselves, to your recomfiture.
>
> (422–25)

The word *bury* carries the double sense of a ritual of interment and a sexual entrance. The two are crossed in Richard's mind because he supposes that grandchildren, the children he will sire when he "buries" young Elizabeth, will replace the mother's dead princes. In his dreams, at least, Richard Crookback wants to put his dick into the Tudor dynasty. That won't be allowed. The time to come on Bosworth field will eject him from that "nest of spicery."

After his failure with the master stroke of time to come, Richard can improve on his vow only by worsening the penalties to be incurred. He restates the "so thrive I" formula associated with Edward's peaceable kingdom and spells out what will lie in store, should his vow prove false, for the time to come:

> As I intend to prosper and repent,
> So thrive I in my dangerous affairs
> Of hostile arms! Myself myself confound!
> God and fortune, bar me happy hours!
> Day, yield me not thy light, nor, night, thy rest!
> Be opposite, all planets of good luck,
> To my proceeding if with dear heart's love,
> Immaculate devotion, holy thoughts,

I tender not thy beauteous, princely daughter.
In her consists my happiness and thine;
Without her follows to myself, and thee,
Herself, the land, and many a Christian soul,
Death, desolation, ruin, and decay.

(397–409)

In the last four lines, Richard, still cunning, shifts from oath to prophecy. If Elizabeth will not believe an oath-swearer, maybe she will be persuaded by a foreteller, especially one whose vision makes the only possible future happiness for himself, herself, her daughter, their country, and many a Christian soul rest on the proposed marriage. Elizabeth will leave the scene bewildered, or pretending to be bewildered, apparently consenting to bear Richard's suit to her daughter. But I think she knows self-confounding when she sees it. The last act of the drama will soon edit and reformulate the prophecy that might have impressed her with Richard's persistent resourcefulness. In "her," in young Elizabeth, does in fact consist the future happiness of everyone listed—save Richard. Edward IV's fantasy of a good world purged of enmity reemerges, much improved, as Tudor England. Richard has already ejected himself from that future in the conditional oath-curses preceding his prophecy. He has himself himself confounded.

With these oaths Richard seals his fate, precisely as Buckingham had. The formulation that first appeared in Elizabeth's "Thy self is self-misus'd" now reappears in "Myself myself confound." He will fail in arms, fail in happiness; the sun will not rise the morning of the battle, and the night before it will bring him no rest; his opponents will be aglow with good luck. Richard brings the end of the play on himself, a great deceiver broken at last by the very structure of an oath, which turns out to be, in the world of the play, a well-contrived instrument for demonstrating human trustworthiness.

That, I think, is Shakespeare's trumping irony at the end of this rising comic catalogue of a desperate man's desperate measures. To gain hard-won trust, wary and suspicious trust, one finally has to risk calling down curses on oneself—and therefore, if there is a just God witnessing our oaths, to defeat and destroy oneself. The career of a deceiver in this oath-swearing society is ultimately self-confounding.

There are, to put this another way, at least two truths about an oath. Truth 1 is the good faith and fidelity of the swearer. Truth 2 is the truth of the oath structure itself. Is there a witnessing God to deliver the specified curses in the event of falsehood and bad faith? Although the glamorously wicked character of Richard has encouraged the audience to waver between oath-respect and the bias of the world, the play ultimately comes down to an oath's truth. When Truth 1 fails, Truth 2 proceeds as requested. Machiavelli and Nietzsche can get loose in Shakespeare's world, but in *Richard III* there are traps in place to destroy them. I hope to have demonstrated that one of these is an oath.

Hard upon the second wooing scene, Richard awakens to his famous attack of conscience. It is almost as if the terrible and self-defeating oaths he has just sworn compel him to open an inward place, a location in the self, appropriate to their seriousness. It is almost as if he has interalized the skeptical voice of Elizabeth. With full awareness, at last, he again himself himself confounds:

Give me another horse! Bind up my wounds!
Have mercy, Jesu!—soft, I did but dream.
O coward conscience, how dost thou afflict me!
The light burns blue; it is now dead midnight.
Cold fearful drops stand on my trembling flesh.
What do I fear? Myself? There's none else by;
Richard loves Richard, that is, I am I.
Is there a murderer here? No. Yes, I am!
Then fly. What, from myself? Great reason why,
Lest I revenge? What, myself upon myself?
Alack, I love myself. Wherefore? For any good
That I myself have done unto myself?
O no, alas, I rather hate myself
For hateful deeds committed by myself.
I am a villain—yet I lie, I am not!
Fool, of thyself speak well! Fool, do not flatter.
My conscience hath a thousand several tongues
And every tongue brings in a several tale,
And every tale condemns me for a villain:
Perjury, perjury, in the highest degree;
Murder, stern murder, in the direst degree;
All several sins, all us'd in each degree,
Thronging to the bar, crying all, 'Guilty, guilty!'
I shall despair. There is no creature loves me,
And if I die, no soul will pity me—
And wherefore should they, since that I myself
Find in myself no pity to myself?
Methought the souls of all that I had murder'd
Came to my tent, and every one did threat
Tomorrow's vengeance on the head of Richard.

(5.3.178–207)

Much has been written about the duality, the dialogue of self and self, in the first half of the speech.[28] Formerly the doubleness in Richard was that of apparent saint and hidden devil. There has been no sign of schism in the partnership; Richard has indeed loved Richard, and no one else, and feared no one, pitied no one. "I that have neither pity, love, nor fear" (*3Hen6* 5.6.68). But here the saintly exterior, once mere façade, seems to develop a mind of its own and refuse the villain both recognition and love: "O no, alas, I rather hate myself."

Why this self-hatred? Why the unprecedented despair of "alas"? Why this sudden fit of misrecognition and dishonesty? "I am a villain—yet I lie, I am not!" It must be the struggle of a man awakening to conscience, a man whose new capacity for self-accusation is coming on so quickly that the gut response of his former self, full of prideful self-love, is just to say "No," "I love myself," "I lie, I am not [a villain]." Words have not changed. They are the same words. "I am determined to prove a villain," we heard him say in his opening soliloquy. But now words have the weight of moral judgment buckled onto their backs. "I am I." Imagine an actor phrasing it "I am *I*?!" Richard is struggling for honest self-apprehension in this new atmosphere of felt moral meaning.

After all the complex things have been said about the first half of the speech, its simple power waits for us in the terrific contrary proverbs of "Fool, of thyself speak well! Fool, do not flatter." Not flattering is exactly the process we have been discussing: the reunion between language and morality. He has ever loved himself, ever spoken well of himself, even when using words like *villain* about himself. But now conscience speaks the word. He feels the sting of abhorrence it prompts in ordinary God-fearing Elizabethan speakers of the English language. The new self-indicting voice has to fight the old fool, the flatterer, long mindful of the "good"— the worldly good, the commodity—he was doing for himself. The new voice is simply that of conscience, for whom *good* has another sense, just as *villain* has another feel. After "Fool, do not flatter" Richard, winning the battle for honest self-apprehension, lets conscience have its say.

In his suggestive essay "Conscience and Conscious" in *Studies in Words*, C. S. Lewis wrote of how a root meaning "knowing with" or "privy to," pointing at some rudimentary form of self-awareness, gradually headed toward "guide," "judge," and "law-giver."[29] Richard's conscience has interiorized an entire trial.[30] Like all legal systems, the one in his mental kingdom hands down a verdict. There is honest testimony at this "bar," which has been variously interpreted as the wooden rail in a courtroom marking off the area around the judge's seat, or as a Roman tribunal, the platform on which magistrates had their chairs of office. It scarcely matters so far as the metaphorical identity of the thronging tongues is concerned. His confessing sins are witnesses, sworn witnesses no doubt, who truthfully, without perjury and without pity, tell their tales of self-accusation, "crying all, 'Guilty, guilty!'"[31]

The paired crimes of perjury and murder, wandering through the play since Clarence's death, come home to Richard's conscience. Clarence stood guilty of one of each— one perjury, one murder. Brought home to Richard, they are nightmarishly multiplied and raised to the highest degree of malicious intent. This inward trial burdens certain words, *charges* and *judgments*, with all the moral authority available in this world: "Perjury, perjury, in the highest degree;/

Murder, stern murder, in the direst degree." It has been a long career. But against whom has Richard been guilty of perjury? He has doubtless broken every oath he has ever sworn and has doubtless sworn many oaths. He probably swore one to Edward IV at his coronation. But we did not see that oath being sworn. He is of course "subtle, false, and treacherous" (1.1.37), and in that sense his whole career could be considered a prolonged experiment in the varieties of perjury. Then, too, there were, as I have emphasized, the false oaths to Elizabeth. But the marriage at issue, the "time to come," never came about, and to that extent his perjury in the second wooing scene remains conditional, however great its literary and dramatic impact. In real dramatic time, in the time during which we have known Richard, he has not committed much in the way of formal perjury. Buckingham is given to understand that he has a promise, but even here Richard avoids the more binding formulae (3.1.194–98). Why, then, the intense charge in the court of his conscience? What is perjury "in the highest degree"?

The profoundest perjury of which Richard has been guilty is against himself: the refusal to tell the truth about himself in the depths of his conscience, the self-flattering refusal through which he fights in the first half of the speech. In asides and soliloquies he has said of himself all the words that can be used to condemn him, but severed from their (as we might call it) conscience meaning. Only the outrage of *that* lie, a lie against God, a lie against the inward court of the self, a lie against the morality inhabiting our common language, can explain the otherwise mysterious priority given to the sin of perjury in Richard's soliloquy. It is the lie that has made possible his tickling self-love. It is the lie that has made him, up to now, unconscionable.

The final lines seem to advance the metaphor of the inward trial, in that the victims themselves, "the souls of all that I had murder'd," move us on from judgment to punishment: "and every one did threat/Tomorrow's vengeance on the head of Richard." But these lines also loop back to the dream from which Richard awakened at the beginning of his soliloquy, where the murdered souls were before us on the stage, enacting contrary dreams, as Richard and Richmond slept. Now we know from the opening of the soliloquy that Richard's dream, which he associates with "Tomorrow's vengeance," ended on the battlefield: "Give me another horse! Bind up my wounds!" A true foreseeing. Tomorrow's loss, the vengeance of his victims, the vengeance of God, has been previewed in dreams. Inasmuch as these dreams inspire his attack of conscience, that, too, must belong to vengeance and punishment. Conscience requires that Richard for a moment see himself as his victims see him.

No flattering perjury obscures the second half of the speech. God's vengeance on the head of Richard is a brief episode of honest morality. I cannot help appreciating here a design that no audience could possibly apprehend, even if they saw *Henry VI, Part 3* and *Richard III* scrunched together, which of course they did not in Shakespeare's day. "No," Richard told his father in his first characteristic irony, "God forbid your grace should be forsworn." In handling the case of this false seemer, God finally *does* forbid it. Richard must behold his conscience swearing to the inward judge in himself the truth about himself. A first irony spun into a last irony: this can only bespeak Shakespeare's incomparable intellectual plotting. According to the Elizabethan homily on perjury, the secrets of a perjured conscience closed to the judges of this world will stand revealed at the ultimate trial:

> And although such perjured men's falsehood be now kept secret, yet it shall be opened at the last day, when the secrets of all men's hearts shall be manifest to all the world. And then the truth shall appear, and accuse them: and their own conscience, with all the blessed company of heaven, shall bear witness truly against them.[32]

From this perspective, his episode of bad conscience brings home a foretaste of his full and complete judgment. He who flaunted his indifference to the fear of God in swearing deceitful oaths must for a moment feel, on the eve of his defeat, the sting of that fear.

I have shown, and surely am not the first to do so, that Richard's dreams and the conscience they arouse can be interpreted as divine judgment. He is one of those villains who would jump the life to come. "God take King Edward to his mercy," he joyfully remarks, "And leave the world for me to bustle in" (1.1.151–52). But in such cases we still have judgment here, here in the temporal kingdom and here in the inward kingdom of conscience.

By the same token, however, it might seem as if divine judgment can be interpreted as Richard's dreams and the conscience they arouse. The soliloquy offers the possibility of reducing the entire Christian heft of the play to some mix of psychology, sociology, philosophy, and politics: modern thought in the modern world, oaths without curses, curses without risks, Truth 1 without Truth 2.

Richard takes this very tack in his last word on the dread of an honest conscience. Himself again, he strikes back at God's inward morality play:

> Let not our babbling dreams affright our souls;
> Conscience is but a word that cowards use,
> Devis'd at first to keep the strong in awe.
> Our strong arms be our conscience, swords our law.
>
> (5.3.309–12)

Man made conscience, and man can beat it. What we have here is more than a reassertion of Richard's character, for the lines also imply that the apparently providential machinery of the enacted dreams and the midnight soliloquy are merely episodes in the psycho-social history of conscience. Richard strikes at the *meaning* of the play. Though he will lose the forthcoming battle, Richard might still enjoy a victory over the interpretation of his defeat. In his eyes, it can mean no more than the stronger winning over the less strong, and all its providential overtones just another example of the ideological mystifications "Devis'd at first to keep the strong in awe."

The tradition of Machiavelli, Hobbes, and Nietzsche would, on this reading, inherit the play. But it seems to me a lie to translate Shakespeare entirely into the terms of modern worldliness. At this point in his career, Shakespeare understands oaths in their full Christian context: Truth 2 undergirds Truth 1. His grandfathers probably swore the Oath of Succession. His final play, *Henry VIII*, which ends with the christening of Elizabeth, might be considered a belated subscription to that oath and certainly looks for all the world like a reaffirmation of the Tudor patriotism of the first tetralogy.[33] If we do our best to get inside the dramatic world Shakespeare intended to create, then look around for ourselves, we realize that his art is not yet ready to submit without remainder to our post-Christian analysis of power. He just eyes us, warily.

With promising still in mind, Shakespeare designed the second tetralogy, beginning with the elaborately dismantled oaths in *Richard II*. Over the next three plays, Hal establishes himself as a master of promising. His first soliloquy reveals promises made to himself. Their unfolding comprises the dramas to come. Falstaff wants Hal to promise him security and preferment during his reign—an assurance that something like the rejection scene will never happen. But the prince, waiting to redeem his prodigal time, makes no promises to Falstaff and every now and then, most memorably in the tavern theatrics of *Henry IV, Part 1*, act 2, scene 4, forewarns him of the inward promises awaiting their austere fulfillment. He solemnly vows before his father ("This in the name of God I promise here" [3.2.153]) that Hotspur will be divested of his honors. In the next play he again swears before his father ("God witness with me" [2*Hen*4 4.5.149]), with specified curses, that he believed the king to be dead when he reluctantly took the crown. *Henry V* concludes the second tetralogy with two interwoven promises, political and personal: his treaty with France and his troth-plight with Katharine. He is as true, and crafty in his truth, as Richard is false, and crafty in his falsehood.

3

Obligation in Venice

〜〜

*T*he management of the double plot in *Merchant* has been much admired. Shakespeare probably began with a prose novella in Ser Giovanni's *Il Pecorone*. Here he found the basic idea of a Venetian merchant who signs a flesh bond with a Jew in order to finance a young man's courtship of the Lady of Belmont. The young man tries three times to bed the lady but twice fails because he drinks a glass of drugged wine. On the third attempt, warned to avoid the wine, he succeeds. Shakespeare discarded the Belmont plot of *Il Pecorone* and in its place substituted, though with interesting variations, a story about gaining a spouse through a choice among gold, silver, and lead caskets found in the *Gesta Romanorum*, an ancient collection of romances and folk tales.[1]

Johnson declared that the "union of two actions in one event is, in this drama, eminently happy."[2] In the manner of nineteenth-century criticism, H. H. Hudson marveled at "what a wide diversity of materials this play reconciles and combines":

> The greatness of the work is thus hidden in its fine proportions. In many of the poet's dramas we are surprised at the great variety of character: here, besides this, we have a remarkable variety of plot. And, admirable as may be the skill displayed in the characters individually considered, the interweaving of so many several plots, without the least confusion or embarrassment, evinces a still higher mastership. For, many and various as are the forms and aspects of life here shown, they all emphatically live together, as if they all had but one vital circulation.[3]

In 1962 Sigurd Burckhardt, using the language of the New Criticism but returning unwittingly to Hudson's praise of "one vital circulation," discovered the play's "controlling metaphor" in the circularity of its plot:

> One of Shakespeare's apparently most fanciful plots proves to be one of the most exactingly structured: it is what it should be: the play's controlling metaphor. As the subsidiary metaphors of the bond and the ring indicate, *The Merchant* is a play about circularity and circulation; it asks how the vicious circle of the bond's law can be transformed into the ring of love.[4]

Like the rings of Bassanio and Gratiano, like ducats and journeys, the plot is in fact circular—or really twice circular. The double plot completes a circle in the trial scene, then begins a second one. Chains of promises fast bind the two circles. I hope to reveal the excellence "hidden" in the play's "fine proportions," while proving that something more substantial than a metaphor controls the "exactingly structured" circularities of its plot.

I have evoked the terms of harmony, but I am well aware that no play in the canon has been subject to more diverse readings, has occasioned more confessions of discordant aesthetic experience, than *Merchant*. Shylock is the question, at least for modern interpreters. Empson found a space for the comedy in one of his types of ambiguity, "a generous skepticism which can believe at once that people are and are not guilty."[5] A. D. Moody, feeling with Hazlitt that Shylock is wronged by hypocritical Christians, tried to discern how the unruly irony of the play might be preserved in a somewhat coherent apprehension of the last act. The main danger, as he saw it, is that when the Christian characters recongregate in Belmont during act 5, "what they offer for our diversion ceases to please, for the heart is sensible of its connection with evil."[6] In 1972 Norman Rabkin stopped trying for harmony, at least of the conventional sort. His famous essay attacked our "bias toward rationality" in searching for a single coherent "meaning" of such a disparate and unsettling play.[7] The rings of provisional minimeanings tripped by disparate signals never stop, fuse, harden, and make sense but just keep on expanding, until we get a play that is circular almost in the manner of Nicholas of Cusa, its center everywhere and nowhere, its circumference an infinite expanse wherein responses and counter-responses bombinate. I hope we do not have to say goodbye to our rational bias for coherent meaning simply because there are tricky binaries in *The Merchant of Venice*.

Though Shylock is a disturbing character, he belongs to the exacting structure of the plot.

As a measure of how overheated some of the commentary on this play has always been, especially so in recent years, we might look briefly at an influential essay by René Girard. He fixes on a moment between Gratiano and Nerissa in act 3. After the marriages have been arranged in Belmont, Gratiano is, as usual, brimming with gusto for popular sports:

> *Gra.* We'll play with them the first boy for a thousand ducats.
> *Ner.* What! and stake down?
> *Gra.* No, we shall ne'er win at that sport and stake down.
>
> (3.2.214–16)

Gratiano suggests to Nerissa that they wager a thousand ducats with Bassanio and Portia over which couple has the first boy. Nerissa, never having seen so much money, cannot imagine how they might come up with "stake down"— that is, put the stakes down, one thousand ducats on the line. Thinking of Elizabethan proverbs like "as stiff as a stake," Gratiano replies that they cannot go "stake down" and expect to win at *that* sport.[8]

For Girard, this bit of bawdy festers with unpleasant implications. He quotes the first line of this passage, then mesmerizes himself with irony:

> Gratiano's baby will be two thousand ducats cheaper than Antonio's pound of flesh. Human flesh and money in Venice are constantly exchanged for one another.

People are turned into objects of financial speculation. Mankind has become a commodity, an exchange value like any other. I cannot believe that Shakespeare did not perceive the analogy between Gratiano's wager and Shylock's pound of flesh.[9]

Granted, metaphors of wealth and idioms of finance pile up like mountains of ducats in the Belmont plot. "Who chooseth me, must give and hazard all he hath," the lead casket is inscribed, and *hazard* is a key word in the mercantile capitalism of Venice, denoting not just the hazard of sending out a trading ship full of goods but also the goodness of mercantile profits, profits earned from hazard as opposed to the riskless profits made by usurers. Shakespeare was deliberately departing from the inscription in his main source: "They that choose me, shall find [in] me that God hath disposed."[10] In making this change, Burckhardt maintained, Shakespeare freed the old story "from a pious falsification. For its meaning was that it sprang from a series of ventures, of hazards; it was propelled by the risks Antonio, Bassanio, Portia, and up to a point, Shylock were willing to take. Its ethic was that of venture capitalism raised to the moral level."[11] Perhaps so, though I think Shakespeare may have had something older and more durable in mind.

"Marriage is destiny," as the Elizabethan proverb went.[12] Portia terms the casket game "the lott'ry of my destiny" (2.1.15). You always take a chance when giving all of yourself in exchange for all of someone else. You always take a chance on the vows. The word *wed* is cognate with Dutch, Icelandic, Old German, and German words meaning "wager."[13] Gratiano, not Girard, has the spirit of the moment. I think Shakespeare could tell the difference between a jesting wager and a "merry bond" concealing lethal hatred. I think he could tell the difference between an anticipated son and an attempted murder. Possibly Girard gets confused at the level of visual image. But I think Shakespeare knew the difference between a baby boy emerging from its mother's body and a pound of flesh being cut from a man's chest.

What is the seed of *Merchant*'s plot? Where does its double story begin? Shakespeare is quite precise, unusually precise, about this. We know that some years back, while Portia's father was still alive, Bassanio came to Belmont in the company of the Marquis of Montferrat (1.2.108–10). There was no talk of a casket choice in those days; the elaborate will was a deathbed inspiration (27–28). Portia took to him. "He of all men that ever my foolish eyes look'd upon, was the best deserving a fair lady" (112–13): this is Nerissa speaking, but her mistress thinks him worthy of the praise. As Portia's memory of the visit implies, nothing was said between them. Bassanio has already confirmed the silence: "sometimes from her eyes / I did receive fair speechless messages" (1.1.163–64). She looked on him with foolish eyes as a deserving romance hero, and he looked on her as the sender of "fair speechless messages." There must have been promise in that mutual beholding.

Now that Portia's father is dead, and his will is being obediently executed, Bassanio has heard the tales of well-bred young men streaming into Belmont from the deserts and seas. He has had some thoughts and as a first step toward putting them into action, has made an appointment with Antonio the merchant. The play opens with Antonio's mysterious melancholy, his "want-wit sadness" (6). Salerio (in Q1 Salerino, Salaryno, Salarino) and Solanio (in Q1

Salanio), who must have been named by the creator of Launcelot Gobbo, cannot help him to identify this enigmatic depression.[14] He is not worried about his goods being at hazard on the treacherous sea, though in terms of the plot, he should be. When Bassanio enters, the other men give way and disappear as if by intuition: the true source of the melancholy has arrived on the scene.

After they pass a few words about the long-winded Gratiano, Antonio gets down to business with Bassanio, and the double plot is conceived in one pregnant question:

> Well, tell me now what lady is the same
> To whom you swore a secret pilgrimage—
> That you today promis'd to tell me of?
>
> (119–21)

Two promises, both Bassanio's. One he "swore" to the Lady of Belmont, from whom, back when, he received speechless messages. The other he merely "promis'd" to Antonio, and now he meets his obligation in meeting him here today, on this stage at this moment, to tell him about the sworn vow of secret pilgrimage—how it bears on Antonio, the friend to whom he is already indebted. In the difference in majesty between "swore a secret pilgrimage" and "you today promis'd to tell me of" we can already sense the hurt, envious love for Bassanio that Antonio is too noble to admit to his friends, perhaps even, at this point, to himself.

The entire first circle of the play emerges from the propulsive force of these two promises. The vow sworn to Portia takes Bassanio to Belmont, casket choice, and marriage. But he cannot fulfill that vow without keeping the promise to meet Antonio. He must first be outfitted properly for the pilgrimage, and that means incurring a new debt. The promise kept to Antonio leads to another loan, which leads to the flesh bond with Shylock, which leads to Antonio's imprisonment and finally to the great courtroom scene at the end of act 4. The Venetian trail is a trail of credit and debt—the same transaction, passed along from Bassanio/Antonio to Antonio/Shylock and from Antonio/Shylock to Shylock/Tubal, who should get credit for being the supreme financier of the comedy. The Belmont trail is a trail of oath and vow—the same oath and vow, in effect, passed along from Portia's father to Bassanio to Portia, then ultimately back from Portia to Bassanio in the ring vow.

Each stage along the way, as the two plots unfold and arc back together in the trial scene, is marked by another promise, another variety of obligation. I ask you to think again of Antonio's opening remarks to Bassanio. Bassanio at that moment is a man sworn to go to Belmont, just now keeping a promise to Antonio, and about to secure a loan. The play is absolutely *driven* by obligation.

We'll stay in Venice for now. In terms of the double plot, Bassanio would seem to be the most divided of the characters. His secret pilgrimage to Belmont results in nuptial obligation to Portia; his kept promise in Venice results in a new—in fact, doubled—financial obligation to his friend Antonio. He stands between marriage and friendship, and one of the main tasks of the play is to sort out the competing claims of these two kinds of human bond. Until the end, however, we never see Bassanio himself in a state of conflict. In Belmont he is entirely the suitor/husband. In the trial scene he is, seduced by Antonio's plight, entirely the friend.

The display of complex inward division seen elsewhere in this cast, in Portia and Shylock, we find in Antonio, not Bassanio.

This interpretation of Antonio has been spurned by some of the play's best critics, Danson in particular.[15] He argues that Antonio's initial melancholy signifies his malice toward Shylock. Explaining the melancholy as a sign of hurt love for Bassanio constitutes in his view "the psychosexual explanation": the play is betrayed to Freudianism, which is presumed to lie outside the spirit or historical vista of Shakespearean drama. Freud may have some things to answer for, but he cannot be blamed for having invented the conflict between friendship ties and marriage ties, which must be a strong candidate for social universality. Did Freud write *The Two Gentlemen of Verona*, the *Sonnets*, and *Othello*? Today many people, male and female, gradually or abruptly lose some or all their friends when they marry. Moreover, the conflict that might be in Bassanio, but is instead in Antonio, can be fully elucidated in Elizabethan terms.

I think the opening scene of the play would have put its original audience in two minds:

> My purse, my person, my extremest means
> Lie all unlock'd to your occasions.
> . . . .
> You know me well, and herein spend but time
> To wind about my love with circumstance,
> And out of doubt you do me now more wrong
> In making question of my uttermost
> Than if you had made waste of all I have.
>
> (*MV* 1.1.138–39, 153–57)

Antonio demonstrates his love in the form of bottomless credit. Bassanio has available every last ducat in Antonio's pocket, plus whatever Antonio can raise on credit. There is both love and foolhardiness here. Words meant to express the depth of friendship—"extremest means," "made waste of all I have"—hover in air, waiting for the plot to deliver their ironic sense. The Renaissance produced an extensive literature on the nobility of male friendship, and Elizabethans, certainly those in the aristocratic portion of Shakespeare's audience, would have recognized that ideal in Antonio.

"Among friends all things are common," declared a Ciceronian proverb. But on whether "all things" included money, the friendship literature is mostly negative. Montaigne exalts male friendship to the very perfection of society, well above all other relationships, including marriage. Whereas friendship is freely and voluntarily enjoyed, marriage is "a bargain to which only the entrance is free—its continuance being constrained and forced, depending otherwise than on our will."[16] The plot of the comedy has, as we will see, absorbed this wisdom and seeks in its way to temper, while by no means denying, the weight of marital obligation. "A single dominant friendship dissolves all other obligations" (142), Montaigne continues, which is an ideal, and indeed a false ideal, as Portia will teach at some length in act 5. But part of this ideal for Montaigne is that business affairs stand apart from friendship: "all associations that are forged and nourished by pleasure and profit, by public or private needs, are the less beautiful and noble, and the less friendships, in so far as they mix into friendship another cause and object and reward than friendship itself" (136). It is just this mixture we find in Antonio. We might also bear in mind Polonius's still famous dictum about wise socializing: "Neither a borrower nor a lender be" (*Ham* 1.3.75). *Merchant* opens with one of each.

The sheer folly of Antonio unlocking to Bassanio his purse and person, a pun that perfectly captures the mixture of which Montaigne disapproves, is masked in part by the way Shakespeare invests Antonio with the morality of the Elizabethan usury tracts.[17] To loan without interest, in these haranguing pamphlets, represents neighborliness, charity, a proper regard for divine law and social good. Antonio's anti-Semitism is to a large degree drawn from the fervent, if unrealistic, condemnation of the usurer in these tracts: the asocial miser profiting from the misfortunes of his neighbors, breeding barren metals unnaturally, substituting contractual bonds for gifts of charity. Inasmuch as the audience is meant to enjoy the humiliation of Shylock, it must also be meant to admire the ideal charity of Antonio's unlocked purse. But ordinary prudence would caution against opening the "extremest means" of one's purse to a friend, however loved. As always, I look to the proverbs. On the one hand, "A friend in need is a friend indeed" and "A friend is never known till a man hath need." But on the other, "Who lends to a friend loses double" and "When I lend I am his friend, when I ask I am unkind."[18]

The passage usually put in evidence by critics who discern in Antonio a demonstration of martyred love for his friend is the account of Bassanio's departure for Belmont:

Sal. I saw Bassanio and Antonio part,
Bassanio told him he would make some speed
Of his return: he answered, "Do not so,
Slubber not business for my sake Bassanio,

But stay the very riping of the time,
And for the Jew's bond which he hath of me—
Let it not enter in your mind of love:
Be merry, and employ your chiefest thoughts
To courtship, and such fair ostents of love
As shall conveniently become you there."
And even there (his eye being big with tears),
Turning his face, he put his hand behind him,
And with affection wondrous sensible
He wrung Bassanio's hand, and so they parted.
Sol. I think he only loves the world for him,—

(2.8.36–50)

The dividedness in Antonio becomes palpable in gesture. Bassanio is to forget Antonio, forget the Jew's bond, and sail off to Belmont in an undivided state of mind, a "mind of love" for Portia. Bassanio is to be cleared for comedy, devoted wholly to merriness, courtship, and heterosexual love.

Antonio seizes the divided thoughts that might trouble his friend and hoards them secretly in himself. His weeping face is turned one way, his carefree hand, shaking Bassanio's, the other. Bassanio sees the devoted friend, unconcerned about his own fate. Antonio keeps to himself, at least for now, unknown and unappreciated, the sorrow of sacrificed love. He only loves the world because Bassanio is in it. Off to Belmont, Bassanio is no longer in his world. Ergo, he does not love it—hence his melancholy at the beginning of the play, when he merely suspected his friend's departure, and the full maturity of that sorrow in the hidden tears at his actual departure.

One recalls the passage in *Twelfth Night* where Viola,

disguised as Caesario, tells Orsino the story of her sister, who "never told her love,"

> But let concealment like the worm i' th' bud
> Feed on her damask cheek: she pin'd in thought,
> And with a green and yellow melancholy
> She sat like Patience on a monument,
> Smiling at grief. Was this not love indeed?
>
> (2.4.111–16)

Petrarchan love was the standard of the period. It often took place in solitude, recording tempests of emotion without much contact with its actual object. But the Petrarchan poets did indeed tell their love, over and over, in poems. The perfection of disinterested love would be complete concealment. Until, imprisoned, he sends his letter to Belmont, Antonio aspires to this purified Petrarchism.

Does Antonio grasp at this point in the play that he stands in extremest hazard with respect to Shylock's bond? We have reason to think not. Another consequence of his melancholy self-savoring of not only losing Bassanio but being so great a friend as to finance his own wound, is a blithe disregard for the malice Shylock bears him. Bassanio negotiates the initial arrangements. Antonio's entrance prompts Shylock's famous aside:

> How like a fawning publican he looks!
> I hate him for he is a Christian:
> But more, for that in low simplicity
> He lends out money gratis, and brings down
> The rate of usance here with us in Venice.
> If I can catch him once upon the hip,

I will feed fat the ancient grudge I bear him.
He hates our sacred nation, and he rails
(Even there where merchants most do congregate)
On me, my bargains, and my well-won thrift,
Which he calls interest: cursed be my tribe
If I forgive him!

(1.3.36–42)

Some of what Shylock resents in Antonio is the open, public, unconcealed manner in which the merchant has scorned him. He insults him in the place where business is done, in the Rialto, "(Even there where merchants most do congregate)." In public he calls him dog, in public he spits on his Jewish gabardine. "In the Rialto you have rated me / About my moneys and my usances" (102–3). Shylock seems fairly to be telling Antonio that locked within himself, expressed fully only in an aside, lies a scorn for Antonio greater even than Antonio's for Shylock. But a complacent Antonio never hears the undercurrent. He does not regret the spitting; he assures Shylock that he will spit again, loan or no loan. That self-satisfaction must be at once maddening to Shylock, the very thing he detests, and gratifying to Shylock, in that his scheme demonstrates and depends on this lack of emotional empathy.

We may put this blindness down to a confidence in his wealth: Antonio has so many ships out that some of them are bound to come in. But there is something more peculiar in his innocence. Antonio is willing to "break a custom" and pay interest on the three thousand ducats. Shylock, hatching his revenge, declares that he would be friends with Antonio, have his love, "Forget the shames that you have stain'd me with" (135). Should the money not be repaid in three months, he will receive, not interest, but "an equal pound / Of your fair flesh, to be cut off and taken / In what part of your body pleaseth me" (145–47). Moreover and ominously, in this transaction, unlike the loan Bassanio secured from Antonio, a Christian's word is *not* his bond. There must be a writ; Antonio is to meet Shylock "forthwith at the notary's."[19] Because the bond is written down, a proper capitalist contract, it can be made public and submitted to the law.

No doubt that feature of the revenge appeals to Shylock. All those public insults born in "suff'rance," "with a patient shrug" (104–5), can be returned in as public a fashion as they were given, returned to an enemy with seemingly no idea that his public execrations might breed in private a revenge bent on enjoying the same shameless openness as the wrongs that have nourished it. Antonio shakes the hand of Bassanio while hiding his grieving face. Shylock makes a merry deal with Antonio while hiding in an aside his vengeful face. In this symmetry there is already a latent sense that Antonio's hidden demonstration of love dovetails with Shylock's for-the-time-being hidden revenge against Antonio. Financing Bassanio's marriage is a great gesture of disinterested love. Dying to finance it will perfect the sacrifice, elevating his disinterest to a sublime Christian *amicitia*.

The portrayal of Shylock is, I suppose, unquestionably laced with anti-Semitism. But I confess that I am not sure precisely what *anti-Semitism* means when applied to this play. Maybe the word is justified by our knowledge that Elizabethan Christians were still given to immodest dramatizations of the superiority of their religion; that mercy stands higher than justice in both testaments; that blaming usury on Jews was a sad piece of scapegoating; that making a stock villain of the rich vengeful Jew created a general climate that eventually permitted worse things. Because the vice of anti-Semitism, however vaguely apprehended, infects the traditions behind Shylock, it is no wonder that the criticism of the play so often charges the Christian characters with scapegoating hypocrisy.

After a fashion, some rough awareness of such hypocrisy belongs to the genre. Historians of Christian drama speak of a metaphorical "Jewishness," in which the Jewish villain can sometimes bear to the audience an image of Christian sins.[20] An apt example might be Shylock's usury. Though there are occasional flourishes of anti-Semitism in the usury tracts, their authors realize full well that the moneylenders ruining England are Christians—not just rich merchants, goldsmiths, and monopolists, but farmers, craftsmen, and tradesmen who happen to have a little more money stashed away than their neighbors. By 1598 the English aristocracy was heavily in debt, dependent for its survival on credit financing; tenant farmers and local craftsmen could not manage from year to year without loans available only at interest. Many were the Shylocks, and the clients of Shylocks, in Shakespeare's audience.[21]

In the closest and most important source for the character, Marlowe's *The Jew of Malta*, the feeling of hypocrisy produced in the audience by the villain passes beyond metaphorical Jewishness to a proud demand for mutual self-recognition. All too often, critics of *Merchant* have dismissed Marlowe's Barabas as a caricature of pure evil, while giving Shakespeare credit for steering the stereotype part way, or all the way, to humanity. That is to simplify considerably the relationship between the two works. Barabas, from the cosmic perspective characteristic of Marlovian irony, repeatedly forces the audience to see themselves inside out:

> It is no sin to deceive a Christian,
> For they themselves hold it a principle,
> Faith is not to be held with heretics;
> But all are heretics that are not Jews.
> This follows well.
>
> (2.3.306–10)²²

The very logic of the passage demands a transposition: "For us Christians, all are heretics that are not Christians, and we hold it a principle. . . . This follows well." In the hands of a greater and more humane writer, this rough empathy, indicting the hypocrisy of the audience by compelling them to see Barabas as Barabas sees themselves, might be transformed into

> I am a Jew. Hath not a Jew eyes? hath not a Jew hands, organs, dimensions, senses, affections, passions? fed with the same good, hurt with the same weapons, subject to the same diseases, healed by the same means. . . . if you prick us do we not bleed? if you tickle us do we not laugh? if you poison us do we not die? and if you wrong us shall we not revenge?—if we are like you in the rest, we will resemble you in that. If a Jew wrong a Christian, what is his humility? revenge! If a Christian wrong a Jew, what should his sufferance be by Christian example?—why revenge! The villainy you teach me I will execute, and it shall go hard but I will better the instruction. (3.1.52–66)

As Shylock, transposing, moves from "you [Christians]" to "us [Jews]," the audience, transposing, moves from "us [Christians]" to "you [Jews]." The ultimate task of this plea for parity is the justification of revenge, and that, too, is Marlovian. The idiom "it shall go hard" is surrounded on either side by sentences using the word *will:* the promise, the vehemence and hardness of the revenge, fills the word *shall.* The phrase may well have been received by Shakespeare's original audience as a quotation from Marlowe, whose Barabas twice, at emphatic moments, declares "it shall go hard."[23]

Hardness and all, the speech works. The response of François Victor Hugo is still instructive for understanding well-intentioned misreadings of the play:

> This sublime imprecation is the most eloquent plea that the human voice has ever dared to utter for a despised race. Whatever be the dénouement, it is hereby justified. Let Shylock be as implacable as he may, assuredly he will no more than equal his instruction. Even granting that he obtains it, a pound of Antonio's flesh will never outweigh, in the scales of reprisal, the millions of corpses heaped in the Christian shambles by a butchery of thirteen centuries.[24]

We are now well over a century beyond Hugo. History since Shakespeare has made it steadily more likely that, hearing the famous speech, we too will conclude that Shylock could not possibly better the instruction. Under the pressure of this dismal history, we tend to find the ironies of *Merchant* either intolerably divisive or else misread in the shallowly

satisfying direction of pointing all the ironies toward Belmont or Christian Venice.

If we exempt Aaron and Tamora in *Titus Andronicus*,
Shylock is Shakespeare's first serious attempt at villainy
since Richard III. Whatever uses, good and bad, he may
have had in the course of post-Elizabethan history, he takes
his first coherence—and the one I am most interested in discovering—from the context of Shakespearean drama. The
proud claim to "better the instruction" has classical precedent in revenge tragedy. Scelera non ulcisceris/nisi uincis,
"You do not revenge a crime unless you surpass it," declares
Atreus in Seneca's *Thyestes*; or as he puts it toward the end
of the tragedy, "Crime should have a limit, when the crime
is wrought, not when repaid."[25] In revenge tragedy, the excess of the revenge over the initial wrong often produces an
effect of moral doubling between the revenger and the villain: coming second, after a first atrocity, the revenger seems
to be owed his excess, and the result is a sense of moral
equivalence. The best-known doubling in revenge tragedy
is that of Hamlet and Claudius, though in this instance other
factors sponsor the conviction that these "mighty oppo-
sites" stand on the same psychic ground.[26] As our discussion of Marlowe suggests, we might expect a doubling effect
of some sort in a revenge story about a Christian and a Jew.

Thinking of "give and hazard all," the inscription on the
lead casket, Auden remarked that "we have seen two characters do this. Shylock, however unintentionally, did, in
fact, hazard all for the sake of destroying the enemy he
hated, and Antonio, however unthinkingly he signed the
bond, hazarded all to secure the happiness of the friend he
loved."[27] This is revenge comedy, not revenge tragedy. Shylock's revenge is in excess of his wrong. In place of moral

doubling we find an oppositional twinning of emotion. The excessive love of a friend, turned around, is the excessive hatred of an other. The two characters are doubled in the irrational extremity of their guiding passions: every bit as much as Antonio loves Bassanio, Shylock hates Antonio. Their bonded collusion—Antonio's martyred resignation, Shylock's determined revenge—produces the hard comedy of the trial scene.

As with Richard III, Shakespeare creates distinctive ironic effects with Shylock's oaths. Serious revenge in Shakespeare almost always (we will encouter the exception of Iago in our next chapter) yields a vow. Shylock's initial one concludes his aside when Antonio enters to negotiate the bond: "cursed be my tribe/If I forgive him!" Right at the beginning of Shylock's revenge stands the first of his refusals to be merciful. Why take such an oath? Why call down on one's fellows, in the event of breaking it, such a curse? Vowing, for Richard, including the lethal oath of the second wooing scene, is of course a form of deceit intended to achieve his own ends. But Shylock's vow has the traditional aim and solemnity: a dangerous commitment of the will, intended to firm it against any chance of future wavering.

He clearly knows that if he goes through with this scheme, all of Christian Venice will ask for mercy. Some appeals will be direct, some subtle. "Shylock the world thinks, and I think so too," the Duke will begin at the trial, that in the last hour "Thou'lt show thy mercy" (4.1.17–20). Isn't the public revelation of his hatred for Antonio enough? When Shylock begins with an oath not to forgive, he anticipates such strategies and even anticipates being moved by them, since the hook of mercy will be baited with all sorts of desirables. But he has anticipated and refused in advance those inducements and imprecations by making a promise, presumably with his God as his witness, and specified as his punishment for breaking it a curse on his tribe. As Hazlitt said, Shylock is "*a good hater*."[28] This is, we will see, the key that unlocks the trial scene.

The revenge plan itself involves pretending a forgiving friendship with the Christians he is now financing. Though he turns down with contempt a first dinner invitation from Bassanio (1.3.29–33), he accepts a later one. Shylock marks this change in plan with a broken oath: "By Jacob's staff I swear/I have no mind of feasting forth tonight:/But I will go" (2.5.36–37). The immediate consequence is that Jessica, left alone in Shylock's fast-bound house, shut up against masquing and music, absconds with Lorenzo, a casket of jewels, and at least a bag of his ducats.[29]

Burckhardt calls attention to the conspicuous freedom of the couple.[30] Unlike Portia, Jessica feels herself under no obligation whatever to her father or his faith. She and Lorenzo take the money and run—to Genoa, then somewhere else, then finally to Belmont. They give us the impression of heedless self-creation. When Tubal relays to Shylock the knowledge that Jessica traded for a monkey a ring given to Shylock by his dead wife Leah, the old moneylender has one of his most poignant moments: "thou torturest me Tubal,—it was my turquoise, I had it of Leah when I was a bachelor" (3.1.110–11). Set in context with the Belmont plot, which shows off the pious obedience of a daughter to her father and the seriousness of ring vows, nothing could indicate more sharply the (for the moment) blasé freedom of this couple. The world begins with them. They make themselves up.

But they are not entirely exempt from the ubiquitous pressure of promising in the comedy. If Lorenzo comes to take her, Jessica says, he will "keep promise" (2.3.20). In their duet of allusions to famous literary couples at the beginning of act 5, they seem with increasing irony to invent themselves in relation to literary precedents. But at the end of this wit match they are joking about vows, providing a thematic prelude to the ring business to follow.

The other reason traditionally given for the Lorenzo/Jessica subplot is its provision of a strengthened motive for Shylock's revenge.[31] Shylock noticeably hardens with the loss of daughter and ducats. Nothing is going right. Indeed, the curse specified in his first oath has fallen on his head: "the curse never fell upon our nation till now, I never felt it till now," he confides to Tubal. The only good fortune on the horizon is Antonio's bad fortune. "I thank God, I thank God" (3.1.93). Bereft, frustrated, feeling for the first time a curse on his nation, Shylock sends Tubal to "fee me an officer." Antonio must be arrested. The law must be invoked. Shylock has determined to bring an action. His revenge, Antonio's self-sacrificing love: all is to be made public now, placed in the hands of the law, a dreaded system of rigorously enforced obligation the same, or so it is said, for Jew and Christian alike. During the arrest of Antonio, Shylock repeats five times in his sixteen lines that "I'll have my bond." Embedded in this repetitive determination, a first look at his manner in the trial scene to come, we find its motive: "I have sworn an oath, that I will have my bond" (3.3.5). The play gives us reason to believe that the loss of Jessica, jewels, and ducats produced in Shylock either a new oath or a sworn rededication to his first one.

We now turn to the other half of the plot's first circle.

Like Antonio, Portia begins the play "aweary of this great world" (1.2.1–2), but she knows exactly what she is weary of: the "great world" in the form of a queue of high-born suitors, some of whom just loiter for a while and never play the casket game. The word *choose* is an irritation, for it names what her father's "will" has denied to her "will." "I may neither choose who I would, nor refuse who I dislike, so is the will of a living daughter curb'd by the will of a dead father: is it not hard Nerissa, that I cannot choose one, nor refuse one" (22–26)? The word *curb'd* derives from equestrian tack; in *Measure for Measure* laws are "The needful bits and curbs to headstrong jades" (1.3.20), where "jades" are willful horses held in check by a curb chain attached to the bit and passing round their lower jaw.

As she exercises the one freedom remaining to her, which is the power to dislike the suitors, we realize how much confidence Shakespeare must have in his exactingly structured plot. He shrinks the entire Venetian plot to an epitome and tosses it out toward the end of a string of witticisms. Portia dislikes the young English baron for being unable to speak Italian, for wearing items of apparel drawn from the fashions of too many countries, and for learning his behavior "everywhere"—which seems to mean that he is a common bully. When Nerissa asks what Portia thinks of "the Scottish lord his neighbor," she replies, "That he hath a neighborly charity in him, for he borrowed a box of the ear of the Englishman, and swore he would pay him again when he was able: I think the Frenchman became his surety, and seal'd under for another" (1.2.75–79). This is the kind of transaction evolving in Venice—a borrowing, a debt, a standing surety, and beneath the metaphor, here as there, violence among males. But the father's will that curbs her own choosing bespeaks an older form of promising, a matter of oath and honor rather than credit and debt.

When Bassanio arrives a couple of acts later, Portia's will stirs, and as her once speechless messages to Bassanio are at last released out loud, we hear the conflict between her will and her curb:

> I pray you tarry, pause a day or two
> Before you hazard, for in choosing wrong
> I lose your company; therefore forbear a while,—
> There's something tells me (but it is not love)
> I would not lose you, and you know yourself,
> Hate counsels not in such a quality;
> But lest you should not understand me well,—
> And yet a maiden hath no tongue, but thought,—
> I would detain you here some month or two
> Before you venture for me. I could teach you
> How to choose right, but that I am forsworn,
> So will I never be,—so may you miss me—
> But if you do, you'll make me wish a sin,
> That I had been forsworn. Beshrew your eyes,
> That have o'erlook'd me and divided me,
> One half of me is yours, the other half yours,—
> Mine own I would say: but if mine then yours,
> And so all yours; O these naughty times
> Put bars between the owners and their rights!
> And so though yours, not yours—prove it so,
> Let Fortune go to hell for it, not I.
>
> (3.2.1–21)

Though Portia is still loyal to the obligation of obeying her father's will, a new vow to a new man, a husband, is aborning. She *does* "wish a sin" in wanting to be free from the "bars" of these "naughty times." Witty and whimsical though she be, psychological and moral conflict runs throughout the speech. I paraphrase roughly: "It is not love, but it is not hate. A maiden hath no tongue, no say in this matter, but a maiden now speaks. If I taught you the right casket to choose, I would be forsworn, but if you were to choose the wrong one, I would wish to be forsworn. I am divided by your eyes, half of me yours and half of me yours—but I have misspoken, and half of course is mine. Finally I am yours and not yours, caught between two vows, a dead father and a living suitor." The *it* in the phrase "prove it so"—meaning "if it prove so"—must refer to "not yours," since Fortune can go to hell in that case, whereas if Portia tells him the right casket, she will go to hell.

Rein in, let go. The curb and the will, the old obligation and the new obligation struggling to be born, are so thoroughly at odds here that I am inclined to accept as authorially intended the stage tradition, rejected by most academic critics of the play, that Portia does in fact offer hints to Bassanio in the music she orders before his casket choice.[32] For such would be a perfect solution to the conflict so patent in this speech: just as she is "though yours, not yours," so she will teach him, though not teach him, "to choose right."

As has been pointed out, the rhyme words in the first stanza of the song (*bred, head,* and *nourished*) cry out for lead.[33] Where is fancy bred and nourished?

> *It is engend'red in the eyes,*
> *With gazing fed, and Fancy dies*

In the cradle where it lies:
Let us all ring Fancy's knell.
I'll begin it. Ding, dong, bell.

(67–71)

Fancy here means pretty much what *passing fancy* means today, or what *fancy* meant and still means today in *A Midsummer Night's Dream*'s "fancy-free"(2.1.164). It is an attraction born in the eyes, "with gazing fed," that once it has run its course dies in the eyes: a person looks deserving, right, irresistible, then after a time he or she just looks ordinary, wrong, altogether resistible. We can see immediately how this view of fancy bears on the attraction between Bassanio and Portia, which began in "speechless messages" from her eyes and a "deserving" look in his eyes. We can also see immediately how the song bears on the casket choice. Gold and silver appeal to the eye, like a brief lover's fancy. The song gives Bassanio a strong clue as to which casket he should choose, and it gives us a strong clue as to the point and purpose, the symbolic meaning, of the choice of caskets.

The details are of some interest, if only because Shakespeare, elaborating his sources, invented the entire legal rigmarole surrounding the caskets. Portia's father was "ever virtuous," a holy man (1.2.27). One of his dying thoughts was a scheme for arranging from the grave a virtuous marriage for his daughter and heir. Normally in comedy the imposition of the will of a *senex* on his daughter's marriage choice is joyfully thwarted. But the complex obligation mechanism devised by this virtuous father does the job, arranging the right marriage and fulfilling the comic genre. Before a suitor chooses a casket, he must swear an oath—

three oaths, to be exact. Arragon provides the fullest account:

> I am enjoin'd by oath to observe three things,—
> First, never to unfold to any one
> Which casket 'twas I chose; next, if I fail
> Of the right casket, never in my life
> To woo a maid in way of marriage:
> Lastly,
> If I do fail in fortune of my choice,
> Immediately to leave you, and be gone.
>
> (2.9.9–16)

Presumably, in swearing this triple oath, in choosing to play at all, a suitor also swears implicitly that he will marry Portia if he selects the right casket. Portia, similarly, must marry a suitor so sworn if he does select the right casket. Both Portia and a winner, that is, are sworn to swear marriage vows. The same symmetry between Portia and the sworn suitors also holds good in the case of a wrong choice. If suitors select the wrong casket, they cannot marry anyone; if suitors select the wrong casket, Portia cannot marry anyone. She cannot choose; suitors, once they take the triple oath, have no choice beyond the casket, getting either the right one (marriage to Portia) or the wrong one (no marriage to anyone).

The outside of each casket contains an inscription. The chooser of the golden one gains what many men desire, of the silver what he deserves. Both of these entice; their choosers are going to get something. But the inscription on the leaden casket tells its chooser that he must give and hazard all he has. It alone of the caskets "threatens" (2.7.18), as Morocco says, later echoed by Bassanio: "thou meagre lead/Which rather threaten'st than dost promise aught" (3.2.104–5). So the inscriptions on the outsides of the caskets, what the suitors must choose among, contain two promises of gain and one threat of hazardous giving.

Inside each casket the father has placed both an object and a poem. All three are judgmental: two spurning judgments, one accepting judgment. The three insides (two spurning, one welcoming) and the three outsides (two welcoming, one spurning) are in symmetrical opposition. The poem in the golden casket, placed in the eyesocket (remember fancy born and dying in the eye), is written from the point of view of the casket itself, which turns out to be not a jewelry box, a "casket" in that sense, but the miniature image of a gilded tomb: "Many a man his life hath sold/But my outside to behold,— /Gilded tombs do worms unfold." That is in part how Morocco made his mistake; the lead casket looked like a common grave: "it were too gross/To rib her cerecloth in the obscure grave" (2.7.51–53). He should have chosen the undisguised grave, toward which all our hazards tend, and not the gilded one promising the desire of all men. The poem inside the silver casket stands next to the picture of a fool's head, and is written mockingly in the person of that foolish head: "Take what wife you will to bed,/I will ever be your head:/So be gone, you are sped" (2.9.70–72). Silver hair does not a wise man make. Arragon, having made the apparently wise observation that true honor is a matter of desert rather than blood, gets what he deserved. If true to his oath, he will never take a wife to bed. What is being tested here?

The obligation mechanism of the casket game might be termed a Comedy Machine. Portia's father was "ever virtuous," and that virtue must have included good vowing between him and his wife. An absolute pride in those marriage vows is what led him to construct the Comedy Machine. It tests whether a man is fit to make marriage vows at all, which is why the sworn penalty for failure is never to marry. There are other implications, of course. Gold and silver are, as Kermode put it, "breeding metals," the stuff of currency.[34] Lead, on the other hand, is base (2.7.50; 2.9.20), heavy, a metal of which utensils are made, a metal mixed with tin in producing pewter.[35] But the focus is on good promising. A man who fancies what every man fancies may stray to this bright creature or that bright object. A man who wants what he deserves is not likely to care much about what his wife deserves. The lead casket represents obligation, the long haul—fidelity till death do us part. Corpses were wrapped in lead.[36]

Just before Bassanio makes his choice, his idle metaphor about wanting to choose right away, since in the state of anticipation he lives "upon the rack," prompts in Portia a sudden suspicion about whether the vow he would like to give her is commensurate with the vow she would like to give him:

> *Por.* Upon the rack Bassanio? then confess
> What treason there is mingled with your love.
> *Bas.* None but that ugly treason of mistrust,
> Which makes me fear th'enjoying of my love,—
> There may as well be amity and life
> 'Tween snow and fire, as treason and my love.
> *Por.* Ay, but I fear you speak upon the rack
> Where men enforced do speak any thing.

Bas. Promise me life, and I'll confess the truth.
Por. Well then, confess and live.
Bass.   "Confess and love"
Had been the very sum of my confession:
O happy torment, when my torturer
Doth teach me answer for deliverance!

(3.2.26–38)

In this telling badinage, Portia becomes the torturer looking for a confession of treason. The proverbial wisdom
about male vows has, at least in verbal play, taken over.
They will say anthing to get their way. Portia probes for
treason. Bassanio's only treason, he assures her, is "mistrust" about making the wrong casket choice. But if he is
on the rack, will he not say anything? The "liar paradox"
in the actual torture of a suspected traitor is that the torturer looks for a confession that he cannot believe once he
gets it, because torture has been necessary to secure it in the
first place. One says anything the torturer wants to hear in
order to stop the pain. The quibble on "confess and live"
and "confess and love," far from creating credibility within
the torture-for-treason metaphor, exacerbates the suspicion. Being taught by one's torturer the "answer for deliverance" is precisely what makes such a confession suspect.

The song about fancy beginning and ending in the eyes
follows this badinage. Bassanio, reasoning about the caskets, hits upon the suggested moral: exterior ornament, appealing to the unwary eyes, hides unsavory truths in this
false world. He will hazard all on lead. The poem in the lead
casket, placed next to the heart-stoppingly powerful portrait of Portia, clarifies the game. Since its enticements begin

and end in the eye, it is the very image of fancy. Once he gathers his senses, he moves from image to language, fancy to vow, and exits the Comedy Machine a winner.

Before him lie immediate riches and immediate beauty, but chained by marital vows to a lifetime of leaden obligation:

> You that choose not by the view
> Chance as fair, and choose as true:
> Since this fortune falls to you,
> Be content, and seek no new.
> If you be well pleas'd with this,
> And hold your fortune for your bliss,
> Turn to where your lady is,
> And claim her with a loving kiss.
>
> (3.2.131–38)

This is a new poetic voice, not a personfication of the casket (like the golden poem) or the object in the casket (like the silver poem). This, from the grave, is the voice Portia's father, the inventor of the comedy machine from which Bassanio now at last is free—free, that is, to "Be content, and seek no new," free to "hold your fortune [the one he has now gained] for your bliss [your one and only bliss from now to the end of your days]." There is gold and silver aplenty, beauty aplenty, but there is also obligation. Lead is a base metal: obligation always, sooner or later, weighs.

Bassanio does not know what to say. He will say nothing until "confirm'd, sign'd, ratified by you" (3.2.148). The metaphor implies, it is worth noting, that written documents are the most obliging, most binding of promises—a point to figure with some prominence in the Venice plot. To bring Bassanio back to the reality implicit in the leaden casket, Portia must make a spoken vow equivalent to being signed, sealed, and delivered. And so Portia does, giving and hazarding all she has in one of Shakespeare's loveliest promises:

> You see me Lord Bassanio where I stand,
> Such as I am; though for myself alone
> I would not be ambitious in my wish
> To wish myself much better, yet for you,
> I would be trebled twenty times myself,
> A thousand times more fair, ten thousand times more
>   rich,
> That only to stand high in your account,
> I might in virtues, beauties, livings, friends
> Exceed account: but the full sum of me
> Is sum of something: which to term in gross,
> Is an unlesson'd girl, unschool'd, unpractised,
> Happy in this, she is not yet so old
> But she may learn: happier than this,
> She is not bred so dull but she can learn;
> Happiest of all, is that her gentle spirit
> Commits itself to yours to be directed,
> As from her lord, her governor, her king.
> Myself, and what is mine, to you and yours
> Is now converted. But now I was the lord
> Of this fair mansion, master of my servants,
> Queen o'er myself: and even now, but now,
> This house, these servants, and this same myself
> Are yours,—my lord's!—I give them with this ring,

Which when you part from, lose, or give away,
Let it presage the ruin of your love,
And be my vantage to exclaim on you.

(3.2.149–74)

I have imposed on the reader the burden of the entire speech because it is the summit of the Belmont arc of the plot's first circle. It replays the entire casket game. Portia is first all gold and silver, what every man wants and every man would like to think he deserves. Then at the end, like lead, she threatens. He must wear the ring, the token of an oath stipulating a curse on him who breaks it: "the ruin of your love" and "my vantage to exclaim on you." Here begins the second circle of the double plot, born like the first out of a double promise: hers to him, and should he place the ring on his finger, his to her. She is indeed her father's daughter. The moment she is free from his complex obligation mechanism, she creates her own.

It could be argued that when, after the trial scene, a disguised Portia requests Bassanio's ring, she does not really want it; she is testing him for fidelity to the ring vow and hopes that he will refuse to give it away. But the mistress of Belmont is a tricksy, fun-loving spirit. Her climactic "vantage to exclaim on you" anticipates the witty entertainment of the last act.

Shakespeare excels in the representation of doubled or divided minds. The body of the speech looks to be both an ideal of wifely vowing and an ideal of male wish fulfillment with regard to wifely vowing. More so than in any other Shakespearean promise, Portia's gift of herself as a wife is mixed in with wishing—wishing to be "much better" just for herself, but "trebled twenty times better" for the sake of him, "A thousand times more fair, ten thousand times more rich," beyond accounting virtuous, beautiful, well-quartered, befriended; and where she falls short, happy that she may learn, happier that she can learn, happiest that she will be directed, lessoned, schooled, and practised by Bassanio, her lord (using the word is thrilling!), governor, and king. Portia is the sum of perfect submission combined with immeasurable good wishes.

But as the play will make clear, all of this, though fully meant, is also fully meant in another sense. Being bound by a will has taught Portia a confidence in her own will. If we look back from the end, we realize that she knows herself to be fair enough, rich enough, virtuous enough, lessoned, schooled, and practised enough, in love enough, for any Bassanio anywhere. It is *he* who must have the lessons, *he* who must prove his worth to her. What was left unresolved in the exchange about tortured confession must now be dealt with. The ring has been offered. The curse has been specified.

It is hard to grasp so much wish fulfillment. Bassanio scarcely remembers what she has said. He is like the crowd after a prince had made a happy annoucement—a "bussing pleased multitude," but thoughtless in its elation, "a wild of nothing" (180, 182). Still, he chose the lead casket, and he got her last point:

> but when this ring
> Parts from this finger, then parts life from hence,—
> O then be bold to say Bassanio's dead.
>
> (183–85)

Now he really has hazarded all. She specified as curses for ring removal only the "ruin" of his love and a "vantage to exclaim" on him. How can he prove himself worthy of such a gift as she has just shown herself to be? He does not have the wealth. He does not have the eloquence. But he does have his life, his most precious possession, and that is precisely what, Antonio-like, he wagers. Bassanio's promise has symbolically shut himself in the lead casket. He leads, from this moment on, a life of obligation.

But there is more than one obligation in Bassanio's life. A letter arrives from Venice. Antonio, arrested and facing forfeiture, has broken his silence at last. He now wants recognition of a quite particular sort:

> Sweet Bassanio, my ships have all miscarried, my creditors grow cruel, my estate is very low, my bond to the Jew is forfeit, and (since in paying it, it is impossible I should live), all debts are clear'd between you and I, if I might but see you at my death: notwithstanding, use your pleasure,—if your love do not persuade you to come, let not my letter. (3.2.314–20)

The wording of the letter, which claims that it must not be the decisive factor, could not be more careful. Antonio begins by calling in a debt. The credit that sent Bassanio from Venice is now, as debt, to bring him home to witness Antonio's death, at which point "all debts are clear'd between you and I." Having called in his marker, Antonio then proclaims that he is playing a different game for higher stakes. The second "if" clause cancels the first. The mixture of credit and friendship, obligation and love, evident from the beginning in Antonio, is now put into hierarchical order.

Love, not the clearing of the debt, must bring Bassanio to Venice. The letter adds its own love test for males (are you fit to love a man who loves you?) to the casket game (are you fit to take marriage vows?) and the ring vow (are you fit to keep marriage vows?). If we think back to the two promises at the first meeting between Antonio and Bassanio, from which the double plot arose, Antonio has here requested a renewal of the second promise, the promise to him, the promise that Bassanio meet him at a time and place in Venice.

Bassanio has already told Portia that he is "nothing," penniless. It took the whole bankroll, three thousand ducats, to get him to Belmont. But he must now reveal that he is less than nothing, a man in debt whose creditor faces the forfeit of a pound of flesh.[37] Bassanio, guilt-stricken, sees in the letter an image of Antonio's sacrifice for him: "The paper as the body of my friend,/And every word in it a gaping wound/Issuing life-blood" (263–65). Portia sends her husband-to-be off to Venice with bags and bags of Belmont ducats, but not before they go to church and make it official. *Then* he may go, "For never shall you lie by Portia's side/With an unquiet soul" (304–5). Sending him off to Venice and the pressing affairs of his friend leaves open the matter of yet another hierarchical ranking. If love between friends stands above the obligation of debt, as Antonio's letter states, what is its standing with respect to the obligation of marriage?

That the answer, blending the moods of the play, is to be both serious and comic, we can already predict. Antonio is willing to sacrifice, so that Bassanio can go to Portia, a pound of his flesh. Now Portia is willing to sacrifice, so that Bassanio can return to Antonio, her wedding night. Ergo, Portia's pound of flesh is Bassanio's. . . . I leave it to the reader to balance this comic equation, which anticipates the bawdy joke in *Merchant*'s final line. When Lorenzo praises her appreciation for "god-like Amity" (3.4.3), Portia replies that her lord's great friend "Must needs be like my lord": "If it be so,/How little is the cost I have bestowed" in saving him from hellish cruelty (18–21). How little, but how much! The consummation of a daughter's long obedience and a marriage's deep vows!

So the first circle of the double plot closes in the trial scene, one of the most enduring theatrical successes in all Shakespeare and one of the problems most bedeviling to his modern critics. The scene has been read in convincing detail as an allegorical reenactment of medieval Atonement plays such as the *Processus Belial*.[38] Portia is New Testament Mercy. Shylock is the devil of Old Testament law. Critics often want to work in "the letter" and "the spirit" here, casting Shylock as the first and Portia as the second, but since Portia discovers mercy in being zealously literal about the meaning of the bond, the initial casting has to undergo some fancy switching. Antonio, if one goes all the way, is Christ-like:

> In offering to meet the demands of strict justice (in accordance with the Old Law) Antonio will pay in blood the price of his friend's happiness; and it cannot be extravagant to argue that he is here a type of the divine Redeemer, as Shylock of the unredeemed.

> *The Merchant of Venice*, then, is "about" judgment, redemption and mercy; the supersession in human history of the grim four thousand years of unalleviated justice by the era of love and mercy. It begins in usury and corrupt love; it ends with harmony and perfect love. And

all the time it tells its audience that this is its subject; only by a determined effort to avoid the obvious can one mistake the theme of *The Merchant of Venice*.[39]

I would not wish to mistake the obvious, and the scene obviously does have an allegorical dimension. But the allegory is not free of context. Shakespeare drops the scene into a play that already has patterns in process, ideas in motion, and characters at work, words busy with meaning and meanings coupling with meanings.

"I pray you tarry," Portia advised a Bassanio eager to choose the right casket. Before allowing mercy to triumph over justice with full emblematic seriousness, the play has time to sacrifice allegory to the hungry gods of comedy.[40] Antonio may sound like "our Redeemer" in saying "Let me have judgment, and the Jew his will" (4.1.83). But this Christlike resignation to divine justice is coupled with a demonstration to Bassanio that nothing could exceed such love—a demonstration that threatens to ravage with grief the new marriage between Bassanio and Portia. In this passage, the allegory seems clear and true until comedy gets hold of it:

> I am a tainted wether of the flock,
> Meetest for death,—the weakest kind of fruit
> Drops earliest to the ground, and so let me;
> You cannot better be employ'd Bassanio,
> Than to live still and write mine epitaph.
>
> (4.1.114–18)

Why should Bassanio think of consummating his marriage? He could not be better employed than in composing something like Fulke Greville's "An epitaph upon the Right Honorable Sir Philip Sidney," which proclaims that "Sidney is dead, dead is my friend, dead is the world's delight," and promises that the author will "spend my ever dying days in never ending grief."[41] Antonio wants to pass his fatalism on to Bassanio in the form of some acknowledgment that the friendship tie, at least in the case of a friend so Christian as Antonio, takes precedence over the marriage tie. Shylock is not the only one who wants his justice. When Antonio gets his own justice, as we will soon discover, the plot begins its second orbit.

In the Atonement dramas, as in Atonement theology, God is in a true legal bind. He framed the law, he made known the punishment. He must either condemn man or condemn his own justice. In the words of Milton's God, "Die hee or Justice must."[42] It is only through the device of substitution, putting Christ in the place of man, that the Atonement can be accomplished. Things are a little different in the fairy-tale courtroom of *Merchant*. There is no legal conundrum here. Shylock can at any moment withdraw his action. The very pleas for mercy presuppose this ability. This seems a simple point, but if we are to appreciate the full meaning of the scene and enjoy its mixture of comedy, psychological realism, and allegory, we must bear that fact in mind.

For why does Shylock not withdraw his bond? Because he craves the law, he stands for law, he must have his bond. He says it over and over, but the allegorical equation of Shylock with law does not in truth answer the question. Despite appearances, despite the allegorical signals, Shylock does *not* stand for the law. It seems as if Shylock, Antonio, and all of Venice are caught up in the blind, even-handed impersonality of the law, *jus civile* being in Venice almost the equivalent of *jus gentium*. But this picture of things, common to much of the play's criticism, is not exactly accurate.[43]

Shakespeare is not hiding anything; I am not alluding to a hidden meaning. What I have in mind is right there in Shylock's words when he refuses the Duke's initial plea for mercy:

> I have possess'd your grace of what I purpose,
> And by our holy Sabbath have I sworn
> To have the due and forfeit of my bond.
>
> (35–37)

We heard of this self-imposed compulsion during the arrest of Antonio. Shylock has sworn an oath by what he holds sacred, a successor oath to the one he swore at the end of his first aside. Anticipating pleas for mercy, anticipating his own self-interested desire to give in to pleas for mercy, he has sworn an oath not to relent. It is to this oath, over and above the law, that he is loyal.

When Portia, disguised as the young legal scholar Baltha-zar, arrives in the courtroom, her dialogue with Shylock neatly evokes the three caskets. In this most disciplined of comedies, we can count her pleas to Shylock for mercy. One:

> *Por.* Then must the Jew be merciful.
> *Shy.* On what compulsion must I? tell me that.
>
> (178–79)

On no compulsion, because, in the play's most famous line, "The quality of mercy is not strain'd"—not, that is to say, constrained. Portia here unveils one of the great determining binaries in this comedy about obligation. Fancy, Bassanio's "secret vow of pilgrimage," the love between Antonio and Bassanio, mercy: these are not obliged, not constrained. But debt, the nest of obligations in the casket game, the love between Portia and Bassanio, the ring he wears, the bond between Antonio and Shylock, the stipulations of the law and the verdict of the court based on those stipulations: these are "strained" indeed. The plot is still looking for the right synthesis of these oppositions. How, in particular, can Portia justify her *must* in "Then must the Jew be merciful"? Why be merciful? Because, reworking the silver and gold caskets, no man deserves mercy (194–95), and for that reason all men pray for mercy. Portia has exposed a lacuna in the "Hath not a Jew eyes?" speech. Somewhere toward the end of it Shylock might have interpolated something like this: "If a Christian does not wrong a Jew, what is his pride? mercy! If a Jew does not wrong a Christian, what should his pride be by Christian example?—why, mercy!" But Shylock has constrained himself not to entertain such an addition. This avenue of thought has been closed off by a sacred oath, and Shylock replies: "My deeds upon my head! I crave the law." That first choice of phrase was portentous. Shylock's oath is about to deliver its ironic truth.

Two, turning from high-minded self-interest to financial self-interest:

> *Por*. Shylock there's thrice thy money off'red thee.
> *Shy*. An oath, an oath, I have an oath in heaven,—
> Shall I lay perjury upon my soul?
> No not for Venice.
>
> (223–26)

Shylock is offered thrice the original figure: the factor of three may be intended to remind us, as this part of the play is meant in general to remind us, of the casket choice. But financial reward will not make Shylock bear the consequences of breaking an oath already deposited in heaven. The vow has locked him into claiming the forfeited flesh: should he relent, he would stand guilty before a higher judge, God himself, of the crime of perjury. So he again rejects the profit all men want.

Three, combining one and two:

> *Por.*   be merciful,
> Take thrice thy money, bid me tear the bond.
> *Shy.* When it is paid, according to the tenour.
> · · · · · · · · · · · · · · · ·
> Proceed to judgment: by my soul I swear,
> There is no power in the tongue of man
> To alter me,—I stay here on my bond.
>
>   (229–31, 236–38)

Again the sworn soul is the sticking point. *That* is why Shylock stands for law, stays on his bond. He has traded the noncompulsion of mercy for the compulsion not to be merciful. He has made the vice of revenge into the virtue of obedience to a sacred vow. Three times he has chosen the leaden casket of obligation.

And so, true to his vow, he gets his judgment. There is a power to alter him, if not in the tongue of man, then in the tongue of woman. All of the problem comedies—and *Merchant* should be considered the earliest of them—have scenes that are either trials or trial-like.[44] All of them, save the unique *Troilus and Cressida*, feature plot tricks that critics find unsatisfactory but audiences usually applaud.[45] One of these devices, familiar in folk tales and fabliaux, scholars have termed the "bed-trick." Bertram in *All's Well That Ends Well* thinks that he goes to bed with a Florentine damsel when in fact, as it turns out, he has consummated his marriage and sired his first son. Angelo in *Measure for Measure* thinks that he goes to bed with Isabella when in fact, as it turns out, he has consummated his old, unfairly vacated precontract with Mariana.

In the first of his problem plays, Shakespeare has rigged the entire Venetian plot with a "bond trick." Antonio and Shylock sign a bond for three thousand ducats thinking that, if the principal is not paid after thirty days, and the bond is enforced, Antonio must forfeit a pound of flesh, when in fact, as it turns out, they have signed a bond that, when enforced, forfeits Shylock's life and fortune to the Venetian state. Both of them forgot that man is flesh *and* blood. Like Morocco and Arragon, they saw only the outside, the flesh.[46] It is not customary in drama for revengers to ignore the matter of blood in their plotting: "O, from this time forth / My thoughts be bloody or be nothing worth," Hamlet exhorts himself in one of his last Senecan moments (4.4.65–66). The comic villain of *Merchant* forgets blood, and therefore his thoughts turn out to be "nothing worth." Shylock's revenge from the very beginning *was* the gift of mercy. In tragedy, serious revengers swear oaths. In comedy, serious revengers swear trick oaths concealing their defeat. Shylock's insistence on the leaden casket of obligation was ironically the right choice—for Antonio!

The Venetians will be merciful. Shylock can have his life. He can have half his fortune, the other half being held in trust by Antonio. But then Antonio, as the wronged party, makes the two mercies dependent on three stipulations. The half of the money held in trust must be willed to Lorenzo upon Shylock's death. Shylock must become a Christian. He must leave his own half of the fortune, at his death, "Unto his son Lorenzo and his daughter" (385).

The conversion to Christianity, which all modern readers and playgoers find difficult to swallow, is in Shakespeare's comedy the final irony of the truth of an oath. Shylock has sworn by what is sacred to refuse mercy and have his bond. But since the bond-trick transforms the whole vengeful scheme into charitable mercy, he therefore loses what is sacred to him. That might seem a tricky formalism, so Shakespeare makes the violation of Shylock's vow as literal as any spiritual prosecutor could wish. After Balthazar has reinterpreted the letter of the pound of flesh, Shylock, his sacred vow forgotten, will settle for the best cash offer: "I take this offer then,—pay the bond thrice / And let the Christian go" (313–14). His punishment for breaking the vow of faith turns out to be forced conversion to another one. I understand that Shylock as I have analyzed him does not float free from a theatrical and theological tradition; perhaps his oath is just an interesting version of the stereotypic "hardheartedness of the Jew." But I think Shakespeare's character makes sense in the genre of revenge tragedy, once we have adjusted it for comedy, and I find his almost-to-the-end loyalty to an oath that places his obedience both beyond the law and beyond good-hearted appeal coherent in dramatic terms.[47] The same could be said for his last-minute violation of it.

In any case, things could be worse, as the hooting Gratiano reminds us. Shylock's soul is now public knowledge, and his prolonged isolation is at an end.[48] There will be two godfathers at his christening. Antonio and Bassanio? "I am content" (389). An actor may say the line as despairingly or angrily as he can. But perhaps the point is that Shylock, though the occasion seems to demand it, is not about to utter any more vows and curses.

The trial scene is a love test for Shylock. He fails. At the end of act 4, our last moment in Venice, Portia sends a still-disguised Nerissa off to Shylock's house to get a signature on his will. To be chased down by paper, by *that* paper: the law's revenge.

In the trial scene Shakespeare skillfully bonds the opening of the second plot circle to the closing of the first. Bassanio demands that "Balthazar" accept some token of gratitude. He offers the young scholar three thousand ducats (4.1.407–8)—a significant sum, and a matter to which we will return. Portia will instead have the ring, the one that Bassanio has sworn to wear until the day he dies. This is, as it were, the love test of "Balthazar": "And you in love shall not deny me this" (425)! Bassanio refuses, at which point Antonio transforms a test of Bassanio's love for Portia/Balthazar into a test of Bassanio's love for Antonio. Symbolically, and more blatantly than ever, Antonio elevates friendship above marriage:

> My Lord Bassanio, let him have the ring,
> Let his deservings and my love withal
> Be valued 'gainst your wife's commandment.
>
> (445–47)

The young scholar has saved Antonio's life and augmented his fortune. When added to "my love withal," there seems rather a great deal of Antonio weighing against "your wife's commandment." Bassanio yields up his ring. This misprision about the value of a wife's commandment must be playfully yet exactingly corrected in the final act. When the wives again meet the husbands in Belmont, the ring will circle back to Bassanio's finger, closing with renewed promises the second round of Shakespeare's doubled double plot.

If that were all, the new husbands' violation of their ring vows would be solely against the letter of their oaths, and act 5 might become as trivial and anticlimactic as it is sometimes claimed to be.[49] But at the height of tension in the trial scene, after Shylock has refused all three of Portia's pleas for mercy, just before she will reveal the comic meaning of the bond, the husbands break the spirit of their vows.

Antonio for the first time makes mention of Bassanio's wife, imploring his friend to deliver her a message:

> Commend me to your honourable wife,
> Tell her the process of Antonio's end,
> Say how I lov'd you, speak me fair in death:
> And when the tale is told, bid her be judge
> Whether Bassanio had not once a love:
> Repent but you that you shall lose your friend
> And he repents not that he pays your debt.
>
> (269–75)

The passage initiates a comic calculation. Since Portia will be alive when she makes the judgment of "Whether Bassanio had not once a love," she must perforce conclude that the love shown Bassanio by his dead friend exceeds the love shown Bassanio by herself. How can she compete with death as a love proof? So long as Portia lives, she is doomed to come in second in this love competition; just to gain parity, she would have to concoct a noble self-sacrifice. Antonio has the angles figured.

Nor will he have to wait until he looks down from heaven to enjoy this imaginative triumph over his friend's other beloved. Bassanio, sensing what is wanted, gives it right now. He can do the judging for himself:

> Antonio, I am married to a wife
> Which is as dear to me as life itself,
> But life itself, my wife, and all the world,
> Are not esteem'd above thy life.
> I would lose all, aye sacrifice them all
> Here to this devil, to deliver you.
>
> (278–83)

To give his life for his friend would be an even bargain, life for life. Moreover, giving up his life would entail giving up "all the world." What he adds to this competitive demonstration of love, the element that makes his devotion to Antonio exceed Antonio's devotion to him, is the sacrifice of "my wife." In his thoughts, he kills off Portia to trump Antonio's demonstration of amity! Would he, to turn things around, imaginatively sacrifice Antonio to prove his love for Portia? We have reason to doubt. Balthazar immediately catches the drift: "Your wife would give you little thanks for that/If she were by to hear you make the offer" (284–85). Nor will she, overhearing the uncensored truth about her husband's friendship like a goddess in disguise, give him thanks for that.

Gratiano, comically seconding Antonio's vow, fixes on the feature isolated by Balthazar, the sacrificing in thought of one's wife: "I have a wife who I protest I love,—/I would she were in heaven, so she could/Entreat some power to change this currish Jew" (286–88). Gratiano's vow, unlike its noble model, has the virtue of practicality. He will not give up his own life—no point in that. If one is going to kill off, in thought, one's wife, one might as well think of something the dead woman could do to alleviate the situation on this earth! The role of begging mercy from God in the great beyond is not, unsurprisingly, to Nerissa's taste: "'Tis well you offer it behind her back,/The wish would make else an unquiet house" (289–90). One of the hardest Elizabethan marriage proverbs declares that "A dead wife is the best goods in a man's house." Or another just as hard, and more to the point at this moment, "A wife brings but two good days, her wedding day and death day."[50] Here we have two husbands who have enjoyed only half their wedding days, having postponed consummation in order to attend to Antonio's plight, and already they have wished for the death days of their wives! This will indeed make for an unquiet house, or rather an unquiet patio, when the women claim their privilege of "exclaiming" on them in act 5.

Shylock, a better judge of fidelity than some of the play's critics, also disapproves of the casual thought-killing of wives in these wishes for an endangered friend:

These be the Christian hubands! I have a daughter—
Would any of the stock of Barabas
Had been her husband, rather than a Christian.

(291–93)

With the scoffs of the two wives ringing in our ears, we have no reason to question the rightness of Shylock in thirding the two women. We also recall the esteem in which he held the turquoise given him by Leah. Once the keeper of a ring vow, and now in this trial obedient to another oath, Shylock understands fidelity. This is his obviously sympathetic moment in the trial scene: he points the satirical finger that Gratiano will later point repeatedly at him. Through his disapproval of the Christian husbands Shylock does, after all, have an imaginative stake in the ring judgments of act 5, so often said by critics to forget him altogether.

The wife-eliminating wishes, followed by the forfeiture of the rings, give substance to the forthcoming ring game. There will be another trial, another comic victory over legality. But the play, so bound up with obligation and so concerned with testing male obligation in particular, suggests a couple of other rationales for the ring game.

First and most obviously, we are inside a comedy, however dark and problematic. Marriage vows are its *telos*. In this particular comedy, they have come into a conflict with male friendship both personal (the love between Antonio and Bassanio) and conceptual. Love stands above and beyond the obligation of debt, or so Antonio has sought to demonstrate. But marriage requires a fusion of obligation and love, fidelity and amity. It is strained. Obligations wear down and bear down. Youth fades. Love comes to Bassanio in a leaden casket.

Launcelot Gobbo belongs to the comedy, and he gives voice to a not altogether unhappy concession about marriage vows heard in every single one of Shakespeare's comedies, in one tone or another. The cuckoo sings. No one knows for sure who his father is. Wives stray and husbands leave bastards here and there. Will Kempe, the famous clown who played the part of Launcelot, must have had the audience in stitches with lines like "being an honest man's son, or rather an honest woman's son, for indeed my father did something smack, something grow to; he had a kind of taste" (2.2.14–17), or had the audience nodding its assent as he slips into inverted proverb with "it is a wise father that knows his own child" (73–74). I associate this blooming buzzing confusion in which marriage vows are broken all the time with Shakespeare's youth in Stratford. This is country humor, country wisdom.

At a somewhat higher, more urban level of social awareness, we have Gratiano. When Lorenzo and Jessica break their promise to appear at a certain time and place, Gratiano and his friends are kept waiting. In the ensuing conversation, he rises to a height of eloquence found nowhere else in his speeches. He expounds, in effect, the leaden casket:

> *Gra.* And it is a marvel he [Lorenzo] out-dwells his
>   hour,
> For lovers ever run before the clock.
> *Sal.* O ten times faster Venus' pigeons fly
> To seal love's bonds new-made, than they are wont
> To keep obliged-faith unforfeited!
> *Gra.* That ever holds: who riseth from a feast
> With that keen appetite that he sits down?
> Where is the horse that doth untread again
> His tedious measures with the unbated fire
> That he did pace them first?—all things that are,
> Are with more spirit chased than enjoy'd.
> How like a younger or a prodigal
> The scarfed bark puts from her native bay—
> Hugg'd and embraced by the strumpet wind!
> How like the prodigal doth she return

With over-weather'd ribs and ragged sails—
Lean, rent, and beggar'd by the strumpet wind!

$$(2.6.3–19)$$

The text may be defective here.[51] No one has been able to explain in a satisfactory way all of the details in Gratiano's little oration. But the initial context is clear enough. It is a "marvel" that Lorenzo is not on time, for one would ordinarily expect earliness from the swearers of "new-made vows," whereas lateness and slowness are the leaden attributes of "obliged faith."

Taking his cue from this contrast, Gratiano suggests a universal principle of biological entropy. As eating lessens appetite, consummation lessens desire. The association of cloyed appetite with male sexuality appears commonly throughout Shakespeare.[52] Cleopatra is the exception that proves the rule: "other women cloy / The appetites they feed, but she makes hungry, / Where most she satisfies" (2.2.236–38). Gratiano, beyond ken of the troublesome miracle of Cleopatra, supposes that sexual appetite, unlike hunger, never returns to its original vigor. Even in horses headed back to the stables we observe tedium and dampened spirit. Then he launches an extended metaphor joining the biblical story of the prodigal son's departure and return (from Luke 15, here minus the happy ending) to the disastrous journey, bravely out and barely back, of a ship. It has been suggested that this conceit, leaning on the biblical parable, tells the story of a young aristocrat whose fortune is wasted on strumpets; he ends his days "lean, rent," in poverty or disease. But sailing has been connected to capitalist hazard since the opening of the play, and capitalist hazard in turn connected to wooing, marrying, vowing. An observed difference between new and old marriage vows elicits the speech.

In the extended metaphor illustrating a principle that "ever holds," we might be hearing the story of Everyman's marriage. The chase, the courtship, the comedy, is played out with vivacity. On their wedding days people set sail like brave ships, tricked out in their finery, only to return at the end of marriage's voyage—to the church? to a funeral?—somehow like the prodigal, beaten and beggared, without any energy left for "obliged faith." Just plain aging no doubt wears us down, sometimes burdening the intimacy of marriage with longstanding mutual resentments. As Dryden observed in the song at the beginning of *Marriage a-la-Mode*,

> Why should a foolish Marriage Vow
>   Which long ago was made,
> Oblige us to each other now
>   When Passion is decay'd?
> We lov'd, and we lov'd, as long as we could,
>   Till our love was lov'd out in us both:
> But our Marriage is dead, when the Pleasure is fled:
>   'Twas Pleasure first made it an Oath.[53]

But the context in *Merchant* suggests that obligation is also a culprit: things once done with zest can lose their flavor when done to meet an obligation. The proverb about a wife providing her husband with two good days, marriage and death, offers a harrowing illustration of the Gratiano Principle.

This interpretation would help to explain why, as first the casket choice and later the ring game of act 5 imply, a man must enter into marriage with his eyes open to the tomorrows of obligation. At least he will know from the beginning what "ever holds" for "all things that are," including the couples of comedy.

Shakespeare's comedies end just before or soon after marriage—at the eager moment of "new-made vows," not at the relatively dispirited times of "obliged faith." What can a comedy do to lay in stores of good fortune against a lean future?

End well. Act 5 of *Merchant* is a wonderful tour de force, a *Merchant* in miniature that gathers in the meanings of the play and prepares them for domestication. "Let us go in," Portia advocates in her final speech (5.1.297). Beginning with intimations of world harmony, act 5 ends in a sexual quibble packed with the shapeliness and good order of the entire play. Marriage, like act 5, joins the harmonics of the mind to the couplings of the body.

Richard Levin has mocked the apparent simplicities of "thematic" criticism. Richard Rorty has chased from the stage a conspiracy of out-of-date metaphysical presuppositions dedicated to making interpreters say that a literary work is "about" something.[54] Half of me knows there is nothing to discover, while the other half brims with the joy of it. I hope the happy part can still say that the theme of *Merchant* is promising, and add to the piles of evidence the fact that act 5, after its neoplatonic prelude, talks about nothing else.

The main business is to adjudicate the lingering issue of the status of friendship relative to marriage while trying the new husbands for oath-breach. Bassanio introduces Antonio to his wife as the man "To whom I am so infinitely bound" (135). Portia firmly emends this, putting a modest cap on infinity: "You should in all sense be much bound to him, / For (as I hear) he was much bound for you" (136–37). Unable to wait any longer, Nerissa begins the chiding, though we only hear Gratiano's first explanation. He gave the ring to the judge's clerk, "Would he were gelt that had it for my part." This comic reprisal on the male member continues throughout the wit play of the second couple. These new emplotted ironies head toward Gratiano giving his penis to Nerissa and Nerissa getting a penis from Gratiano—the completion of their interrupted wedding day. All the witticisms of act 5 flow into the watershed quibble waiting at the completion of the comedy.

Now Portia starts to chide. Gratiano, to be plain about it, was to blame:

> To part so lightly with your wife's first gift,
> A thing stuck on with oaths upon your finger,
> And so riveted with faith unto your flesh.
>
> (167–69)

As Nerissa had earlier claimed, the issue is not the loss of the ring itself but the "value" (151) of the ring, the oath that "riveted with faith" the ring to the finger. Fidelity is what has been lost. In a ten-line passage where every line ends with *ring* except for one in the middle, which hangs out the unmelodic word *displeasure,* Portia puts Bassanio on the rack. He is under a strong temptation to lie, or to invent some desperate stratagem, as he reveals in an aside: "Why I were best to cut my left hand off, / And swear I lost the ring defending it" (177–78). The mock trial even has the thought of sacrificed flesh. First the penis of the clerk, and now, more nobly, the ringless hand of the offender.

She mounts a series of jests about marital oath-breach. If

the learned judge is held so dear by Bassanio, Portia will "not deny him any thing I have,/No, not my body, nor my husband's bed" (227–28). The superb doubleness of Portia's wit, naughty but nice, combines a glance ahead at nuptial consummation with a chiding threat that infidelity in the husband will breed a vengeful infidelity in the wife. Portia jestingly pictures a marriage gone bad in terms reminiscent of an Ovidian elegy:

> Lie not a night from home. Watch me like Argus,—
> If you do not, if I be left alone,
> Now by mine honour (which is yet mine own)
> I'll have that doctor for my bedfellow.
>
> (230–33)

In the climactic joke of this sort, Portia and Nerissa matter-of-factly beg pardon that they went to bed last night with the doctor and his clerk. The play does not record a reaction speech from Bassanio. Gratiano, however, voices his comic indignation: "What, are we cuckolds ere we have deserv'd it" (265)? What can comedy do to fortify good vowing? What but make a jest of bad vowing, of domestic revenge, jealous surveillance, casual cuckoldry. Elizabethan audiences must have enjoyed seeing the comic couples absorb a touch of Launcelot. In this play of solemn obligations, subjecting bad vowing to good humor seems a relief, a blessed sanity come just in time to mock the triumph of leaden rigidity.

"I am th'unhappy subject of these quarrels," Antonio confesses. After all, *his* competitive love, *his* hidden jealousy, *his* blind embrace of the flesh bond, and *his* insistent love tests make up the backstory of the lost rings. Bassanio has already admitted that he offered three thousand ducats to the learned judge, who nevertheless preferred the ring. As we noted before, this has to be a significant sum, precisely what Bassanio borrowed from Antonio to finance the first generative promise in the play. However, by the time this amount was offered to Balthazar, Antonio and Shylock had given it a new sense. Both of them measured their grand passion by a pound of flesh—the excess or "interest" over and above the monetary figure. When Portia turned down the money and demanded the ring, she created a private love test in which her husband's ring became the equivalent of Bassanio's suprafinancial devotion to her: her pound of flesh. She indeed got it, but only after Antonio demanded that Bassanio relinquish the token as a demonstration of Bassanio's love for him. Portia must now take care of that interference, of the whole matter of friendship.

Calling his "friends" (241) to witness, Bassanio tries to swear a new oath to his wife:

I swear to thee, even by thine own fair eyes
Wherein I see myself—

Whereupon Portia interrupts, and someone, at last, sees a doubleness in Bassanio:

Mark you but that!
In both my eyes he doubly sees himself:
In each eye one,—swear by your double self,
And there's an oath of credit.

(243–46)

Portia is not entirely joking here. As we have seen, Bassanio earned this Donne-like appraisal during the trial scene, when his wish for his friend's life sacrificed hers. The accused husband completes his oath: "Pardon this fault, and by my soul I swear/I never more will break an oath with thee" (246–47). "But why," Antonio must be thinking, "should Portia believe my undeniably ringless friend?"

At this point Antonio defines his correct position in the life of a married Bassanio:

> I once did lend my body for his wealth,
> Which but for him that had your husband's ring
> Had quite miscarried. I dare be bound again,
> My soul upon the forfeit, that your lord
> Will never more break faith advisedly.

(249–53)

Portia was right about Bassanio's swearing; his oath of credit is indeed sworn by a doubled self. Antonio's first bond put his body in the place of Bassanio's lost fortune. His second bond puts his soul in the place of Bassanio's lost faith. He swears on his own credit that Bassanio will never again "break faith advisedly"—that is to say, on his advice, as was the case with surrendering the ring. In the future he will advise fidelity.

Antonio's friendship is now properly aligned with, and subordinate to, Bassanio's marriage vow. His first expression of love sought to demonstrate its superiority to the marriage-tie. His final expression of love seeks to guarantee that tie. Antonio has come around. A sacrificial need to risk himself for the sake of his friend's debts has found its proper role in Belmont.

Portia accepts the guarantee, activating the binding legal force in *shall:* "Then you shall be his surety: give him this,/ And bid him keep it better than the other" (254–55). The ring then travels from Portia to Antonio to Bassanio. "Here Lord Bassanio, swear to keep this ring," Antonio says. I imagine Antonio putting it on Bassanio's finger, who then gestures at the audience with his hand: back on, back to me! Bassanio went to Antonio to secure Portia. Now Portia goes to Antonio to secure Bassanio. As obligation comes to rest on the hand of Bassanio, the second circle of the plot closes. He enters into the spirit of the jest: "Sweet doctor, you shall be my bedfellow,—/When I am absent then lie with my wife" (284–85). One last gentle rain of good fortune (three ships in for Antonio, half the Shylock estate promised to Lorenzo and Jessica), and Portia is ready to go in. She imagines that the conversation will continue on in the mansion— a trial where the "inter'gatories," the witnesses, "will answer all things faithfully." And the play ends.

Well, almost. Is there not to be some intimate testimony inside the mansion? It is left to a suddenly rhyming Gratiano to bring the comedy down to earth:

> Let it be so,—the first inter'gatory
> That my Nerissa shall be sworn on, is,
> Whether till the next night she had rather stay,
> Or go to bed now (being two hours to day):
> But were the day come, I should wish it dark
> Till I were couching with the doctor's clerk.
> Well, while I live, I'll fear no other thing
> So sore, as keeping safe Nerissa's ring.

Lovers ever run before the clock. Gratiano has also received his ring, though without the ceremony lavished on Bassanio. I imagine him holding his hand up to the audience as he says his closing lines—with a ruder gesture than Bassanio made, since he is the one destined at the very end to reveal the bottommost meaning of a man's finger thrust through a ring.[55] The two rings, symbolic of the plot, are now worn by self-certified happy males, both of them filled with a sexual desire in union with their vows. They can now enact fidelity.

Some of my students refer to the act punningly evoked at the end of *The Merchant of Venice* as "the wild thing." Shakespeare's wild thing: a little bit of nature surrounded by a whole lot of designed obligation; a little bit of animal ringed by promises, vows, oaths, tests, debts, bonds, laws, judgments, and wills.

4
Ironic
Vows

~ ~

Running through *Othello* is a sequence of five quasi-trials. In act 1, Othello and Desdemona come before the Venetian Senate to answer the charges of Brabantio; in act 2, Othello dismisses Cassio after the brawl on Cypress, with Iago acting as a reluctant but effective witness; in act 3, Othello and Iago try Desdemona on charges of adultery; in act 5, Emilia is a star witness in the trial of Othello and Iago and is murdered for her truthful testimony; finally, in the second half of 5.2, the quest for judgment moves to the interior of the hero's soul, who variously assesses himself in his last speeches, ending with a suicide that is both a vehement condemnation and a landmark gesture in the history of romantic extravagance.

The first of these trials, setting the tone of the entire play, is heavy with omens. The idea of his daughter loving Othello seems to Brabantio beyond preposterous: "For nature so preposterously to err,/(Being not deficient, blind, or lame of sense,)/Sans witchcraft could not" (1.3.62–64). Othello will remember these words when giving voice to his first doubting thought about Desdemona: "And yet how nature erring from itself—" (3.3.231). "Ay, there's the point," Iago interrupts. Elaborating on the improbability of Desdemona's love for the rest of the temptation scene, he convinces his general that Desdemona is a case of erring nature rather than exceptional love. Brabantio, finding no ease for his "bruis'd heart" (1.3.219), transfers his sense of betrayal to Othello in a nasty parting shot: "Look to her, Moor, have a quick eye to see:/ She has deceiv'd her father, may do thee" (1.3.292–93). "She did deceive her father, marrying you," Iago will repeat (3.3.210), already in the process of turning "may do" into "is" by giving Othello "a quick eye to see." He adds a tainted urgency to Brabantio's "Look to her": "Look to your wife, observe her well with Cassio;/Wear your eye thus, not jealous, nor secure./. . . look to 't" (3.3.201–4).

"Yet she must die, else she'll betray more men" (5.2.6), Othello declares in the murder scene. This is a difficult line, which we will revisit later on. But surely Othello has at least two men in mind, Brabantio and himself; killing her will choke off the string of betrayals. Brabantio's parting shot has given his son-in-law what becomes, by the end of the tragedy, a motive for murder.

So the tragedy, even before it arrives at Cypress, is already heavily freighted with irony. But recent criticism has loaded the opening scenes of the play with such a weighty cargo of its own invented ironies that the ship of the plot is virtually sunk in the harbor. The lovers are said to begin their marriage lacking virtually all fruits of blessed condition: self-esteem, oedipal maturity, autonomous selfhood, a nonvisual and therefore nonpornographic epistemology, and any protection whatsoever against foul trends in early modern English ideology. As quickly as the productive system of modern literary theory can emit naïveties, they are cast into the word-processed seethe of contemporary *Othello* criticism.

Stanley Cavell's discussion is both typical and influential. The play opens with Iago's poisoned evocation of old black Othello tupping young white Desdemona. It would appear, however, that the consummation of the marriage must wait until the first night on Cypress. Since it is interrupted by a brawl and squeezed into the rapid lapse of the double-time scheme, skeptical minds can doubt its completeness or satisfactoriness. Perhaps the wedding night, having been as bestial and indecent as Iago foretold, trips the murderous jealousy? "My guiding hypothesis about the structure of the play," Cavell reveals, "is that the thing *denied our sight* throughout the opening scene—the thing, the scene, that Iago takes Othello back to again and again, retouching it for Othello's enchafed imagination—is what we are shown in the final scene, the scene of murder."[1] Sex, I guess, is murder. That the sexual act should be denied our sight seems so much a matter of course in the theatrical traditions of planet earth that one is a bit surprised to come upon an influential commentator who really claims to experience it as a denial. That *Othello*'s structure rests on the equivalence of intercourse and murder in its hero's tormented mind seems a hysterical abstraction from the texture of the play.

Not that Cavell is entirely without evidence. Does Othello strangling Desdemona "in her bed, even the bed she hath contaminated" resemble the sexual act? Undoubtedly. Far more so, certainly, than in Cinthio, where the Moor and the

Ensign beat her to death with a sock full of sand, then knock down part of the ceiling to make it look as if a rafter collapsed on her head.[2] "Good, good, the justice of it pleases," Othello observes when Iago suggests the strangling, about which Othello seems to waver (see 5.1.35–36). Then again, Shakespeare's Moor does not lose sight of the difference: "Be thus, when thou art dead, and I will kill thee,/And love thee after" (5.2.18–19). The many readings of *Othello* in terms of dubious consummation and sexual anxiety make heavy weather of porno-violent images "denied our sight." On the surface of the play, Brabantio flings a quite specific worry at Othello—an anxiety about the reliability of her marriage vow.

If anything signficant is denied to a curious audience in the first act of the tragedy, it is the vows of Othello and Desdemona. They triumph before the Venetian Senate without repeating them or giving any specifics about the form or circumstance of their spousals. "My parts, my title, and my perfect soul,/Shall manifest me rightly" (1.2.31–32). Surprisingly enough, they do, and without any show of bona fides. "I have married her," Othello tells the Senate. "Here's my husband," Desdemona soon declares, again withholding details. The substance of *Othello* is the drama of attacking, doubting, testing, defending, keeping, breaking, and defiling these unrepresented promises. No doubt the marriage took place. But all we know is that Desdemona was spirited away from her father's house by gondola and sequestered in an inn named the Sagittary.[3] Their actual promises remain shrouded in silence—and that may well be the point. For once they are exchanged, marriage vows cease to be a historical event. They rather inhere, moment after moment, in an ever repeated act of mutual faith. Desdemona's honor, Iago notes, is "an essence that's not seen" (4.1.16). Such is the strength of marriage, but also, the drama contends, its fragility.

Getting married under Elizabethan law was both easy and difficult.[4] The first stage was trothplight, an exchange of vows. Even if this exchange took place in private, the couple was assumed to be married so long as their vows were tendered in the present tense. But of course private vows were readily subject to legal challenge, should one of the partners wish to back out or one of the families object to the match. For this reason trothplight normally occurred before witnesses, at least before a priest, and signed documents oftentimes accompanied the oral vows. After the posting of the banns, trothplight was solemnized in a church ceremony before the assembled dearly beloved.

Whatever the time or place in which his dramas were set, Shakespeare habitually assumed matrimony to be governed by these Elizabethan procedures. Well aware that *marriage* covers a spectrum of legal bonds from the weak to the unassailable, Iago warns Othello that he must be, in view of Brabantio's opposition, "fast married":

Are you fast married? For be sure of this,
That the magnifico is much belov'd,
And hath in his effect a voice potential
As double as the duke's; he will divorce you,
Or put upon you what restraint, and grievance,
That law (with all his might to enforce it on)
Will give him cable.

(1.2.11–17)

The word *fast* means "securely" but no doubt also alludes in this context to *handfast,* one of the several names for the trothplight ceremony.[5]

The ceremony itself sometimes ended with a clapping, then clasping of hands.[6] Milton's Adam and Eve wander out of paradise "hand in hand." In genealogies of the period, the visual logo of clasped hands symbolizes a marriage.[7] Throughout *Othello* hands are featured players in the psychological drama of jealousy. In this context, we should remember how the joined hands of Hermione and Polixenes trigger in Leontes, almost like a genetically imprinted image, the thought of oath-breach. One moment he remembers his three-month courtship of Hermione, "Ere I could make thee open thy white hand,/And clap thyself my love" (*WT* 1.2.103–4); the next moment the sight of "paddling palms, and pinching fingers" drives him to exclaim "Too hot, too hot" (115, 108). Iago's poisoned suggestions will make the hand of Othello's bride seem to him the forswearing agent of deception and betrayal.

A dumb show of hands, proceeding alongside the spoken text of *Othello*, narrates in body language its story of betrayed idealism. When rehearsing with Roderigo his ability to present a convincing case for adulterous love between Desdemona and Cassio, Iago calls attention to their hands: "Didst thou not see her paddle with the palm of his hand" (2.1.251–52)? Their touches were not, as Roderigo supposes, "courtesy," but "Lechery, by this hand: an index and prologue to the history of lust and foul thoughts" (254–55). Ocular proof will be provided to Othello by the fatal handkerchief, originally passed from the giving hand of Othello ("my first gift" [3.3.443]) to the receiving hand of Desdemona. Maddened with jealousy, Othello will strike Desdemona with one hand, smother her with both. Desdemona's hand appears to him "Hot, hot, and moist," heat and sweat being traditional signs of lust. Her lusty hand requires

> A sequester from liberty; fasting and praying,
> Much castigation, exercize devout;
> For here's a young and sweating devil here,
> That commonly rebels: 'tis a good hand,
> A frank one.
> *Des.*   You may indeed say so,
> For 'twas that hand that gave away my heart.
> *Oth.* A liberal hand; the hearts of old gave hands,
> But our new heraldry is hands, not hearts.
>
>   (3.4.36–43)

Milton, also alive to the mute poetry of manual gesture, will remember this passage when his Eve feeds the forbidden fruit to Adam "With liberal hand."[8] The main idea here is that Othello believes himself to have married in the squalid Venice whose "country disposition" has been described by Iago (3.3.205–8), a time and place of "new heraldry," where palpable hands are given (outward signs of vowing) but invisible hearts are not (being full of deception). We can understand the contrast by recalling the "old" form of handfast represented in *The Tempest.* "Here's my hand," says Ferdinand. "And mine, with my heart in't," Miranda replies, sealing their vows (3.1.89–90). Othello will ultimately want to be remembered "as one whose hand, / Like the base Indian, threw a pearl away." Then he returns his hand, instrument of vowing and revenging, to its pre-Desdemona glory, a valiant warrior's hand dedicated to punishing the enemies of Venice, and judges himself with its death stroke.

"Iago's essential achievement," in McAlindon's formulation, lies in "the undoing of all the words, vows ('a frail vow betwixt an erring barbarian and a super-subtle Venetian' [1.3.354–55]), tokens (a strawberry-spotted handkerchief) and gestures (shaking or kissing the hand) that constitute the fabric of human relations"—relations, I would only add, based on promising.[9] What we witness is the systematic "unhanding" of Othello from his trothplight, freeing him to conspire, to make new vows based on the false belief in her infidelity, and ultimately to punish.

The arch-villainy of Iago, which usually appalls critics of the play but sometimes wins their admiration, has many facets—a resentment of gentility, a disparaging view of women as sexually voracious, envy of Cassio, a gnawing hatred of the Moor, a savoring of his artist's power to plot and deceive. But the connective tissue is a deep-seated conviction in his superiority, and this trait bears to some extent upon promising. Imposing loyalty oaths in order to secure the new institution of the Anglican church, Tudor authorities were counting on fear: a false oath invited the wrath of God. But they were also banking on self-esteem. Swearing an oath—making a promise of any kind—creates a new virtue, fidelity, which infuses the will with moral pride. One might have held a certain truth, or behaved a certain way, without the impingement of a promise, but once the promise is in place, the holding or the behaving becomes an example of the new virtue of being faithful.

Richard pretends to be the ideal subject, the man of conscience presupposed by an oath-administering society. In the difference between this public persona and the ruthless manipulator, stripped of the fears and self-esteems Christian government presupposed, we behold the glimmerings of a new kind of self-respect. For Richard surely loves himself. His is the arrogance of one who has seen through pieties of the will; fidelity, no longer an ethic governing conscience, becomes a worldly instrument for satisfying his will. Iago is thus a development of Richard, a man in whom self-esteem has cut loose from the piety of being faithful to latch onto the brilliant iconoclasm of being pure will out for satisfaction, not virtue. Shylock, in this regard, is a more old-fashioned villain. He makes a sacred vow to prosecute the letter of his bond; piety and revenge come into alliance. When circumstances conspire against him, and he offers to relinquish his pound of flesh for a cash settlement, he breaks his vow and suffers accordingly. Richard by contrast is a new-fangled character, but Shakespeare pulls him back into the old assumptions of an oath-administering society, linking his comeuppance to the truth of an oath he himself considers to be no more than an instrument of his will.

Iago is close to being a new man boasting of a new, post-promising worldview. He uses promises to lead Cassio, Desdemona, and Othello by their noses to an ironic fate—ironic in large part because that end, though achieved through promises, is, as McAlindon says, the "undoing of all . . . vows." But he himself, in his soliloquies and his conversations with Roderigo, never vows. Othello grandly promises to take revenge on Desdemona, and Iago vows his assistance. But Iago, when we suppose him to be speaking in his own person, never promises to take revenge on Othello. He simply does it. This villain's inner life proceeds without reference to piety.

When Iago declares, in his definitive formulation of the split between public duty and private self-serving, "I am not what I am," he confirms the wisdom of a longstanding ambivalence about public swearing: there are indeed fearless men, men without conscience, men whose self-esteem does not derive from virtue, for whom the public investment in oath-taking is, so to speak, a God-sent opportunity to thrive. It seems emblematic that Iago's main speech on the will should begin with a contemptuous dismissal of virtue:

> Virtue? a fig! 'tis in ourselves that we are thus, or thus: our bodies are gardens, to the which our wills are gardeners, so that if we will plant nettles, or sow lettuce, set hyssop, and weed up thyme; supply it with one gender of herbs, or distract it with many; either to have it sterile with idleness, or manured with industry,—why, the power, and corrigible authority of this, lies in our wills. If the balance of our lives had not one scale of reason, to poise another of sensuality, the blood and baseness of our natures would conduct us to most preposterous conclusions. (1.3.319–30)

The traditional metaphor of moral and spiritual gardening devolves before our eyes: the language of ethical renovaton is here being used to exhort Roderigo to do whatever it takes to bed Desdemona. There is still something called reason, able to direct the will to its satisfactions, but this reconfigured reason belongs to "the power and corrigible authority" of the sovereign will. What Iago terms reason is no more than the capacity to scheme: by showing will the paths to success, "reason" prevents it from lapsing into base despair.

In Iago we find what is only nascent in the more mythi-
cal contours of Richard—a largely realistic portrait of a
prideful immorality generating its self-esteem, its sense of
superiority, from the very dismissal of virtue, duty, loyalty,
honesty, fidelity. His Nietzschean will prides itself on not
becoming encumbered with promising. At the end of the
play, Othello demands an explanation; he would know
"Why he hath thus ensnared my soul and body" (5.2.299).
What, for a man like Othello, would constitute an explanation? He might well expect to hear something like his own
story, an account of how Iago, believing himself wronged,
vowed to take revenge on him. For Iago, however, will is
the only justification. He simply *wanted* to destroy Othello,
and reason showed him how to do it. "Demand me nothing, what you know, you know" (304). Inasmuch as Iago's
will stands revealed in Othello's tragedy, there is nothing
more to say, no higher court of justification, and Iago's
words are in fact the first honest thing he has said to Othello
in the entire play. They confront each other like alien beings
from different worlds, though they derive from two poles
of the same historical process. For Othello, it must seem
demonic cruelty in Iago to say that he already knows the
explanation. For Iago, it must seem an ongoing stupidity in
Othello to think that he does *not* know the explanation.

A villainy beyond promising, and a virtue inconceivable
without promising, pass like ships in the night in *Othello*.
But there is one tragic difference between them: vice understands what makes virtue tick, while virtue can never grasp
the unimaginable inner workings of vice. A villainy this
complacent, this complete in itself, has its fascinations.
However, I am finally more interested—I think the play is
more interested—in the acid baths of irony in which the

well-intentioned promises of the virtuous characters are repeatedly dipped.

The absence of detail about marriage vows gives a sinis-
ter emphasis to the vows we actually witness at the pivotal
moment of the tragedy. "Patience I say, your mind may
change" (3.3.459), Iago remarks after Othello has called
out for blood. Dropping to his knees, a murderous Othello
compares his "bloody thoughts" to the ever running, never
ebbing tides flowing from the Black Sea to the Sea of Mar-
mara and through the Dardanelles into the Aegean.[10] He
will not look back. His course is set "due on" to vengeance.
He will not succumb, as Iago has suggested he might, to the
weakness of "change"—to what Othello calls "humble
love" and Iago has termed "patience."

But like Shylock, Othello must anticipate a future moment in which he will be tempted by mercy or at least
stymied by indecision, for he redoubles this statement of certain direction with a private vow. A promise is necessary to
assure his certain course:

> Even so my bloody thoughts, with violent pace
> Shall ne'er look back, ne'er ebb to humble love,
> Till that a capable and wide revenge
> Swallow them up. Now by yond marble heaven,
> In due reverence of a sacred vow,
> I here engage my words.
>
> (464–69)

His last two and a half lines formally "engage," put under
the obligation of a sacred vow articulated in the present
tense, his prior future-tense description of bloody thoughts
rushing into the swallowing sea of bloody deeds. Iago,

dropping to his knees beside Othello, seconds the vow in giving up his "excellency" of "wit, hand, heart, / To wrong'd Othello's service."

They proceed to divide the task. Othello's occupation being gone, Iago is through his vow of service "my lieutenant" in an altogether new sense: second-in-command on the field of vengeance, his duty the killing of Cassio within three days. Othello himself, "wronged Othello," will find some means to kill the "fair devil." It is the marriage of a deceived mind with a false mind, to be consummated in murder and admitting no impediments. Iago's "I am your own forever" (486) is reminiscent of Hermione's promise during her trothplight with Leontes: "then didst thou utter / 'I am yours forever'" (*WT* 1.2.104–5). The marriage vows kept in the dark in act 1 now come forth, perverted, in the linked revenge vows of Othello and Iago.

We can already discern the irony of the absent wedding vows at the beginning of the play. Just as Othello predicted, the Venetians do believe his title and trust that he is "fast married": the one who does not trust the marriage turns out to be (nudged by Brabantio, led by Iago) Othello himself. Engaging his words in a sacred vow, he formally disowns his faith in Desdemona's troth. His replacement for that loss is a trothplighting dedication to punish her in concert with honest Iago. But the playwright sharpens to an even finer point the ironies of promising in his tragedy. For Desdemona also makes a vow on Cypress. She demonstrates (to the eyes of the audience) her meticulousness as a promise-keeper and (to the eyes of her husband) her wantonness as a promise-breaker.

Escaping Brabantio's "guardage" (1.2.70) to marry Othello, Desdemona leaves everything behind. No attempt was made to secure the consent of her father. She risks his displeasure, and when she gets it, bears the burden as one of her own choosing. She acted with "downright violence, and scorn of fortunes" (1.3.249). Her primary duty of obedience has shifted from father to husband (180–89); Brabantio would not have her reside with him while Othello goes to war, nor would she impose on him again (240–43). But another choice between divided loyalties emerges on Cypress. As Iago quite rightly says, after suggesting that Cassio pursue his cause through Desdemona, "'tis most easy/The inclining Desdemona to subdue,/In any honest suit" (1.3.330–32).

Her vow to champion the suit of the dismissed Cassio makes it clear that, for "inclining" Desdemona, keeping promises is a point of great moral pride. Cassio can be "well assur'd" that she will keep him "in a politic distance" (3.3.11–13). This is not assurance enough for Cassio, who still fears that his cause will be forgotten. Desdemona is happy to augment her assurance with a formal promise:

> before Emilia here
> I give thee warrant of thy place; assure thee
> If I do vow a friendship, I'll perform it
> To the last article; my lord shall never rest,
> I'll watch him tame, and talk him out of patience;
> His bed shall seem a school, his board a shrift,
> I'll intermingle every thing he does
> With Cassio's suit; therefore be merry, Cassio,
> For thy solicitor shall rather die
> Than give thy cause away.
>
> (19–28)

It almost goes without saying that Shakespeare loved irony. But the sustained profusion of ironies in *Othello* is remarkable even by his standards. Nearly everything that is said, by foreshadowing the lethal deception of the hero, loses its immediate contextual innocence and acquires tragic ominousness. Her vow to Cassio will indeed "intermingle" with her vow to Othello, infecting the most intimate places of her marriage. She really will die, in part, for not giving his cause away.

This meeting with Cassio at the beginning of the long temptation scene prompts Iago's "Ha, I like not that" (35). So the hook of deception has already been nibbled on when Desdemona begins her first attempt to win Othello to Cassio's cause: "I have been talking with a suitor here," she says (43), and the second, ironic, tragic, Iago-tainted sense of *suitor* appears to penetrate Othello's ear, who asks obtusely, as if unable to connect the man he has just seen parting from his wife with the ironic sense of *suitor*: "Who is't you mean" (45)? She means Cassio of course, who served as a go-between during courtship, who spoke well of Othello when she herself was disposed against him. Othello will hear no more of this, not now. He sends her away after granting a concession to her insistent advocacy. "Prithee no more, let him come when he will, / I will deny thee nothing" (76–77).

When she next renews her suit, the handkerchief has been lost. Othello looks upon her hand with deceived eyes and beholds a moist devil. Oblivious in her innocence, Desdemona demands the fulfillment of his promise. "What promise, chuck?" "I have bid Cassio come speak with you" (3.4.45–46). At this point, claiming a runny nose, Othello asks for the handkerchief. Instructed about its importance and sharply interrogated on its whereabouts, she tries to stifle the subject with a white lie or maybe just a fervent hope ("I say it is not lost"), and returns to her vowed advocacy. "This is a trick, to put me from my suit,/I pray let Cassio be receiv'd again" (85–86). As she proceeds to sing Cassio's praises, an enraged Othello three times interrupts her with "The handkerchief!"

The ironies of the scene have their comic side.[11] Demonstrating to her own satisfaction good faith in her vow to Cassio, she simultaneously, faithful act after faithful act, demonstrates to Othello the infidelity in her vow to him. They have opposed pictures of the situation, and the pictures turn on kept and unkept promises. She sees herself being loyal to a vow while her husband tries to wheedle out of a promise. He sees a fidelity to Cassio that ever more flagrantly means infidelity to him. She hears neither the full force of his jealousy nor the tainted meanings in her own ambiguous words. He neither hears the hapless force of her innocence nor recognizes her deafness to his intensifying jealousy. The audience has a third and different picture. It understands both of their pictures and hears single pieces of language breaking off into two disparate zones of interpretation. "Zounds!" is Othello's exit line, at least in Q1. The conjunction, in his eyes, of Desdemona's loyalty to Cassio and disloyalty to him produces a blasphemous oath—a swearing against the God whose truth stands behind all swearing.

When Ludovico arrives with a letter asking Othello to resign his command to Cassio, Desdemona again returns to the "unkind breach" between her husband and his former first lieutenant. She hopes "To atone them, for the love I bear to Cassio" (4.1.228). Othello in the meantime is raging away, maddened by her ill-concealed confessions of betrayal: "Fire and brimstone!" When she learns the contents of the letter, which if followed to the letter would reinstate Cassio and successfully conclude her advocacy, she cannot suppress her pleasure—indeed, she expresses it with an asseveration, lest anyone be in doubt: "By my troth, I am glad on't" (233). For Othello, of course, that gladness fairly screams out her troth to Cassio and untroth to him. This latest example of her stubborn dedication to Cassio's welfare issues in a blow. An epithet goes with it, twice repeated a moment later: "Devil!" One of the keys to Desdemona's "inclining" character is her ardent oath-keeping.

When the fact of Othello's jealousy has finally broken through to Desdemona, she again meets with Cassio. Even now her main concern is that Cassio believe she was true to her vow of friendship. Though unsuccessful, she has advocated her cause to the point of recklessness and will do still more, holding Cassio's interests above her own:

> So help me every spirit sanctified,
> As I have spoken for you, all my best,
> And stood within the blank of his displeasure
> For my free speech: you must awhile be patient;
> What I can do I will, and more I will
> Than for myself I dare, let that suffice you.
>
> (3.4.123–28)

"So help me every spirit sanctified" is an oath implying that, if she speaks falsely, every sanctified spirit should *not* help her. Clearly she does not expect this oath alone, though a serious one, to bear the main brunt of persuasiveness here. Cassio is to believe her because she who was, before the Venetian Senate, "subdued/Even to the utmost pleasure of my lord," has for Cassio's sake incurred his displeasure. As a vow-keeper, Desdemona is impeccably obedient. As a vow-giver, she leaves implicit, and therefore unsaid, the curses wound up in her promises. Her character as a vower bears on the tragedy.

About the character of Desdemona, as about that of Othello, there are varying opinions.[12] One of my favorite Shakespeare critics, A. P. Rossiter, not at his best on this play, mounts a furious moral tirade, availing himself of whatever sermonizing zeal he can find in the alien vocabulary of psychoanalysis, "omitting as much of Oedipus as I can, and saying *nothing* of homosexual patterns or pseudo-patterns," to indict the character of Othello, of anyone who ever admired Othello, and finally of "this pathetic, girlish, nearly-blank sheet, Desdemona."[13] Easy to dismiss this as a fit of pique brought on by the achingly ironic twists of the plot; "nearly-blank sheet" is no doubt a most unfortunate phrase. But there *is* something exasperating about the character of Desdemona.

We sense it, for example, when she and Emilia have their conversation about cuckolding husbands. Would a wife do such a thing for all the world? Emilia, entering into the spirit of this hypothetical, states that she surely would, and uses an asseveration that in other circumstances would simply be emphatic: "By my troth, I think I should, and undo't when I had done it" (4.3.70–71). But since the issue here is fidelity to the troth of marriage, her "By my troth" comically undoes itself. Emilia would "undo't" in the sense that, having acquired the world through adultery, she would then make her husband the monarch of it. Desdemona, however, cannot get past the sheer wrongness of the doing: "Beshrew me if I would do such a wrong,/For the whole world"

(77–78). She has not understood the force of Emilia's point, which involves imagining not only that one is adulterous but that one really does, as the fantasy reward for one's adultery, rule the world. The older woman has to spell it out: "Why, the wrong is but a wrong i' the world; and having the world for your labour, 'tis a wrong in your own world, and you might quickly make it right" (79–83).

There are several things that a good woman might say here. Emilia has invited her to imagine ruling the world and from this perspective to realize that might, custom, and the disposition of pragmatic earthly power actually do, in their way and in their sphere, make right and wrong. Desdemona could reply that this is so in the world, yet there is another world, and in it an observing God, whose right and wrong have nothing to do with this-worldly pragmatics. But she is not this sort of good woman. Desdemona refuses to play the imaginative game of ruling the world. She will not taint her mind by conceding anything to the determining power of earthly authority. She literally can't get into it, can't imagine that even Emilia is into it: "I do not think there is any such woman" (83).

We might well suspect that Desdemona here reveals a temperamental refusal to imagine herself a man. Surely that imaginative leap must be entailed in the ability to fantasize about ruling the world, since males in Shakespeare's plays do in fact rule it. Emilia will later say in her version of "Hath not a Jew eyes?" that adulterous women who do resort to "some revenge" are but instructed by their husbands: "The ills we do, their ills instruct us so" (103). Again, the ability to participate in this thought-experiment and imagine oneself an adulterous woman, rests on a knowledge of maleness. Desdemona declares that "Men are not gods"

(3.4.146), but she shies away from the sordid consequences of their earthliness, and indeed a few lines after uttering this prudent declaration recovers her idealization of Othello: "Now I find I had suborn'd the witness,/And he's indicted falsely" (151–52). This purity of imagination will obviously handicap her in trying to convince a man: you have to know your audience. Along the same lines, she faces the moral issue of adultery wholly oblivious to earthly pragmatism. When Iago says that "out of her own goodness" he will "make the net/That shall enmesh 'em all" (2.3.352–53), he has in mind a specific aspect of her goodness, not a general virtue common to all good people.

A. C. Bradley, another favorite not at his best on this play, betrays some of Rossiter's exasperation in saying that Desdemona is "helplessly passive." He goes on to explain that "she is helpless because her nature is infinitely sweet and her love absolute."[14] True, she is somewhat passive in not figuring out that Othello suspects her with Cassio; she might have asked Emilia about the handkerchief. But what we have traced thus far looks more like helpless activism—helpless because (and perhaps Bradley's Victorian vision of a woman all sweetness and wholly loving implies this) she lacks an imagination of the jealous male psyche realistic enough to grasp how profoundly her words and actions are being misunderstood by her husband. Having no picture of Othello's picture, she is unable to translate her innocence into an effective pragmatic denial. One definitive shape of the play's ironies: Othello is too trusting to imagine a deceitful Iago; Desdemona is too trusting to imagine a jealous Othello.

I am about to propose a definition of how an audience might find its own privileged comprehension of these ironies reflected in the play itself. I realize that this can be only an approximation, occupying the audience intermittently at best. But Iago, who can imagine the vulnerable trusting of both Othello and Desdemona, represents from the beginning an irresponsible pleasure-seeking in the audience that enjoys this deliciously evil irony. Emilia, who imagines an Othello, a Desdemona, *and* an Iago, then ultimately discovers their tragic convergence, comes by the end to represent the responsible side of the audience that deplores this painfully ironic evil.

By the time Othello confronts Desdemona with direct accusations in the so-called brothel scene (act 4, scene 2), he can no longer be turned around by ordinary protestations. Jealousy feeds on itself. That is, when a predisposed Othello makes a jealous, tainted interpretation of one of Desdemona's innocent remarks, his jealousy receives a confirmation. He is that much more likely to hear a tainted meaning in her next innocent remark, and so on, ever deeper into self-deception. Dismissing Emilia as if she were a procuress in a brothel, Othello demands of Desdemona "Why, what art thou" (4.2.34)? "Your wife, my lord, your true and loyal wife," she honestly replies, defining herself by reference to her marital vows. Othello seizes on this reference to swearing:

> Come, swear it, damn thyself,
> Lest, being like one of heaven, the devils themselves
> Should fear to seize thee, therefore be double-damn'd,
> Swear thou art honest.
>
> (36–38)

Anticipating a vow of innocence, he has already interpreted it. Simply to be dishonest is damnation. To be dishonest and falsely to swear honesty is to be "double-damn'd." A false oath, added to the crime, will destroy her resemblance to an angel and make claiming her an easier task for the devils. What he says of the devils he also means of himself: a keen sense of Desdemona's beautiful innocence, the image he loved and married, intrudes now and then on his jealous hatred for her, right to the moment of murdering her. How can she reply to "Swear thou art honest"? How can she possibly vow her innocence, when that vow has itself been predefined as the full revelation of her wickedness? It's a double bind. Double-damned if she does, damned if she doesn't.

"Heaven does truly know it" is her first attempt, and Othello simply throws it back in her face, jealous side out: "Heaven truly knows, that thou art false as hell." Desdemona harks back to the letter putting Cassio in command. Perhaps Othello is enraged because her father might have played a role in securing that order? If so, her father has become her enemy as well (45–48). We can see that she is still some distance away from an apprehension of the real situation. She understands, because she lived through it and made a definitive choice, the conflict between obligation to her father and obligation to her husband. Hence, attempting to grasp matters, she supposes that Othello might think she was in league with her father in removing him from command. This obtuse reconstruction of his feelings inspires another of Othello's characteristically self-pitying rants. He is a man disposed toward stoic patience. He could bear the slings and arrows of outrageous fortune—diseases, shames, poverty, hopeless captivity, scorn—but not letting foul toads "knot and gender" in "there, where I have garner'd up my heart, / Where either I must live, or bear no life, /

The fountain, from the which my current runs, / Or else dries up" (58–63).

The word *there* must allude not just to her vagina, as so many recent critics assume, but to her womb as well.[15] His adulterous wife cheats him of the "life" of lawful issue. This speech is one of the few before act 5 to stir the ethic of honor. Female honor, the chastity of the wife, as Hermione says to her jealous husband in *The Winter's Tale*, "'Tis a derivative from me to mine" (3.2.44). Her honor assures the honor of the bloodline, issuing in children who know their mother and father, parents who know their sons and daughters.[16] "I hope my noble lord esteems me honest," Desdemona says (4.2.66), at last attuned to her husband's poisoned picture.

"Alas, what ignorant sin have I committed?" As always, misfortune dogs her words; her name derives from a Greek word meaning "ill-starred."[17] Since *committed* is a common euphemism for "committed adultery," she has, as it were, ignorantly committed a sin in her very question about ignorant sinning. Othello sees only a brazenness that ought to be intolerable to the universe: "what committed,—/ Impudent strumpet!" The charge is out in the open now, unmistakable, and there follow two questions and two answers backed up with vows. "Are you a strumpet?" "No, as I am a Christian." She rests her marital faith on her religious faith. There may be a curse implicit in the vow. If she is lying about being faithful, then she is lying about being a Christian and implicitly invites the wrath of God for her false claim to religious faith. "What, not a whore?" "No, as I shall be sav'd." The second vow strengthens the implications in the first. Falsity here would mean a willful loss of salvation.

Even Othello seems for a moment impressed: "Is't possible?" Granted, the line may be read in two ways. Is it possible, since he knows her to be false, that she could lie under threat of damnation? Then again, what I take to be the actual meaning, Othello could be reassessing his confirmed and reconfirmed picture of things. Could she possibly be faithful? Is all this whorishness only in his mind?

I take this to be the meaning because it produces the most delicious, most painful irony. Her vow has stopped him in his tracks. She has heard the accusation; there has at last been direct communication; she has staked her salvation on her fidelity. Another misfortune is about to land. We have to see things from Desdemona's point of view. It is only with evident reluctance that she has suffered her ignorance of the cause of his wrath to be stripped away. Openly called a strumpet and a whore, she has twice vowed that she is not. Desdemona has not wanted to come to this place; there is in her mind no reason why she should. *Just having to suffer through this moment* must be a malign fate, punishment for some ignorant and obscure sin. So she says, misfortune now fairly nipping at the heels of her words, "O heaven, forgiveness." Her little prayer, seeming to a jealous ear to confess the very sin she is denying, brings Othello back to his self-deceived senses. "I cry you mercy," he says, answering her prayer with the ironic rage of a renewed conviction in her guilt, "I took you for that cunning whore of Venice,/ That married with Othello" (90–92). The moment of reconsidering is gone. They will scarcely talk again until her murder.

Standard vowing almost turned the tables. Curses were implicit in her vows, but left unsaid. Her disavowals lacked bite.[18] What if she had tried a harder form of vowing, staking her truth on her faith in God, then specifying the curses to which she would be subject should her vow be false? It is, ironically, Othello who, throughout the play, makes the curses explicit. "Fire and brimstone!"—"Devil!"—"Therefore be double-damn'd"—"Would thou hadst ne'er been born"—and finally, to Emilia on his way out of the brothel scene, "you, mistress / That have the office opposite to Saint Peter, / And keeps the gates in hell." But Desdemona herself seems to shy away from the element of cursing in the structure of a vow. Goodness, not fear, seems to her motive enough for promise-keeping.

It is among the supreme ironies in the play that the hard sort of vow, the vow with curses expressed, the vow that might have made Othello more than for a moment uncertain of himself, Desdemona in fact offers, soon after Othello has departed, to Iago. Othello knelt before heaven in swearing his sacred vow of revenge. Swearing a sacred vow of her innocence, Desdemona kneels before Iago:

> O good Iago,
> What shall I do to win my lord again?
> Good friend, go to him, for, by this light of heaven,
> I know not how I lost him. Here I kneel:
> If e'er my will did trespass 'gainst his love
> Either in discourse of thought or actual deed,
> Or that mine eye, mine ears, or any sense,
> Delighted them in any other form,
> Or that I do not yet, and ever did,
> And ever will (though he do shake me off
> To beggarly divorcement) love him dearly,
> Comfort forswear me! Unkindness may do much;
> And his unkindness may defeat my life,
> But never taint my love. I cannot say "whore":
> It does abhor me now I speak the word;

To do the act that might the addition earn
Not the world's mass of vanity could make me.

                                    (4.2.150–66)

Iago will be the go-between, the new Cassio, in a second courting of Othello.

Why does this irony arise? Why does she swear for Iago, but not for Othello, a vow (and on her knees, too) that convincingly details her innocence, defines her love, and specifies the "comforts" she puts at risk should she not be true? The answer must lie in her feeling that Iago is "another person" in a sense that Othello is not. She has not made a marriage vow to him, and therefore, in her mind, he stands in need of a more convincing promise. Her wifely fidelity, on the other hand, requires little defense beyond restatement before her husband. He, after all, *has* her fidelity. She is his. Her relatively weak vowing before Othello is a sign of her innocence—of the invisible strength of her faith. But Othello, as his speeches repeatedly note, is no longer Othello: his occupation is gone, his faith is gone, his love is blown to the winds. Nothing could make Desdemona *be* a whore. But she ought to be considering: what could make me be *thought* a whore?

This is the tack taken by Emilia, as she thinks her way toward the knowledge of the audience:

Why should he call her whore? who keeps her com-
    pany?
What place, what time, what form, what likelihood?
The Moor's abus'd by some outrageous knave.

                                    (139–41)

One practical thing to do is to seek out "some outrageous knave." The audience agrees and can also, in view of the brothel scene, imagine another wise thing to do. Desdemona should abandon the native plain style of innocence and deny the charge before her husband with full use of the great Renaissance rhetoric of serious vowing. How exasperatingly ironic that she should do precisely that to prove her innocence to the "outrageous knave" himself! He who, next to herself, already knows it best of all!

Because she cannot imagine how Othello could call her a whore, because she cannot even imagine that adulterous women exist, Desdemona goes to her death without ever comprehending the jealousy that is its cause. But if she cannot understand a jealous man, she can understand, in the context of courtship rather than marriage, a faithless one. The mass of Elizabethan platitudes about the unreliable vows of courting males has indeed come within her ken. Her famous "Willow Song" is on one level a beautifully confused attempt to understand her mysterious and unwarranted fate.

The scene has been compared to Ophelia chanting "snatches of old lauds / As one incapable of her own distress" (*Ham* 4.7.176–77). Desdemona is not, like Ophelia, "Divided from herself and her fair judgment" (4.5.85), but there is a similarity between Desdemona's song and Ophelia's St. Valentine's ballad (48–66), in that both songs are sung by females who have encountered, in courtship, the unreliability of male vows. Ophelia also dies, as if foreshadowing the "Willow Song," when climbing out on the "pendant boughs" of a "willow . . . askant the brook" to weave garlands. The undersong of thwarted female love in Shakespearean tragedy becomes entirely audible in *Othello*.[19]

Othello has commanded her to go to bed and dismiss Emilia. She has on her own initiative asked Emilia to lay the wedding sheets. A mood of undiminished devotion, ready to "approve" even Othello's "checks and frowns" (4.3.19–20), shares her mind with a dark foreboding: "If I do die before thee, prithee shroud me / In one of those same sheets" (23–24). The fierce ironies of helpless innocence that mark her scenes with Othello here soften into pathos.

She fell in love with him as virtually a literary character, the hero of a romance or romantic epic whose adventures inspired her wonder and pity. Now, her marriage gone inexplicably wrong, she turns for wisdom and succor to another work of art, a song, a specific genre of song—a complaint ballad, learned in her childhood from her mother's maid Barbary:

> She was in love, and he she lov'd prov'd mad,
> And did forsake her; she had a song of "willow,"
> An old thing 'twas, but it express'd her fortune,
> And she died singing it; that song to-night
> Will not go from my mind.
>
> (27–31)

Finally appreciating an irony, she seems to understand that Shakespeare is foreshadowing her end. The song will also express Desdemona's fortune—but in the image of Barbary's fortune, which stands aside from hers, separated as a commentary from a text.

"Ludovico is a proper man," Desdemona remarks before singing. He has gone walking with Othello; that might help.

"He speaks well." She must no doubt be thinking particularly of his last words to her, "Madame, good night. I
humbly thank your ladyship," to which she honestly replied, "Your honour is most welcome" (3–4). Emilia may
have some mischief in mind by praising Ludovico and later
voicing her spirited apologia for adultery. But I do not think,
with many critics, that Ludovico represents Desdemona's
nostalgia for Venice, perhaps for that queue of curled dar-
lings she turned down before meeting Othello.[20] It is rather
that she welcomes the honor of hosting Othello's guest and
appreciates its acknowledgement. She hopes that Othello,
when he comes to bed, will also warm to her honor. But the
"Willow Song" is a psychological and spiritual contingency
plan.

Enough versions of the song survive for us to be fairly
sure that it was popular in Shakespeare's day. It probably
was, to the original audience, "an old thing." Shakespeare
has transposed the genders in the song, but not its general
drift. A man sits alone under the sycamore tree, sighing and
crying, his hand on his bosom and his head on his knee.
Though his love has played him false, he will be true to her.
He complains. The willow will be his funeral garland. To
quote a stanza from our fullest version of the ballad, "The
willow wreath weare I, since my love did fleet;/O Garland
for lovers forsaken most meete."[21] The speaker knows that
his death will make him a conspicuous standard-bearer for
all future male complainers. But he reveals a pronounced
ambivalence over the meaning to be assigned to his sor-
rowful death. He means to prove a point, to accuse: "In
grave where I rest mee, hang this [the willow garland] to
the view/Of all that doe knowe her, to blaze her untrue."
Then again, he does not mean to make that point at all: "I

cannot against her unkindly exclaim,/Cause once well I loved her, and honour'd her name." But the last line in the version from which I have been quoting returns in a fuzzy, unclarified way to the idea of demonstrating, through death, one's truth to a false lover: "Thou dost loath me, I love thee, though cause of my death." Is this forgiving or accusatory?

One can hardly think of a song like this one as having had an author. Verses must have been added and subtracted for its many performances. The popular imagination took the song in two directions, toward a quiet, self-enclosed death and toward a hostile, accusatory death.[22] Moreover, the song as it has come down to us lacks, in the second of these directions, a clear motive for the singer's defiant protestation of truth. Adapting three stanzas from the conventional willow ballad, Shakespeare invents a fourth one that supplies this missing motive.

Desdemona's song, interspersed with preparations for bed, is halted before the last stanza, the one Shakespeare seems to have invented, by three interruptions. First she stops herself. Having sung the stanzas out of order, she must backtrack to air the penultimate one. Then the wind knocks, as if to punctuate her own pause. Then Emilia speaks, identifying the wind as the knocker:

> *The poor soul sat sighing, by a sycamore tree,*
>   *Sing all a green willow:*
> *Her hand on her bosom her head on her knee,*
>   *Sing willow, willow, willow.*
> *The fresh streams ran by her, and murmur'd her moans,*
>   *Sing willow, willow, willow.*
> *Her salt tears fell from her, which soften'd the stones;—*
> *Lay by these:—*

Sing willow, willow, willow.
Prithee hie thee: he'll come anon:—
Sing all a green willow must be my garland.
Let nobody blame him, his scorn I approve,—
Nay, that's not next. Hark! who's that knocks?
Emil. It is the wind.
Des. I call'd my love false love; but what said he then?
  Sing willow, willow, willow:
If I court moe women, you'll couch with moe men.
Now get thee gone; good night: mine eyes do itch,
Does that bode weeping?

(39–58)

Genders transposed, the picture of the poor soul in the first two stanzas would be perfectly familiar to the audience. The line that she sings out of order—"Let nobody blame him, his scorn I approve"—also appears in extant versions of the song. In the context of this scene, it reaches back to echo "my love doth so approve him," Othello's checks and frowns having still, for her, "grace and favour in them." But it also reaches forward to the deaths of both the woman in the song and the woman singing the song. Desdemona's murder will be interrupted, like her song, by a knock at the door and the voice of Emilia.[23] Nobody must blame her love, whose scorn she approves even in the form of murder. Desdemona will answer Emilia's "O, who has done this deed?" with her now famous last words: "Nobody, I myself, farewell:/Commend me to my kind lord, O, farewell" (5.2.125–26)!

But that is not all she says when, as if by miracle, she returns to life. Shakespeare has sharpened the ambivalence in the "Willow Song." The scorn is approved; there must be no blame.[24] But when Desdemona sings the correct next verse, the one that should precede blameless scorn's approval, Shakespeare gives the deaths of both women a second meaning: "I call'd my love false love; but what said he then?/If I court moe women, you'll couch with moe men." We must now imagine this verse to have been sung before the choice to die. The motive Shakespeare adds to the defiant direction of the song is heavy with *Othello*, especially as the play has been experienced by Desdemona. The man stands accused of breaking a vow; he has been "false" to the woman in order to have his way with her sexually and now directs his attention to other women. In the song he blithely declares that she, too, will be false. Just as he courts more women, she will—the language deteriorating from high to low in the shift from "court" to "couch"—bed down with more men. If that were to happen, he would be false, she would be false, and therefore no one would be false: his parting from her would be, as it were, a "no fault" oath-breach. For someone to be false, someone must be true. So, in the invented stanza, the singer will die to prove him false—false about her, and therefore false to her. His unapproved scorn will be emphatically disproved by her death.

"Yet she must die, else she'll betray more men," Othello declares, echoing a half-line ("you'll couch with moe men") of the man's speech in the "Willow Song." When Desdemona returns to life after the caesura in her murder, her first words are the accusatory "O, falsely, falsely murder'd" (118). There must be no misfortune in this final chance to declare her innocence. Othello, his sweet revenge turning harsh, has just heard from Emilia that Roderigo has been murdered and Cassio wounded. Lest Othello, Emilia, or the audience think that she might just have been referring to a falsely murdered Cassio or Roderigo, she unambiguously restates her wronged innocence: "A guiltless death I die" (123).

When its last two stanzas are put back in their correct order, the song accurately foretells the sequence of her two as-if-from-the-grave responses to her murder. First justice and defiance: my death proves him false, myself true. Then mercy and self-effacement: let nobody blame him, his scorn I approve. In the murder scene Othello has a mind split between love and jealous hatred. Desdemona, as her song elaborately forecasts, is divided between submission and defiant defense / accusation. It seems reasonable to interpret her mistake over the order of the stanzas as ambivalence over which message should occupy the climactic position.

For she already knows, when singing the "Willow Song," that merely by hurling accusations of infidelity at her, Othello has been faithless to her—has lost his faith in her. Another definitive shape of the play's irony: while Othello thinks he knows that she has been unfaithful to her vow, Desdemona truly knows that Othello has been unfaithful to his vow. The "Willow Song" bears the pathos of this ironic commentary, turning Othello's accusation back on himself. The ballad permits her to understand his jealousy, with a powerful metaphorical rightness, in terms of being played false. As she approaches her death, Desdemona finds in herself, through the song, what might be called a romantic stoicism. Unkindness can do much. She cannot clear away the falseness of the charge. She cannot change the faithlessness of her husband. All she can control is her ambivalent love— the expressions of this ambivalence, and the ordering of those expressions.

During the murder scene Othello, though he rolls his eyes and gnaws his lip, has somehow risen above the base turmoil of raw jealousy. He thinks of himself as doing the work of all the great authorities who administer the system of truth and justice. "It is the cause, it is the cause, my soul," he mutters to himself. Although the word *cause* was probably never entirely free of its belabored philosophical senses, Othello seems to have its legal meanings primarily in mind. As Nowottny explains, a "cause" is an accusation or a charge, the matter about which one sought legal redress, one's case, the adequate grounds for one's action.[25] Othello is the judge. Later in the scene he will be a kind of priest ("confess thee freely of thy sin"). Nor is godhead from his thought ("this sorrow's heavenly,/ It strikes where it does love"). Judge, priest, God: these are the solemn, watchful figures before whom vows are made and false vows punished.

Othello's cause, insofar as it is sexual, cannot be named beneath the chaste stars. But he has another one, more honorable, that can be proudly named. Is it not, in comparison to the degrading rages of jealousy, a source of self-esteem? "Yet she must die, else she'll betray more men." The focus on betrayal supplies the key to the murderer's peculiarly elevated state of mind. As the scene unfolds, Shakespeare has Othello utter a word that has not yet been used in the play. He has kept its moral force in reserve for the climax of his tragedy. "Sweet soul, take heed, take heed of perjury" (51). Bradley may have been right to suspect that Shakespeare had his doubts about the old superstition of damnation awaiting deathbed perjurers, but there can be little doubt that Othello believes it.[26] To his mind Desdemona is a cunning, practiced, inveterate perjurer. "I would not kill thy

soul" (32). For her sake, then, there must be no more false
denials of her falseness. In any case, vowing is no longer of
any avail:

> Therefore confess thee freely of thy sin,
> For to deny each article with oath
> Cannot remove, nor choke the strong conceit,
> That I do groan withal: thou art to die.
>
> (54–57)

Because vowing would put her soul at risk, and because he
is beyond persuasion, certain of her guilt and her due punishment, he pleads for no more pleading promises. Desdemona only half obeys. She reaffirms her innocence, but
without vows. "I never did / Offend you in my life, . . . never
lov'd Cassio, / . . . I never gave him token" (59–62). But to
Othello, these are still lies. Her stubborn perjury pushes him
over the edge from "sacrifice" (killing only her body) to
"murder" (killing both her body and her soul), and I see no
indication in the text that he ever climbs back to the exalted
role of sacrificer:

> O perjur'd woman, thou dost stone thy heart,
> And makest me call what I intend to do
> A murder, which I thought a sacrifice;
> I saw the handkerchief.
>
> (64–67)

He murders her in the fullest sense. For how else can one
kill a "perjur'd woman"?

Throughout the play adultery and perjury are under-
standably confused in Othello's mind. Insofar as adultery en-

tails a violation of the marriage vow, a proof that her promise was a lie, it is akin to perjury. Akin, but not quite the
same thing. Bradley thought there was a difference when he
distinguished "jealousy proper," which is the thought of
adulterous sex, "of another man's possessing the woman he
loves," from "the wreck of his faith and love," which is the
thought of her dishonored vows and lying disavowals.[27]

I want to be as clear as possible on this crucial matter.
Imagine yourself in the position of Othello. Your spouse has
sex with someone else. What is the worse crime he or she
has committed? Is it the sex with someone else? Or is it the
betrayal of the marriage vow? Jealousy fixes on the first.
Honor mulls over the second. Acting as the representative
of wronged husbands everywhere, urging the cause of betrayal and giving a perjured woman her due, Othello tri-
umphs over the chaotic rage of his jealousy. But the rage still
drives him, however disguised as high-minded charity. As
Desdemona pleads for less and less of life—to be banished,
to be spared for one night, for half an hour, for a last
prayer—he chokes off her pleas in the name of shortening
her pain. Othello has added to the deceit inflicted on him by
Iago the finishing touch of perfected self-deceit. The judge,
punishing a faithful wife for loss of faith, demonstrates his
own infidelity. The priest, thinking he consigns a perjured
soul to hell, damns his own to hell. The God, putting out the
light, uncreates the world, and chaos is come again. Thinking to manifest his ideals, Othello subverts and defiles them.

The irony turns. I have maintained that Desdemona has
been exasperatingly impractical in her weak disavowals
during the brothel scene. But Othello's ultimate unwill-
ingness to hear vows, followed by her naked denials, is the
first of several indications in the last scene of the play that

Shakespeare means for us to reflect on the whole system of
promising. Indeed, some of our exasperation with the tragic
end—so inexorable, yet so many ways it might not have
happened—gets channeled into this reflection. Backing up
a statement with an oath is, after all, a form of rhetoric, a
technique of persuasion. It may be done, like Iago's vowing, not just to assure another person of a supposed truth,
but to gain the advantage of his trust. As Shakespeare shows
us in Othello's perfected self-deception, truth—in the sense
of an accurate picture of things—may not finally have anything to do with promising. Vows depend for their force on
a capacity to be persuaded. That capacity in turn depends
on the auditor's faith, which is itself vulnerable, not only to
false vows, but to other kinds of psychological and rhetorical manipulation. Othello's conviction of her perjury is the
exact measure of his own faithlessness. We will return to
these matters when, after the murder, Othello appeals to the
concept of honor.

The spirit of Desdemona's desperate cries ("O Lord, Lord,
Lord!") seems to pass to Emilia ("My lord, my lord!"), who
indeed becomes the representative of her cause and the des-
ignated interpreter of her true last words. When Othello
admits her into the bedroom, Desdemona revives. Her final
testimony that "nobody" killed her has an ironic sense;
Othello is not himself, and in that respect she really is murdered by nobody she knows. But her foremost intention is
surely to exonerate her husband from the guilt of his crime.
Desdemona's "nobody" forgives him, smothers accusation
in a last reaffirmation of her love, and passes on to Othello
her own faithful innocence.

It first appears that Othello will take this unforeseen opportunity to escape detection. "You heard her say, herself,

it was not I." But Emilia is going to reverse Desdemona's idea of the correct order of the stanzas in the "Willow Song." For her, within the terms of the song's commentary on the forthcoming murder, Desdemona *did not* sing the verses out of sequence. She will be loyal to the first two exclamations of her revived mistress, "O, falsely, falsely murder'd!" and "A guiltless death I die." Her death is to be an accusation, a proof of her innocence and an indictment of her husband's falsity. "She said so," Emilia tells Othello, "I must report a truth." Self-effacing submission will not be allowed the triumph Desdemona intended for it. Welcoming Emilia's enquiry into the truth, Othello confesses the murder—the full murder of body and soul. Why shouldn't he? Desdemona's exonerating last words have provided the last of his many confirmations of her perjury: "She's like a liar gone to burning hell, / 'Twas I that kill'd her."

In large part because of Emilia's vehement insistence, the truth comes to light. Up to now, all of Iago's crimes have been committed under cloak of secrecy. Exposed, accused, he stabs Emilia in full view of the assembly of Venetians (we are not sure how many) in the bedroom.[28] How appropriate that Emilia, in her own dying speech, having solved the mystery of Othello's jealousy and accused Othello and Iago, should reprise the song's refrain:

> What did thy song bode, lady?
> Hark, canst thou hear me? I will play the swan,
> And die in music: [*Singing*] *Willow, willow, willow.*
> Moor, she was chaste, she lov'd thee, cruel Moor,
> So come my soul to bliss, as I speak true;
> So speaking as I think, I die, I die.
>
>   (5.2.247–52)

Barbary, Desdemona, Emilia: three women have expired singing the swan song of the willow. As Emilia's latently inquisitional "My lord, my lord" transforms Desdemona's imploring "O Lord, Lord, Lord," so her "*Willow, willow, willow*" completes the refrain missing at the end of Desdemona's hurried rendition of the ballad. After this musical tidying, she turns her address from Desdemona to Othello. Her last three lines profess one last time the defiant sense of Desdemona's death; the devotion of her living voice to her dead lady is proven by her overswearing of Desdemona's last disavowal of infidelity. "So come my soul to bliss, as I speak true" echoes Desdemona's once ineffectual "No, as I shall be sav'd." The oath finally does its work. In her own defiant way, Emilia has commended Desdemona to her kind lord. Speaking as she thinks, thinking as she knows, Emilia then speaks, thinks, and knows death. There are now two corpses on the bed.

No other tragic end in the canon brings home such a devastating rebuke to the hero as a man, an intelligence, a spiritual being. Lear holds in his arms his dead daughter and dies of grief, but the idea of his ultimate responsibility for her death has been softened somewhat by the reconciliation scenes. The final emphasis is on his unbearable loss, not the destruction of his self-esteem. There must be terrible chagrin in falling to a scorned or dreaded enemy. Macbeth is a poor, deluded reader of the significations of his life. But, stripped one by one of his superstitious protections and facing his destined slayer, he only for a speech feels "cow'd" in "my better part of man" (*MB* 5.8.18), and soon lays the steel on Macduff. Unable to keep his vow to burn Rome, Coriolanus returns to his old enemies to be called "boy of tears" and divested of his proud name. His response to these deeply wounding taunts is to take on a stageful of Volscians. No hero is made such an ass, left so bereft of self-importance, as Othello. It is as if *King Lear* ended on the heath after the old fool had murdered Cordelia. "O gull, O dolt,/ As ignorant as dirt" (5.2.164–65): can we imagine any other of Shakespeare's tragic heroes being scolded in this manner, and with perfect justice, by a lady in waiting? When Ludovico asks the whereabouts of "this rash and unfortunate man," Othello implies that attaching "rash" and "unfortunate" to his manhood is excessively humane: "That's he that was Othello; here I am." After Cassio tells the true story of how he came into possession of the handkerchief, Othello addresses himself in the manner of Emilia. "O fool, fool, fool!"

The primary drama in the remainder of the play turns on fluctuations in Othello's self-regard. After discovering his folly, he makes two references to honor. The first represents a nadir of despair in his thoughts about himself:

> I am not valiant neither,
> But every puny whipster gets my sword;
> But why should honour outlive honesty?
> Let it go all.

$$(5.2.244-47)$$

"Honor," considered as reputation, should not outlive "honesty," the interior virtue that ought to underlie an honorable reputation. "Men should be that they seem," as Othello notes early in the temptation scene (3.3.130). Disarmed of his sword, he has just lost his reputation for valor. Having no honest virtue left, he has no reason to worry about reputation—unless he would be, like Iago, an arch-deceiver; or unless he would be comforted by the empty praises Macbeth calls "mouth-honor" (*MB* 5.3.27). So "Let it go all," assigning to the depths of scorn his former image of public greatness.

After Othello has wounded Iago, Ludovico turns to him. "What should be said to thee?" The question invites him to make a contribution to his own external regard, to place an image of himself in the sphere of honor. Othello answers with his second, more puzzling use of the word *honor:*

> Why, anything,
> An honourable murderer, if you will:
> For nought did I in hate, but all in honour.
>
> (5.2.294–97)

"Why, anything" appears to extend the despairing mood of his earlier "Let it go all." Why should honor outlive honesty? Then all of a sudden Othello says that he is an honorable murderer. What are we to make of this troublesome self-congratulation? He knows he was deceived and mistaken. Even so the murder, to his mind, still has merit.

When we are rocked back on our heels in a Shakespeare play, the first thing to do is always to look for the pattern. Stunningly, puzzlingly, Othello lays claim to the mitigation of honor. What is going on here? Structure: the structure defined by the "Willow Song" continues to unfold. The two bequests of accusation and forgiveness left Othello by the death of Desdemona reverberate in his own conscience at the end of the play. Damning self-accusation is his first and primary response; Emilia makes sure of that. But the claim to honor, however ironic it may be, is the sequel in Othello's mind to the exoneration of Desdemona's last words. As

McAlindon correctly says, "The disclaimer of hatred is pal-
pably untrue, and the appeal to honour can remind us only
of a brutal, wounded pride."[29]

Our hostile reaction to "honourable murderer" must be
seen as a judgment, not just on Othello, but on an entire
ethical system that makes keeping or not keeping a promise more important than the acts promises oblige or pro-
hibit. Although promising creates its own atmosphere of
obligation, and its own charged way of describing action
("Don't break your promise"), we can lose sight of the nat-
ural priority of acting or not acting over the keeping or
breaking promises only by succumbing to the lure of some
casuistical formalism; one of the lures may be that perjury
is so cut-and-dried, so congenial to the judicial tempera-
ment of honor, and unlike the raw enraging deed of un-
chastity, no embarrassment whatsoever to the chaste stars
on the roof of the world. William Godwin had a point when
he argued that if we ought to do something, then we ought
to do it, and promising to do it is superfluous: "promises
and compacts are not the foundation of morality."[30] Moreover, he went on to argue, basing promises on ethical deter-
minations can be a dangerous way of husbanding time. By
fixing our will at a certain stage of our knowing and judging, they discourage us from reconsidering our judgment
by taking the time to learn more. Othello's sacred vow of
vengeance, forged in the heat of impatient fury, seems a
prime example of promising as a substitute for prolonged
reflection. His fidelity to that vow must also play a role in
his late claim to honor. Was he not, during the murder, obeying a sacred vow to carry out his vengeance? Were not those
sacred words engaged "by yond marble heaven" (3.3.467),
before whose chaste stars he but a moment before held his

tongue? Irony once more claims the "honourable murderer" and everything that made him possible. It is a case where, as Eliot writes in "Little Gidding," "honour stains."[31]

The pattern of retrieved self-esteem and devastated self-condemnation proceeds to replicate itself. Finding a sword, Othello regains a portion of his lost manhood: "Behold, I have a weapon." He could once have escaped from a force twenty times larger than the one that surrounds him at this minute: "Who can control his fate? 'tis not so now" (5.2.266). Though the Venetians retreat from this rearmed warrior, they need not fear him now. "Here is my journey's end, here is my butt, / And very sea-mark of my utmost sail" (268–69). The only way to regain some scant control over his fate is to end where he stands: the idea of self-murder seems to form in his mind as soon as he grasps his sword. But then he thinks of Desdemona, staring at the corpse he has made of her, and his momentarily salvaged valor dissolves into self-condemnation. It is not a sight he deserves to have: "Whip me, you devils, / From the possession of this heavenly sight" (278–79). His last comment on "Desdemona dead" (repeating with deepened sorrow the "roar" of 5.2.198) is the exclamation "Oh, oh, oh," mingling his love with his guilt, which might remind an audience, depending on the tone and cadence of the actor's delivery, of "Willow, willow, willow." The exclamation also cuts up his wounded name into the stars of the long vowels that bracket it.[32]

In his last lenghty speech, culminating in suicide, he stipulates how he wishes to be remembered. T. S. Eliot was correct in remarking that Othello in this speech is "*cheering himself up*. He is endeavoring to escape reality, he has ceased thinking about Desdemona, and is thinking about himself. Humility is the most difficult of all virtues to achieve; nothing dies harder than the desire to think well of oneself. Othello succeeds in turning himself into a pathetic figure, by adopting an *aesthetic* rather than a moral attitude."[33] But the pattern holds. The suicide that concludes the speech surely *is* a moral judgment, and one that has by no means forgotten Desdemona. Eliot was right about the renewed pride. What he failed to realize, Braden suggests, making the best case possible for a sympathetic response to the speech, is that Othello's recovery in self-esteem is a necessary prelude to the self-judgment of his heroic suicide.[34] What Braden passes over, however, is the degree to which irony infects "one that lov'd not wisely but too well" and "one not easily jealous."

His disparate self-judgments have settled into a balanced composition of condemnation and qualification:

> I pray you in your letters,
> When you shall these unlucky deeds relate,
> Speak of them as they are; nothing extenuate,
> Nor set down aught in malice; then must you speak
> Of one that lov'd not wisely, but too well:
> Of one not easily jealous, but being wrought,
> Perplex'd in the extreme.
>
> (5.2.341–47)

"O fool, fool, fool!" has mutated into "not wisely," whereas the "honourable murderer" returns in "but too well." Then, in a latent chiasmus, honorable love and foolishness reverse positions in the repeated syntactical structure of "not . . . , but." Honor kept him from being "easily jealous": during the murder he managed to suppress jealousy in rectitude.

But his foolishness made him "Perplex'd in the extreme."
As Othello tells it, his is a story of division—foolishness and
perplexity mitigated by love and honor.

Desdemona would believe it. She has ever loved his stories,
and this one is, as the patterns of the last act reveal, her
legacy to him. But I cannot make the separation Othello demands of us when we nothing extenuate, rid ourselves of
malice, and set down things as they are. Honor and foolishness seem to me mixed together, mutually contaminated.
What the self-description obscures is the fact that his honor
was his foolishness and *was*—indeed, still is—the main-
spring of his perplexity. If honor can put a good face on the
murder of Desdemona, it is a dishonest guide who can stew-
ard self-esteem through any conceivable debasement. The
same moral inflation that made Desdemona's murder such
a travesty of righteousness also swells in Othello's partial
rehabilitation at the end of the play. If I am right in con-
tending that Shakespeare himself rigged "honorourable murderer" to release an ironic backlash, then he too, like Emilia,
has chosen to override Desdemona's climactic forgiveness.
Having poisoned his honor with ironic disdain, Shakespeare leaves Othello "in disgrace with Fortune and men's
eyes."[35] The pitiless ironies of his tragedy will not allow Desdemona to have her way.

But our feelings for Othello undergo one last transition.
He reels to the bed, adding his body to its "tragic lodging"
(364). In order to find the vehemence of the blow, he wan-
dered to Aleppo. Suddenly, across gulfs of time and emotion, Othello reenters the play. Shakespeare juxtaposes the
heroic severity of his self-wounding with the amorous extravagance of his death:

I kiss'd thee ere I kill'd thee, no way but this,
Killing myself, to die upon a kiss.

(359–60)

This sort of couplet was occasionally censured in the eighteenth century, which thought Shakespeare a bit too enamored of showy rhetoric. The couplet is a tiny song, another swan song, entranced by the sounds of *kiss* and *kill*. It contains "I kill'd thee" and "Killing myself" within the boundaries of "I kiss'd" and "a kiss." A critic in 1791 regretted that Shakespeare, having "with uniform propriety" carried through the difficult character of Othello, "should at last fall off, and put a trifling conceit in the mouth of a dying man."[36] A conceited couplet to be sure, a couple's couplet, but not a trifling one.

Back in the temptation scene Othello had twice expressed to Iago "the pity of it" (4.1.191–92). Here we advance beyond ethical judgment, beyond the complex snarls of tragic irony, to behold in moving simplicity the full and complete "pity of it." Othello leaves behind the public world, with its concerns over honor and justice, to die in the realm of pathos opened by the death of Desdemona. His suicide is not merely an act of self-judgment. It is also a heartrending attempt to return to the last time he kissed the living Desdemona, the kisses just before her murder, and die on them. In singling out these kisses as the ones he wishes to die on, Othello conceives them on the model of still earlier kisses. When the lovers reunited in Cypress, he defined the joy of the moment as an ideal death: "If it were now to die, / 'Twere now to be most happy, for I fear / My soul hath her content so absolute, / That not another comfort, like to this / Succeeds in unknown fate" (2.1.189–93). When Desdemona replied that their joys should grow rather than crest, Othello said "Amen to that" but continued to dwell on this present content. As if to mark the moment for future reference in the annals of unknown fate, he twiced kissed her: "And this, and this, the greatest discord be / That e'er our hearts shall make!" He is in fact able to create, out of his catastrophe, another moment like to this.

At his death he comes back, not only to the last kisses before the murder, but to these powerful welcoming kisses indexed in his memory. Anticipated death joins, at death, the memory of that anticipation. "And this, and this" becomes "no way but this." Now the word *this* means suicide. Greatest discord has indeed severed their hearts. But he rhymes it with, and ends it with, a kiss, reconnecting in this broken, pathetic way with the moment earlier defined as the summit of his happiness and his ideal of a "most happy" death. The dense, beautifully turned couplet asserts a truth: there truly is no way but killing oneself to be certain of dying on a kiss. Actors and directors have had many successful ideas for staging the end of *Othello*. Still, I cannot but imagine that he falls on the bed, says his two lines, and dies as he kisses her. Shakespeare wrote it that way. The couplet, reaching through time to happy unions with Desdemona, infuses the story of Othello with pity. Ludovico informs us how his story is to be told in the play's last words: "Myself will straight abroad, and to the state / This heavy act with heavy heart relate."

In this "heavy heart" the judicial rigor of irony—expressions of forgiveness alternating with renewed accusations—finally comes to rest in pity.

Epilogue

I think I must by now have said enough about *Richard III*, *The Merchant of Venice*, and *Othello* to lend credence to my initial suggestion that promising is almost always on Shakespeare's mind. He wrote at a decisive moment in the history of promising, toward the end of its High Christian phase and near the beginning of its metaphysically diminished, though still central role in the "contractual" state. In this as in other respects, Shakespeare rose to his historical occasion. Over and over in his plays, promising does the plot work of motivating, linking, convening, destroying, and fulfilling, trying his characters with burdens of obligation and investing his dramas with literary structure. Promising was particularly fertile for Shakespeare as a source of excellent ironies, some of which turn on the historic shift through which he lived. Soon after beginning this book, I knew it should end with the fellowship of secrecy that Hamlet creates by formal oath-swearing after conversing with his father's spirit. But before we visit this brilliant and somewhat puzzling scene, I want to survey our plays yet again, this time with the intellectual history of my first chapter foremost in mind.

British philosophers in the social contract tradition inherited, most immediately from the English Civil War but also from the sixteenth-century reconstruction of the Anglican church, an uncertain view of the relationship between promising and social order. On the one hand, it was clear that the links joining individuals to the state were forged of promises: this was social stability. Societies require trust and cooperation, and promising broadly considered was in an obvious way the main source of these. But what was to prevent the infection of these promises by a plague of deceit? On what did the strength of this network of agreements depend?

Its original moral prestige derived, as Ralegh and many others attested, from individual conscience, with its twin considerations of faith and fear. In the work of Hobbes, faith and fear lost their immediate relation to the ultimate things of salvation and damnation. Faith became an honorable reputation, fear the dread of state coercion. Only the second could secure the stability of promises. But of course it was precisely the apprehension of coercive authority that had led so many individual consciences, whether backed by the clever reasoning of "equivocation" or simply acting out of self-preservation, to swear false oaths. Hume, like Locke before him, sought to work out a more positive account of the benefits of reliable promising. Fear was still the main enforcer, but Hume, neatly collapsing Hobbes's distinction, located fear in the individual's concern for his good name.

A promise-breaker would incur the penalty of bad repute—and consequently, the terrible ostracism of not being permitted to enter into contractual relations.

The broad conception of Richard III's character, framed for deceit, opens out into this philosophical problematic. To all appearances, he seems a man of saintly conscience, but hidden within is a Machiavel beyond faith and to some degree beyond fear, fueling his self-esteem on his ability to achieve through deceitful means his high-pitched ambitions: Richard is the unconscionable monster that made Ralegh uneasy, that Hobbes could dispose of only by granting him, as king, sole sovereignty over his would-be imitators. Some of the old Christian fear survives in Richard. As I have emphasized, he refrains, onstage at least, from swearing false oaths. But the dire comedy of the second wooing scene arises from a situation later stressed in Hume. For Richard's private self is now public knowledge. What oath can he possibly swear that would convince Elizabeth of his good will toward her daughter? As the comic energy of the scene builds, and oath after oath meets only with skeptical contempt, Richard stands forth ever clearer in his solitude: he has been ejected from promising, and since promising defines the social order, there can be in social terms no isolation more profound. Ultimately, dizzy with frustration, he spells out his own defeat. The drama ends with the detailed realization of his self-confounding curse on himself.

Unlike the more or less secular philosophers who would inherit the subject of promising, Shakespeare had a penetrating, richly ironic understanding of its Christian underpinnings. In Richard he shows us with beautiful clarity that the career of deceit must inevitably be self-defeating; with his overmastering drive to be trusted, the deceitful man will eventually speak the oath compelling his own destruction. Machiavelli and Nietzsche have their roles in Shakespeare's world, but there are traps in place to contain them. In *Richard III*, the trap is the truth of an oath.

What does it take to thwart a Machiavellian egoist? All of the answers later to be offered by philosophers appear in Shakespeare's play. It takes legitimate authority to defeat him by force, as in the victory of Richmond. It takes the loss of his good name, as in the second wooing scene. But this play is still loyal to the old Christian restraints of conscience. Until the midnight soliloquy preceding the Battle of Bosworth Field, the language Richard uses in asides and soliloquies to define his villainy glisters with self-love. Indeed, the power of the character—immediately for the first audience, recessively for us today—resides in this magical suspension of language's ordinary ethical sense. He does not feel the moral force of words because his self-esteem originates, precisely, from *not* feeling that force, from *not* being restrained by a cowardly Christian conscience within which that force is both created and registered. He is virtually an impossible human being in Christian terms: the language of moral condemnation is his language of self-love. But in the last soliloquy, the magical suspension of moral sense for a moment lifts, and the old words of self-love enter his mind bearing their customary moral force. His former language is now revealed as a deeply spiritual variety of perjury—a flattering perjury, a lying denial of his unlovable character. It is his foretaste, here in this life, of the judgment to come.

This confident Christian view of promising survives in *The Merchant of Venice*. Shylock makes a sacred vow on his faith to persist in claiming his pound of flesh despite anticipated temptations to relent. When, defeat staring him in the face, he breaks that vow, he soon thereafter loses his faith. The truth of an oath, reworking the ironies of *Richard III* in yet another portrait of villainy, motivates the punishments that fall on Shylock like the ungentle rain of heaven at the end of the trial scene. But promises and obligations weigh on all the main characters of the play: they have no opportunity, in a sense, to choose anything but the leaden casket, which I interpret as a symbol of obligation. Portia must obey the will of her father; her suitors must take oaths to obey the terms of the casket game; Bassanio, who wins that game, must immediately shoulder the obligation of accepting Portia's ring; Antonio, to whom Bassanio is obligated, obligates himself to Shylock in the flesh bond; Shylock yokes his pursuit of justice to a sacred vow. Promises initiate the double plot, and when the two strands meet in the trial scene, broken promises spirit the play back to Belmont.

On the one hand, the whole feel of the drama is different from that of *Richard III*. Solvency and love replace sovereignty and advantage as the touchstones of ambition. Promising does not turn on loyalty to competing political factions, but on the inevitably divided loyalties of people embedded in marriage, friendship, business. Yet the continuity of making, keeping, and breaking promises runs through these obvious differences. In a Shakespearean history, England is always in a sense the main character, its present deeply informed by its past and future. But if we never think of *Merchant* as being about the epic history of Venice or Belmont, its events are in some fashion attached to a personified abstraction. "Civilization" is a comedy's England, and civilization in *Merchant* makes its way by meeting ob-

ligations it receives from the past and reaffirms by sending
into the future.

So profuse are the promises in the comedy that one might
well reflect that nature has been almost wholly sacrificed to
culture. Obligation manifests itself in the outward form of
a leaden coffin destined to encase our animal remains. As
Gratiano suggests, in time "obliged faith" inexorably becomes burdensome, exhausting, dispiriting. Compelled behavior of any kind tends to become irksome to us, all the
more so when we are continually being tested for our ability to rise above such rebelliousness. And how often in this
play is promising used as a test of civilized virtue! Anxiety
is the hydra of civilization. People exact promises in order
to still anxieties about the reliability of others, but promises—so easy to proffer, so easy to break—produce anxieties of their own. Is anybody without a touch of Richard?
Man, the promising animal, is also a lying and inconstant
animal. The anxious use of promising as a test persists until
the very end of the play—right to the brink, that is to say,
of its marriages' sexual consummation.

A modern student of the play, surveying this vast array
of linked obligations, might well think of Nietzsche's diag-
nosis of promising as a pathology of the will, an interior
reenactment of the barbaric ecstasies of cruelty and submission. If he does not, it is probably because the figure of
Portia has the dramatic magic to transform the potential
leadenness of obligation into a golden filigree. The gift of
herself to Bassanio comes with an ecstasy so pure that it
must, we think, belong to an entirely different order from
the dire impositions discussed by Nietzsche. Subverting
tragic justice in the trial scene, she returns to Belmont to

preside over a comic trial of infidelity. Portia, reconciling seriousness and mirth, makes the constrained seem "not strained."

In tragedies, the great sustaining ideals of the Shakespearean hero, often embodied in the ideality of another character (in Gertrude for Hamlet, in Desdemona for Othello, in Cordelia for Lear), lapse into disillusionment. Still, despite the unusual degree and extent of irony in *Othello*, promising remains a potent ideal. Desdemona's sense of herself as a wife under a vow to love, honor, cherish, and obey her husband, although it sanctions a passivity offensive to some modern tastes, is not intended to question the wisdom of marital promising: all her love is behind that vow, and inasmuch as the purity of her love renders her punishment almost unbearably undeserved, the goodness of her marriage vow belongs to the design of the play. Irony in this case serves as a kind of blueprint enabling the audience to shape its emotions to tragic contours.

But irony can also breed doubt and suspicion. When Othello accuses her directly, and Desdemona must swear to her innocence, we face the challenge of a more intellectual, more skeptical form of dramatic irony. Since these are ineffectual vows, lacking altogether in persuasive power, we realize that promising has a rhetorical side—what J. L. Austin would later call its "perlocutionary force." Of what avail is a promise that fails to convince? In act 4, scene 2, Desdemona seems to be reminding Othello of her marriage vow when she should be persuading him of it. Might not a more drastic set of disavowals, specifying curses in the event of falsehood, have stunned Othello into a reappraisal of what he presumes to know? Simply to think of promising as a rhetorical act counts as a considerable concession to the worldviews of a Richard or an Iago: above and beyond their truth, promises have not done their job unless they *seem* reassuring. Truth is not just an affair of the individual conscience. The utter futility of Desdemona as a rhetorician of promising comes to light when she offers her most emphatic, convincing vow of innocence not to her husband but to Iago (4.2.153–66).

This beachhead of skepticism develops into a full-scale invasion when we turn to Othello himself. His vow of vengeance, like other vows found in Shakespeare's tragedies, reveals the obvious but crucial fact that keeping a promise is not itself synonymous with virtue. This promise has a solely defensive function, extricating Othello from an intolerable state of uncertainty and indecision. It cuts short further inquiry into the truth of the charge. By the end of the play, punishing Desdemona allows Othello to exchange the humiliation of the cuckold for the spurious moral grandeur of an "honorable murderer." Something has gone wrong when the simplistic formalism of whether or not a promise has been kept deflects attention from the offending act. From the perspective of mere promise-keeping, Desdemona is simply wrong and Othello simply wronged. But a focus on the deed rather than the betrayed promise might have initiated a different sort of reflection. Why Cassio? Why am I not sufficient to her desire?

Othello cannot bear to dwell on these questions. "It is not words that shake me thus," he says before falling into a faint; mental images of "Noses, ears and lips," of adulterous bodies, whip him into frenzies of madness. The clear difference, I think, is that promise-breaking leads to the loss of Desdemona as an ideal, whereas the act of adultery leads as well to the loss of Othello's own self as an ideal, and the first loss, though shattering, is preferable to the jealous debasement of the second. Thus it is that an honorable murderer, possessed by a high-minded "cause" and hoping to be God-like in his "sacrifice," kills a "perjur'd woman." Thus it is that the end of the play vexes us with the difficult crux of Othello's self-esteem. The restless irony of the work finally takes the form of an extraordinarily systematic ambivalence in judging the hero, as the two messages of the "Willow Song," accusation and forgiveness, anger and empathy, succeed one another through the entire last scene.

Far more than *Richard III* and *The Merchant of Venice*, where promises are to be kept and a false promise gets punished in accord with its own specifications, *Othello* is a work of turbulent moral complexity. Richard, misusing promising, lives outside its ethical sphere, and in the end the social order, centered on that sphere, ejects him. But Othello, from within the ethic of promising, falls victim to subtle prides and self-deceits. *Richard III* derives its providential structure from the truth of an oath. *Othello* prompts us to reflect on treacheries born inside the codes of promising. The testing of *Merchant*, only lately burdensome, evolves into the gruesome mock tests of *Othello*, where the verdict decided in advance can only be reconfirmed. In his mature work, Shakespeare came to the realization that promising, like everything else at the root of our existence, mixes the noble and the base.

Might we get beyond, or at least severely lessen, the institutions of promising? At the end of my *Othello* chapter, having tried to register the full brunt of its excruciating ironies, I alluded to Godwin's idea that promises are superfluous to virtuous deeds, which should be performed because they are virtuous, not because we swear to do them. "I promise" is an unnecessary addition to "I ought." Perhaps Godwin is something of a straw man at this point in my argument. Perhaps I have been so impressed by the self-canonizing urge in Western intellectual prose of the last twenty-five years to be beyond, past, or post many of our traditional social and cultural practices that I automatically assume a sympathy toward Godwin's project in some portion of my readership. Though I habitually regard this would-be difference-making with suspicion, I found myself playing with the idea of a Godwinian transcendence of promising as I worked though the last three acts of *Othello*.

But promising lies so deeply embedded in our moral lives and social orders that uprooting it is difficult to conceive. A newborn babe knows no promises, yet his life is encircled by them—by untold generations of marriage vows, by mortgages, debts, contracts, international treaties, and agreements of all kinds. After he learns the primal concepts of yes and no, he will soon be promising that he will and promising that he will not, and soon thereafter be exacting promises of his own. Promising goes with the turf. Even Godwin was forced to make an exception of "perfect promises," and on the matter of social order would sacrifice laws of property and contract to the higher demands of justice only on the assumption that widespread sincerity might take the place of promise-keeping.[1] There are some "oughts" that presuppose promises, such as "I ought to be true to my spouse," "I ought to tell the whole truth and nothing but the truth when under oath," "I ought to do my best to pay my debts," or "I ought to keep my promises." We can probably discuss the morality of these cases without recourse to promising. Yet when an "ought" proves to be as binding as a promise, is it not a promise in disguise? A key difficulty with Godwin's theory is that he purports to get beyond promises but retains them under other names.

That aside, Godwin leads indirectly to a deeper understanding of promising by encouraging us to weigh "I ought" against "I promise." There is an interesting asymmetry in how these two kinds of resolve customarily undergo revision. Persuaded that an "ought" is wrong or partial, we simply change our behavior. But when we revise our view of the rectitude of a promise, we may still be reluctant to break it: a promise is a promise. Promising amounts to a principle of conservatism in the moral life. In a certain sense, it stands above our moral autonomy. Indeed, it is precisely in view of our capacity for autonomous fluctuation that promises are given and requested. The arguments that seem so persuasive on one day may seem otherwise a few days later. Despite the abuses of promising brought to light in *Othello*, it seems to me that our moral lives are well provisioned in having both relatively autonomous reason to save us from our rigidity and relatively stable promises to save us from our inconstancy.

The formulas of promising, as if by magic, conjure into existence the pressures of conscience. Speaking them, our desire for moral improvement or resistance to moral decline, airy nothings, materialize in the formality of obligation. Time congeals. *Now* becomes decisive. Promising to do something strengthens our motivation, allows our promisees through the gift of trust some respite from raw anxiety, and when the promise is kept satisfies us with a momentary sense of goodness. In search of sound practical wisdom on this matter, we probably cannot better the maxim found in Hugh Plat's *Floures of Philosophie* (1572): "Take good advise before thou promise any thing, but when thou hast once promised then perform it."[2] For better or for worse, shame and self-esteem derive in some measure from the breaking and keeping of promises. Making good on a decent promise is not life's sharpest pleasure but seems to be, on the evidence of human societies, among its most reliable. Another obligation met: take a breather. We have miles to go before we sleep.

The best-remembered passage about promising in Shakespeare occurs on the battlements of Elsinore Castle. Hamlet has just conversed with the ghost of his father. He has received from this supernatural visitor the commandment that, in his early enthusiasm, he will empty the book of his mind to inscribe "all alone" (1.5.102). He actually writes the ghost's last injunction, "Adieu, adieu, remember me," in his tables. "I have sworn't," he says, sworn to remember, and as I understand the moment, to obey, all of his father's instructions. Now Horatio and Marcellus enter. Marcellus will never be seen again. We already know that Horatio is Hamlet's loyal friend and confidant. After trying to break away from these intruders on a private moment, Hamlet faces them with "one poor request." They must never make known what they have seen tonight. In the older versions of the story, this fellowship of secrecy might have had some consequence. But in Shakespeare's play the whole scene, and the "antic disposition" that follows from it, seems on the borderline of the gratuitous.

Our sense of pointless proliferation heightens as the scene unfolds. They say they will not make anything known. Then Hamlet asks them to "swear't." They do so, using the oath "in faith"—swearing, like Desdemona, on their Christian faith. This oath is not good enough. They must swear upon the cross made by the hilt of his sword—a corporal oath, as it were, made when touching the symbol of the faith they have already sworn by. Both protest that they have already sworn. Hamlet insists: "Indeed, upon my sword, indeed." At this point a peculiar scene becomes most peculiar.

"Swear," cries the ghost from under the stage; it may be entertaining to recall that, in a tradition initiated by Nicholas Rowe in 1709, Shakespeare himself took the role of the ghost and would therefore have been the first actor to speak this heavy word.[3] Hamlet has sworn that he will remember. Horatio and Marcellus will be sworn over and over to remember not to speak of what they have seen this night (one oath, one sword swear), of what they have heard (one sword swear), or of what they know about Hamlet, should he ever act strangely (one sword swear). This is the passage everyone remembers. Four times the ghost in the castle, the actor in the cellarage of the theater, yells "Swear!" Once he yells, specifying unnecessarily, "Swear by his sword," as if any other swearing format were currently available. All the while Hamlet greets with wild bouts of humor these ghostly affirmations of his own enthusiasm for a major swearing. "Are you there, truepenny?" A lame translation might be: "Is that you my father, or you my fellow actor? I hear an actor under the stage, but I must, and you two other actors must (have we not sworn to play these roles?) take him to be a most serious ghostly visitor to Elsinore Castle—and an honest one, too, a truepenny, much exercized over swearing." The scene evolves into a sardonic travesty of solemn oath-taking. Have you sworn to keep quiet about anything you saw tonight? You need to be bound again, because you might talk about what you heard tonight. And not done yet, because you might give voice to something you thought about tonight, such as the behavior of a ghost-visited Hamlet. The joke is that the swearing could go on and on, the loopholes in the letter of this or any oath being practically infinite. The urge to perfect a promise issues in its *reductio ad absurdum*.

Controlling human behavior with an oath is like the old tales about stopping a collapsing dam with your fingers. Plug a leak here, and another one springs up there. The solemn oaths and promises supplying the links in the Great Chain of Being are, after all, more fragile than the metaphor of a chain might want to concede. Promises are made to be broken, or if not broken, then somehow got around. Good social order, like a good play, depends on a show of impressiveness. "Swear!" says the bloodcurdling voice of the horrid ghost of murdered King Hamlet. "Swear!" says the funny old mole in the cellarage. Hamlet's humor opens a line of communication from sworn obedience in a serious tragic plot to an uproarious recognition of the folly of sworn obedience. "Oaths are but words," as the saying went.[4] A promise, solemnly enjoined and kept in good faith: so much resting on such a feeble thing. Everybody knows it. Laugh, audience, laugh!

Yet it is by means of this folly that fellowships are formed, for whatever they are worth, and obligations, for whatever they are worth, passed down through the generations. "Remember me" and "Swear" are the ghost's most striking commands. They dovetail. History, remembering at its most sublime, is made of a sense of obligation. If promising does indeed mark the difference between nature and culture, we have inherited a practice from which there is no obvious escape. Whatever can be said against the ethic of promising, it is impossible to see how we could stop making promises, since to do so we would virtually have to promise to stop promising. The scene before us suggests that the mere promising of such a thing, like any really determined promising, might well go on forever, shutting loopholes and multiplying stipulations until the cure seems every bit as arduous and wearisome as the initial condition.

What audiences still take away from this scene, long after the centuries have dulled them to its jokes about porous oaths, is the image of Hamlet making fun of swearing but still doing it, and making fun of the voice of his dead father, who still, imperturbable spirit, cries "Swear!" That serious word, with its great load of human implication, echoes on in the theaters of living memory. A postpromising age? Not, I think, in this world. There is no antidote beyond vigilance for the diseases of promising exposed in *Othello*. Justifiably ambivalent, we remain promising animals.

Notes

Preface

1. These conventional distinctions are set forth in Francis Hutcheson, *A Short Introduction to Moral Philosophy* (Glasgow: Robert Foulis, 1747), 203–8; and with more complexity in his *A System of Moral Philosophy,* 2 vols. (London: Robert Foulis, 1755), 2: 44–103.

2. Frances Shirley, *Swearing and Perjury in Shakespeare's Plays* (London: George Allen & Unwin, 1979). It is remarkable, for example, that Shirley's excellent work is nowhere cited in the Shakespeare chapters of J. Douglas Canfield's *Word as Bond in English Literature from the Middle Ages to the Restoration* (Philadelphia: Univ. of Pennsylvania Press, 1989).

3. Shirley spends a chapter on this issue. I quote from the statute as given in E. K. Chambers, *The Elizabethan Stage,* 4 vols. (Oxford: Clarendon Press, 1951), 4:338–39.

4. Quoted in Felix Schelling, *Shakespeare Biography* (Philadelphia: Univ. of Pennsylvania Press, 1937), 80. Furness was probably thinking of one of Steevens's most famous notes, quoted in S. Schoenbaum, *Shakespeare's Lives,* new ed. (Oxford: Clarendon Press, 1991), 120.

5. *Morgann's Essay on the Dramatic Character of Sir John Falstaff,*

ed. William Arthur Gill (Freeport, N.Y.: Books for Libraries Press, 1970), 70–72.

6. See "Hegel's Theory of Tragedy," in A. C. Bradley, *Oxford Lectures on Poetry* (London: Macmillan, 1950), 69–95.

Chapter 1. *The Promising Animal*

1. *Love's Labour's Lost,* ed. R. W. David, New Arden Shakespeare (London: Methuen, 1951). Throughout, my quotations from Shakespeare come from the New Arden editions, where the plays occupy separate volumes with separate editors. Unless I make use of the editorial matter, I will not cite the volumes from which the quotations are taken but merely identify them in my text by act, scene, and line numbers.

2. On the contrary views of women and female vows, see my *Hamlet's Perfection* (Baltimore: Johns Hopkins Univ. Press, 1994), 63–93; and, reworking some of the same material, "A Woman's a Two-Face: Splitting in Shakespeare and His Age," *Ben Jonson Journal* 1 (1994): 125–46. For later examples, drawn from Milton, the Cavaliers, and the Restoration wits, see my "A Theory of Female Coyness," *TSLL* 38 (1996): 209–22. Commonplaces about unreliable promises during courtship may be found in Robert Burton, *The Anatomy of Melancholy,* ed. Floyd Dell and Paul Jordan-Smith (New York: Tudor, 1927), 711–15.

3. On *flyting* see Geoffrey Hughes, *Swearing: A Social History of Foul Language, Oaths, and Profanity in English* (Oxford: Blackwell, 1991), 47–50. On the motif of wit contests in Elizabethan drama, see M. C. Bradbrook, *Themes and Conventions of Elizabethan Tragedy,* 2d ed. (Cambridge: Cambridge Univ. Press, 1980), 110–12.

4. Plutarch distinguished a friend from a flatterer on the basis that a friend promises to do our bidding if it is possible and within his power, while a flatterer, dispensing with qualifications like the braggart in a comedy, promises to do our bidding beyond all doubt. *Morals,* trans. Philemon Holland (London: Arnold Hatfield, 1603), 101.

5. These proverbs are culled from Morris P. Tilley, *A Dictionary of Proverbs in England in the Sixteenth and Seventeenth Centuries* (Ann Arbor: Univ. of Michigan Press, 1950). Their Tilley numbers are, in the order listed, A24, A149, P602, M885, M1217, N272, S1030, and P605.

6. In *A Supplement to the Oxford English Dictionary,* under "Cross, v.," the earliest citation for "cross my heart" is from 1908, for "cross my heart, and hope to die," from 1926. The *New Dictionary of American*

Slang, ed. Robert L. Chapman (New York: Harper & Row, 1986), gives the meaning as "I am telling the truth: *I love you, baby. Cross my heart.*"

7. "A Hymne to God the Father" in *The Divine Poems of John Donne,* ed. Helen Gardner (Oxford: Clarendon Press, 1952), 51.

8. Walter Burkert, *Creation of the Sacred: Tracks of Biology in Early Religions* (Cambridge: Harvard Univ. Press, 1996), 169.

9. J. L. Austin, *How to Do Things with Words,* ed. J. O. Urmson (New York: Oxford Univ. Press, 1962); subsequent citations appear in the text by page number.

10. It may be of incidental interest here that Wittgenstein, according to a recent biographer, embarked on a lifetime of philosophical work when, at the age of eight or nine, he became fascinated with the question, "Why should one tell the truth if it's to one's advantage to tell a lie?" See Ray Monk, *Ludwig Wittgenstein: The Duty of Genius* (New York: Penguin, 1990), 1.

11. J. R. Searle's "How to Derive 'Ought' from 'Is,'" originally published in *Philosophical Review* 43 (1964), is reprinted in his *Speech Acts: An Essay in the Philosophy of Language* (Cambridge: Cambridge Univ. Press, 1969), 175–98.

12. Those emphasizing the "background of promising" would include A. I. Melden, "On Promising," *Mind* 65 (1956): 49–66; H.L.A. Hart, "Legal and Moral Obligation," in Melden, ed., *Essays in Moral Philosophy* (Seattle: Univ. of Washington Press, 1958), 101–5; and Hart, *The Concept of Law* (Oxford: Clarendon Press, 1961), 42–43; P. S. Atiyah, *Promises, Morals, and Law* (Oxford: Clarendon Press, 1981), 106–22; and "Contracts, Promises, and the Law of Obligation" in Atiyah, *Essays on Contracts* (Oxford: Clarendon Press, 1986), 10–56; the most famous attempt to distinguish promising rules from other rules is John Rawls's "Two Concepts of Rules," *Philosophical Review* 64, 1 (1955): 3–32, which may be traced back to Ludwig Wittgenstein, *Philosophical Investigations,* 1.23 (New York: Macmillan, 1968), 11–12. Charles Fried argues for a more abstract, rational view of promising—the so-called liberal theory of contract—in *Contract and Promise* (Cambridge: Harvard Univ. Press, 1981).

13. Thomas Elyot, *The Book Named the Governor* (London: Everyman's Library, 1962), 172–82, esp. 181, on the prevalent vice of perjury. See also Keith Thomas, *Religion and the Decline of Magic* (New York: Scribner's, 1971), 44, 67–68, and Frances Shirley's *Swearing and Perjury*

in Shakespeare's Plays (London: George Allen & Unwin, 1979), 18–19, 38, 73.

14. *Table Talk of John Selden,* ed. Frederick Pollock (London: Quaritch, 1927), 37; see also his remark at the end of the section on oaths (87).

15. Cicero, *De officiis* 1.7, as translated by Ernest Rhys in *Offices, Essays, and Letters* (London: J. M. Dent, 1909); see also *De legibus* 2.9.22, 2.11.29, 2.16.41, 4.6.7.

16. On the peculiar power of the oath for Romans, see Montesquieu, *The Spirit of the Laws,* trans. and ed. Anne M. Cohler, Basia Carolyn Miller, and Harold Samuel Stone (Cambridge: Cambridge Univ. Press, 1989). Cicero drew morals from the story of Marcus Regulus in *De officiis* 3.4.24; Horace told his story as an admonition to contemporary ill-doers in *Odes* 3.5. Emile Benveniste, *Indo-European Language and Society,* trans. Elizabeth Palmer (Coral Gables, Fla.: Univ. of Miami Press, 1973), 389–98, 407–98, considers Greek and Roman oaths, vows, and laws in relation to Indo-European roots.

17. A useful overview may be found in Alain Renoir, "The Heroic Oath in *Beowulf, Chanson de Roland,* and the *Nibelungenlied,*" in Stanley Greenfield, ed., *Studies in Old English Literature in Honor of Arthur B. Brodeur* (Eugene: Univ. of Oregon Books, 1963), 237–66.

18. This broadside was issued by Stephen Daye in Cambridge, Massachusetts. See Charles Evans, *American Bibliography,* vol. 1 (Chicago: Blakely Press, 1903), 1–2. There is no extant copy of the printed oath. Evans gives a version published in London in 1647.

19. Immanuel Kant, *Groundwork of the Metaphysic of Morals,* trans. H. J. Paton (New York: Harper, 1964), 57.

20. E.M. Forster, *Two Cheers for Democracy* (London: Edward Arnold, 1954), 78. Cited subsequently in my text.

21. Thomas Hobbes, *Leviathan,* ed. Michael Oakeshott (Oxford: Blackwell, 1957), 92. Cited subsequently in my text. Speculations about the origins of society found in the social contract tradition have recently been defended on Darwinian grounds by Daniel C. Dennett in *Darwin's Dangerous Idea: Evolution and the Meanings of Life* (New York: Simon & Schuster, 1995), 453–81.

22. Atiyah, "Consideration: A Restatement," in *Essays on Contracts,* 169–243; and for a fuller historical treatment, his *The Rise and Fall of Contract Law* (Oxford: Clarendon Press, 1979).

23. David Hume, *Treatise of Human Nature,* ed. L. A. Selby-Bigge (Oxford: Clarendon Press, 1978). Hume's view of the origin of promis-

ing has been ably expounded by Annette C. Baier in *A Progress of Sentiments: Reflections on Hume's Treatise* (Cambridge: Harvard Univ. Press, 1991), 243–54; she defends and amplifies Hume in "Promises, Promises, Promises," in *Postures of the Mind: Essays on Mind and Morals* (Minneapolis: Univ. of Minnesota Press, 1985), 174–206.

24. John Locke, *Two Treatises of Government* (New York: Signet, 1965), 374.

25. Tilley, *Dictionary of Proverbs*, P603.

26. Andrew Stephenson's *A History of Roman Law* (Boston: Little, Brown, 1912) attempts to reconstruct the law of the Twelve Tables known to us only through fragments (126–37). Hans Julius Wolff, *Roman Law: An Historical Introduction* (Norman: Univ. of Oklahoma Press, 1951) is not weighed down in technicalities; Barry Nicholas, *An Introduction to Roman Law* (Oxford: Clarendon Press, 1962), will satisfy scholarly readers.

27. Friedrich Nietzsche, *On the Genealogy of Morals and Ecce Homo*, ed. Walter Kaufmann (New York: Vintage, 1967), 39. Cited hereafter in my text.

28. Wallace Stevens, *Opus Posthumous*, ed. Milton J. Bates (New York: Vintage, 1990), 200.

29. Benno Tschischwitz, cited in *Hamlet*, ed. H. H. Furness, 2 vols. (London: Lippincott, 1877), 1: 365–66. I speculate that this speech looms behind several passages in T. S. Eliot (the words that "strain,/ Crack, and sometimes break" in the last movement of "Burnt Norton"; the famous lines about history's "cunning passages" in "Gerontion"); see also "Silence," in Eliot, *Inventions of the March Hare: Poems 1909–17*, ed. Christopher Ricks (London: Faber, 1996).

30. For a full history of this proverb, see Archer Taylor, "'He that will not when he may; when he will shall have nay,'" in Greenfield, ed., *Studies in Old English Literature*, 155–61. Heather Asals, "'Should' and 'Would': *Hamlet* and the Language of the Fathers," *Genre* 13 (1980): 431–39, does not pay sufficient attention to the details of the passage.

31. Gert Ronberg, *A Way with Words: The Language of English Renaissance Literature* (London: Edward Arnold, 1992), 66–71; also G. L. Brook, *The Language of Shakespeare* (London: André Deutsch, 1976), 113–14.

32. H. W. Fowler, *A Dictionary of English Usage* (New York: Oxford Univ. Press, 1950), 729 (s.v. *will*, vb.).

33. *Sir Walter Raleigh: Selections from his Writings*, ed. G. E. Hadow

(Oxford: Clarendon Press, 1926), 70–71. See also Edward to Warwick in *3Hen6* 2.3.33–34 ("I do bend my knee with thine;/And in this vow do chain my soul to thine"); *MSND* 2.2.42; and Sir Thomas Browne, *Christian Morals* 3.19, in *Works*, ed. Charles Sayle, 3 vols. (Edinburgh: John Grant, 1907), 3: 499, where oaths are also said to be "chains."

34. *Certaine Sermons or Homilies Appointed to be Read in Churches in the Time of Queen Elizabeth I*, facsimile of the 1623 edition, ed. Mary Ellen Rickey and Thomas M. Stroup (Gainesville, Fla.: Scholars' Facsimiles, 1968), 47.

35. Erik Erikson, *Identity, Youth, and Crisis* (New York: W. W. Norton, 1968), 96–97, 101–4.

36. See Faith Thompson, *Magna Carta: Its Role in the Making of the English Constitution 1300–1629* (Minneapolis: Univ. of Minnesota Press, 1948); and for translations of the documents into modern English, Richard Thomson, *An Historical Essay on the Magna Charta of King John* (London: John Major, 1829).

37. From "The Life of Mr. Richard Hooker" in Izaak Walton, *The Lives*, ed. Thomas Zouch (Boston: Crosby, Nichols, Lee, 1860), 209–10.

38. Thomas, *Religion and the Decline of Magic*, 96–104.

39. I have been guided on issues concerning the Henrician reform by G. R. Elton's *The Tudor Revolution in Government: Administrative Changes in the Reign of Henry VIII* (Cambridge: Cambridge Univ. Press, 1969), *Policy and Police: The Enforcement of the Reformation in the Age of Thomas Cromwell* (Cambridge: Cambridge Univ. Press, 1972), esp. 217–62 on oaths and other means of enforcement; and "The Reformation in England," one of Elton's contributions to *The New Cambridge Modern History*, vol. 2, *The Reformation 1520–1559* (Cambridge: Cambridge Univ. Press, 1958).

40. Elton, *Policy and Police*, 226.

41. The figure is that given by Philip Hughes, *The Reformation in England*, 3 vols. (New York: Macmillan, 1954), 2: 255.

42. S. Schoenbaum, *Shakespeare's Lives*, new ed. (Oxford: Clarendon Press, 1991), 10; and Eric Sams, *The Real Shakespeare: Retrieving the Years 1564–1594* (New Haven: Yale Univ. Press, 1995), 12. Schoenbaum takes the traditional line that John Shakespeare was absent from church (a good place to find someone) so as not to be arrested for debt; Sams believes that the poet's family (and the poet) was Catholic, and the absence from church is therefore evidence of resistance to reform.

43. J. R. Tanner, *Tudor Constitutional Documents, A.D. 1485–1603*

(Cambridge: Cambridge Univ. Press, 1922), 134; for a similarly formulated oath from 1602, see Roland G. Usher, *The Reconstruction of the English Church*, 2 vols. (New York: D. Appleton, 1910), 2:312–13, and 310–24 generally for Elizabethan documents used as precedents for James I's Oath of Allegiance. Christopher Hill, in *Society and Puritanism in Pre-Revolutionary England* (London: Seeker & Warburg, 1964), 387, describes the anonymous *The Book of Oaths and the several forms thereof* (1649) as in fact containing 416 pages of oaths and the forms thereof; I have not been able to examine this book. For the repeated linking of "conscience" with oath-taking in More's writings, and in Roper's *Life of More*, see the passages quoted in R. W. Chambers, *Thomas More* (London: Jonathan Cape, 1935), 237, 304, 312, 337–38, 339–40, and passim.

44. John Calvin, *Institutes of the Christian Religion*, ed. John T. McNeill, trans. Ford Lewis Battles (Philadelphia: Westminster Press, 1960), 2:390; William Ames, *The Marrow of Theology*, trans. John Eusden (Durham, N.C.: Labyrinth Press, 1968), 268. Milton considered oaths in *Christian Doctrine* 2.5, in *The Complete Prose Works of John Milton*, ed. Don M. Wolfe et al., 8 vols. (New Haven: Yale Univ. Press, 1953–82), 6:684–96, but remained silent on oath-curses.

45. Perez Zagorin, *Ways of Lying: Dissimulation, Persecution, and Conformity in Early Modern Europe* (Cambridge: Harvard Univ. Press, 1990), 163, 171.

46. J. B. Black, *The Reign of Elizabeth, 1558–1603* (Oxford: Clarendon Press, 1936), 325–27; J. E. Neale, *Queen Elizabeth I: A Biography* (New York: Doubleday, 1957), 273–76.

47. Tanner, *Constitutional Documents*, 360–62.

48. As given in Thompson, *Magna Carta*, 208. In 1591 Sir James Morice, an attorney of the Court of Wards, represented Robert Cawdry (*Cawdry's case*) at the Queen's Bench, arguing the illegitimacy of the High Commission's procedures (Thompson, *Magna Carta*, 213, 218–19). He lost the case and continued the argument in *Briefe Treatise of Oathes* (1598, but probably written earlier). The work may be found, with a useful preface on the High Commission's reliance on the ex officio oath, in Leonard J. Trinterud, ed., *Elizabethan Puritanism* (New York: Oxford Univ. Press, 1971), 384–439.

49. On the Oath of Allegiance, see R. C. Bald, *John Donne: A Life* (New York: Oxford Univ. Press, 1970), 203–4, 207–8, 212–18, 222–26. The Oath of Allegiance itself, which contained the formula "acknowl-

edge, profess, testify and declare in my conscience," may be found in
Charles Howard McIlwain, ed., *The Political Works of James I* (Cambridge: Harvard Univ. Press, 1918), 73–74.

50. Ibid., 74.

51. Tilley, *Dictionary of Proverbs*, T244.

52. McIlwain, *Works of James I*, 305. Cf. 2Hen6 3.2.292–93.

53. David Masson, *The Life of John Milton*, 6 vols. (Gloucester, Mass.: Peter Smith, 1965), 3:12.

54. Ibid., 6:124; also Robert Thomas Fallon, *Milton in Government* (University Park: Pennsylvania State Univ. Press, 1993), 37.

55. An entire canto of Butler's satirical epic *Hudibras* (pt. 2, canto 2) is devoted to the black comedy of oath-swearing by oath-breachers. See also Zagorin, *Ways of Lying*, 245–48.

56. *Boswell's Life of Johnson*, ed. George Birkbeck Heil, rev. L. F. Powell, 6 vols. (Oxford: Clarendon Press, 1936), 2: 220.

57. *Table Talk*, 85.

58. *The Sermons and Expository Treatises of Isaac Barrow*, 2 vols. (Edinburgh: Thomas Nelson, 1839), 2:378.

59. The passage quoted is from Samuel Butler, *Characters and Passages from Note-Books*, ed. A. R. Waller (Cambridge: Cambridge Univ. Press, 1908), 292.

60. Locke, *Two Treatises*, 318.

61. The classical examples are Cicero, *De officiis* 1.10.32, 3.29.107; and Augustine, *Letters*, 125.3. William Perkins, *A Discourse of Conscience* (Cambridge: John Legat, 1597), offers a compromise solution, since "some Protestant divines think it [the promise to the highwayman] doth binde: some again think no" (105). The question is addressed by Joseph Hall in *Resolutions and Decisions of Divers Cases of Conscience*, decade 1, case VIII, in *The Works of the Right Reverend Joseph Hall*, 10 vols., ed. Philip Wynter (New York: AMS Press, 1969), 7:289–91; Milton in *Christian Doctrine* 2.5; Hume (glancingly) in *Treatise of Human Nature*, 525; and Adam Smith in *The Theory of Moral Sentiments*, ed. D. D. Raphael and A. L. MacFie (Oxford: Clarendon Press, 1976), 330–33—see the annotation to these pages in Smith for further examples; also Atiyah, *Promises, Morals, and Law*, 22–23. Smith is hereafter cited in my text.

62. See William Kerrigan and Gordon Braden, *The Idea of the Renaissance* (Baltimore: Johns Hopkins Univ. Press, 1989), 177–78, on the relationship between this repeated idealization and the Petrarchan genre.

63. In his edition of *Shakespeare's Sonnets* (New Haven: Yale Univ. Press, 1977), Stephen Booth proposes that "aversion to solemn promises is one of the strong threads running through Shakespeare's work" (530) and cites a batch of passages, none of which prove this indefensible contention or in any way countermand the many solemn, beautiful, fully meant promises in Shakespeare. His commentary on 152 is marred by a fussy complexity that keeps veering away from the heart of the poem. To limit myself to one example, the "deep oaths" here have nothing to do with "mouth-filling, resounding oaths" (532). Booth seems to be confusing the solemn testimonials about the truth of the Dark Lady in 152 with Hotspur's "good mouth-filling oath" in *1Hen4* 3.1.248.

64. John Kerrigan, ed., *The Sonnets and A Lover's Complaint* (Harmondsworth: Penguin, 1986), 368.

65. *The Poems of Sir Philip Sidney*, ed. William Ringler (Oxford: Clarendon Press, 1962), 188.

Chapter 2. *The Truth of an Oath and the Bias of the World*

1. "A treatise of Warres," stanzas 45–46, in Geoffrey Bullough, ed., *Poems and Dramas of Fulke Greville*, 2 vols. (Edinburgh: Oliver and Boyd, 1941), 1:225. On the proverb "Man is a wolf to man," see William Kerrigan and Gordon Braden, *The Idea of the Renaissance* (Baltimore: Johns Hopkins Univ. Press, 1989), 38.

2. On the relation between *A Mirror* and the history play generally, see Lily B. Campbell, *Tudor Conceptions of History and Tragedy in "A Mirror for Magistrates"* (Berkeley: Univ. of California Press, 1936); Campbell, *Shakespeare's 'Histories': Mirrors of Elizabethan Policy* (San Marino, Calif.: Huntington Library, 1947); and M. M. Reese, "Origins of the History Play," in Eugene M. Waith, ed., *Shakespeare: The Histories* (Englewood Cliffs, N.J.: Prentice-Hall, 1965), 42–54.

3. On the idea that Shakespeare essentially created the genre of the English chronicle history play, which would not have seemed credible at the beginning of the twentieth century, see F. P. Wilson, *Shakespearian and Other Studies*, ed. Helen Gardner (Oxford: Clarendon Press, 1969), 23: "So far as we know, Shakespeare was the first popular dramatist to give dignity and coherence to the play on English history." There were of course precedents—John Bale's *King Johan* in particular—but their differences from Shakespeare's histories seem more important than the sim-

ilarities, as suggested by F. P. Wilson in *The English Drama 1485–1585* (Oxford: Clarendon Press, 1969), 38.

4. On Elizabethan Senecanism, see Gordon Braden, *Renaissance Tragedy and the Senecan Tradition: Anger's Privilege* (New Haven: Yale Univ. Press, 1985), 171–223.

5. Other examples of the grief-into-revenge motif in the first tetralogy may be found in *1Hen6* 1.1.17, 86–88; *2Hen6* 3.2.304–7; *3Hen6* 5.4.21–28. It is also prominent in *Titus Andronicus*, for this transformation is generic in revenge tragedy; thus Hieronimo, immediately upon finding Horatio's body in Kyd's *The Spanish Tragedy*, ed. Thomas W. Ross (Berkeley: Univ. of California Press, 1968), 46: "To know the author were some ease of grief,/For in revenge my heart would find relief" (2.4.104–5).

6. For analogues of Henry VI's desire to live in a pastoral world, see Sidney's "Disprayse of a Courtly Life" in his *Poems*, ed. William Ringler (Oxford: Clarendon Press, 1962), 262–64, and "Theorello: *A Sheepheards Edillion*," the second poem in *Englands Helicon*, ed. Hugh MacDonald (Cambridge: Harvard Univ. Press, 1949), 3–6. In *Elizabethan Poetry* (Ann Arbor: Univ. of Michigan Press, 1968), 19, Hallett Smith notes the prominence of complaint in *Englands Helicon*, and in Sidney's contributions to the genre. G. Wilson Knight, *The Sovereign Flower* (London: Methuen, 1958), 20, suggests a link throughout Shakespeare between pastoralism and pity.

7. Cairncross edited *King Henry VI, Part 1* (London: Methuen, 1962), *King Henry VI, Part 2* (London: Methuen, 1957), and *King Henry VI, Part 3* (London: Methuen, 1964). I have quoted his note to *1Hen6* 5.5.30. See also his introduction to that play, xliii–xliv, xlix, and his introduction to part 3, liv–lvi. For a treatment of *truth* as "troth" (fidelity, good faith) in earlier English literature, including full readings of some Shakespeare plays, see J. Douglas Canfield, *Word as Bond in English Literature from the Middle Ages to the Restoration* (Philadelphia: Univ. of Pennsylvania Press, 1989). Though Canfield's book is orderly and well written, he does not get very deeply into Shakespeare on this subject, in part because he assumes that the ethic of oath-obedience was unquestionable and absolutely virtuous.

8. See Cairncross's edition of *3Hen6*, 18, n. to 1.2.18. On the same page can be found the appropriate citations to Marlowe. In one of Shakespeare's sources, Edward Hall's *The Union of . . . Lancastre and Yorke* (1548), the Yorks acquire a papal dispensation to ignore their oath to

Henry VI; Geoffrey Bullough, *Narrative and Dramatic Sources of Shakespeare*, 8 vols. (London: Routledge, 1960), 3: 160.

9. Thomas Nashe, *Works*, ed. T. B. McKerrow, rev. F. P. Wilson, 5 vols. (Oxford: Oxford Univ. Press, 1958), 1:213.

10. In his essay "Of Wisdom for a Man's Self," Bacon observes that servants of the state who follow only the dictates of self-love "set a bias upon their bowl, of their own petty ends and envies, to the overthrow of their master's great and important affairs." Francis Bacon, *Essays and the Advancement of Learning* (London: Macmillan, 1900), 58.

11. For the response of reformed theologians to the Anabaptist refusal to take oaths, see John Calvin, *Institutes of the Christian Religion*, ed. John T. McNeill, trans. Ford Lewis Battles (Philadelphia: Westminster Press, 1960), 1:391, n. 32. Other statements more or less explicitly disowning the Anabaptist view on oath-swearing before temporal magistrates may be found in Arthur C. Cochrane, ed., *Reformed Confessions of the Sixteenth Century* (Philadelphia: Westminster Press, 1966), 96, 182–83, 217–18, 299–300.

12. Charles Hardwick, *A History of the Articles of Religion*, 3d ed., rev. (London: George Bell, 1876), 347. In four parallel columns, Hardwick reprints the Latin and English Forty-two Articles from 1553, the Latin Thirty-nine Articles of 1563, and the English Thirty-nine Articles of 1571; see also 159–77 on the creation and institution of the Articles.

13. William Perkins, *A Discourse of Conscience* (Cambridge: John Legat, 1597), 109. Hereafter cited in the text by page number.

14. *The Prince*, chap. 18, in *Machiavelli: The Chief Works and Others*, trans. Allan Gilbert, 3 vols. (Durham, N.C.: Duke Univ. Press, 1989), 1:65. Behind the character of Richard III lies the fusion of the Vice figure from the moralities with the Machiavel, as found in the prologue to Marlowe's *The Jew of Malta*. For a brief and balanced discussion, see N. W. Bawcutt's remarks in his edition of *The Jew of Malta* (Manchester: Manchester Univ. Press, 1978), 11–15.

15. *Gorgias* 483b–483c, in Edith Hamilton and Huntington Cairns, eds., *The Collected Dialogues of Plato* (New York: Bollingen, 1963), 266. Also Jonson's *Sejanus*, 2.2.24: "'Twas only fear first in the world made gods."

16. Calvin, *Institutes*, 1:388. In 2 *Tam* 2.2.36–65, the Turk Orcanes dares Christ, "if there be a Christ," to revenge himself on perjured Christians; otherwise, Christ would be merely "esteemed omnipotent," and unworthy "the worship of all faithful hearts."

17. Gilbert Burnet, *An Exposition of the Thirty-nine Articles of the Church of England* (London: Knapton, 1759), 497.

18. S. L. Bethell, *Shakespeare and the Popular Dramatic Tradition* (rpt.; New York: Octagon, 1970), 21; Christopher Ricks, *The Force of Poetry* (Oxford: Clarendon Press, 1984), 279. Both critics rely on T. S. Eliot's famous definition of wit in *Selected Essays* (New York: Harcourt, Brace, 1960), 262.

19. On the evolution of the morality play in relation to Elizabethan drama, see Bernard Spivack, *Shakespeare and the Allegory of Evil* (New York: Columbia Univ. Press, 1958); David M. Bevington, *From 'Mankind' to Marlowe: Growth of Structure in the Popular Drama of Tudor England* (Cambridge: Harvard Univ. Press, 1962); and Robert Weimann, *Shakespeare and the Popular Tradition in the Theater: Studies in the Social Dimension of Dramatic Form and Function*, ed. Robert Schwartz (Baltimore: Johns Hopkins Univ. Press, 1978), 98–160.

20. Alexander Leggatt called my attention to this fact in *Shakespeare's Political Drama: The History Plays and the Roman Plays* (London: Routledge, 1988), 32. Moralities featuring the Vice character often did begin with his address to the audience. Wilson, *English Drama 1485–1585*, 64.

21. This is Sonnet 18 ("On the Late Massacre in Piedmont"). Milton's emphasis on wrath and hatred is a main theme in the work of Michael Lieb; see "'Hate in Heav'n': Milton and the *Odium Dei*," *ELH* 53 (1986): 519–39; also David Loewenstein, *Milton and the Drama of History* (Cambridge: Cambridge Univ. Press, 1990), 136–51.

22. J. Kerrigan, *Revenge Tragedy: Aeschylus to Armageddon* (Oxford: Clarendon Press, 1996), 139, and on Milton, 121–27.

23. Keith Thomas, *Religion and the Decline of Magic* (New York: Scribner's, 1971), 504, and on the issue generally, 502–12. On how one's league with God should be formed in love, not hatred, see Thomas Wright, *The Passions of the Minde in Generall*, ed. Thomas O. Sloane (Urbana: Univ. of Illinois Press, 1971), 229–33.

24. For example Calvin, *Institutes*, 2: 912: "the Lord excludes from the number of his children those persons who, being eager for revenge and slow to forgive, practice persistent enmity and foment against others the very indignation that they pray to be averted from themselves."

25. E. E. Stoll, "The Objectivity of the Ghosts in Shakespeare," *PMLA*, n.s., 15 (1907): 231–32.

26. For a contrary opinion on the merits of the second wooing scene,

see Wolfgang Clemen, *A Commentary on Shakespeare's Richard III*, trans. Jean Bonheim (London: Methuen, 1957), 190.

27. Calvin, *Institutes* 2:1256, 1275. In *The Winter's Tale*, the Clown, expecting social elevation from the marriage of Perdita and Florizel, says he will swear to the king that Autolycus is honest. His father declares that he may say it, but not swear it, to which the Clown replies: "Not swear it, now I am a gentleman?" (5.2.159). Cf. *Cym* 2.1.11–12. I assume that the sort of casual swearing and vowing we find in Richard is the aristocratic fashion Shakespeare has in mind in these passages from the romances. For the deterioration of oath-taking to childish or even insane extravagance in France and the Netherlands in the fourteenth and fifteenth centuries, see Johan Huizinga, *The Waning of the Middles Ages* (Garden City, N.Y.: Anchor, 1954), 85–93.

28. Some of which I myself have had a hand in; see W. Kerrigan and Braden, *Idea of the Renaissance*, 67–78. Some of the earlier efforts may be sampled in H. H. Furness Jr., ed., *The Tragedy of Richard the Third* (Philadelphia: Lippincott, 1908), 401–6; see also the "Longer Note" of editor Anthony Hammond in *King Richard III* (London: Methuen, 1981), 340.

29. C. S. Lewis, *Studies in Words*, 2d ed. (rpt; Cambridge: Cambridge Univ. Press, 1994), 181–213.

30. A similar internalization of the legal system is on display throughout Perkins's *Discourse of Conscience*.

31. Morris P. Tilley, *A Dictionary of Proverbs in England in the Sixteenth and Seventeenth Centuries* (Ann Arbor: Univ. of Michigan Press, 1950), C601: "Conscience is a thousand witnesses."

32. *Certaine Sermons or Homilies Appointed to be Read in Churches in the Time of Queen Elizabeth I,* facsimile of the 1623 edition, ed. Mary Ellen Rickey and Thomas M. Stroup (Gainesville, Fla.: Scholars' Facsimiles, 1968), 50.

33. This speech of prophetic celebration is given to Archbishop Cranmer, architect of the Anglican articles. The royal babe "promises/Upon this land a thousand thousand blessings": "Truth shall nurse her" (*Hen8* 5.5.18–19, 28). It seems to me that the speech closes a circuit with Richmond's celebration of "time to come" at the end of *Richard III*.

Chapter 3.   Obligation in Venice

1. These and other possible sources may be consulted in Geoffrey Bullough, *Narrative and Dramatic Sources of Shakespear,* 8 vols. (New York: Columbia Univ. Press, 1961), 1: 463–514.

2. Cited in H. H. Furness, ed., *The Merchant of Venice* (New York: Dover, 1964), 421.

3. H. H. Hudson, *Shakespeare: His Life, Art, and Character,* 4th ed., 2 vols. (Boston: Ginn, 1891), 1: 296. For more recent praise of this sort see Thomas Marc Parrott, *Shakespearean Comedy* (New York: Oxford Univ. Press, 1949), 143; and John Palmer, *Political and Comic Characters of Shakespeare* (London: Macmillan, 1965), 412.

4. Sigurd Burckhardt's *"The Merchant of Venice*: The Gentle Bond" was first published in *ELH* 39 (1962): 239–62; I cite it from James Calderwood and Harold Toliver, eds., *Essays in Shakespearean Criticism* (Englewood Cliffs, N.J.: Prentice-Hall, 1970), 240. Lawrence Danson, *The Harmonies of The Merchant of Venice* (New Haven: Yale Univ. Press, 1978), 11–12, accepts Burckhardt's observation about circularity but promises to put it to a difference use.

5. William Empson, *Seven Types of Ambiguity,* 2d ed. (Harmondsworth: Penguin, 1961), 44.

6. A. D. Moody, "The Letter of the Law," in Thomas Wheeler, ed., *The Merchant of Venice: Critical Essays* (New York: Garland, 1991), 98.

7. Norman Rabkin, "Meaning in Shakespeare," delivered as a paper in 1971 and first published in 1972, is here cited from Wheeler, *Merchant,* 116.

8. See Morris P. Tilley, *Dictionary of Proverbs in England in the Sixteenth and Seventeenth Centuries* (Ann Arbor: Univ. of Michigan Press, 1950), S809.

9. The piece originally entitled "'To Entrap the Wisest': A Reading of *The Merchant of Venice*" and published in 1980, has now been incorporated into René Girard's sublimely footnoteless (a work about envy!) *A Theater of Envy: William Shakespeare* (New York: Oxford Univ. Press, 1991); I quote the passage on 244–45.

10. Bullough, *Sources of Shakespeare,* 1: 514.

11. Burckhardt, *"Merchant of Venice,"* 253.

12. Tilley, *Dictionary of Proverbs,* M682; see the related M271 and W232.

13. See the entries for *wed* in Walter W. Skeat, *An Etymological Dic-*

tionary of the English Language (Oxford: Clarendon Press, 1974); and in C. T. Onions, G. W. S. Friedrichsen, and R. W. Burchfield, *The Oxford Dictionary of English Etymology* (New York: Oxford Univ. Press, 1966).

14. On the names of the Venetian buddies, one of whom appears in Belmont as a messenger (if he is not a third, separate, and similarly named character), see the somewhat useful table in M. M. Mahood, ed., *The Merchant of Venice* (Cambridge: Cambridge Univ. Press, 1987), 179–83.

15. Danson, *Harmonies*, 34–39; and for a contrary view, E.M.W. Tillyard, *Shakespeare's Early Comedies* (New York: Barnes & Noble, 1965). My own sense of the conflict between friendship and married love is close to that of Anne Barton in her introduction to *Merchant* in *The Riverside Shakespeare* (Boston: Houghton Mifflin, 1974), 250–53. I also learned a great deal about vowing in the play from Alice N. Benston, "Portia, the Law, and the Tripartite Structure of *The Merchant of Venice*," in Wheeler, *Merchant,* 163–94, though I do not share her conviction that friendship and love are entirely harmonious.

16. *The Complete Essays of Montaigne*, trans. Donald M. Frame (Stanford: Stanford Univ. Press, 1965), 137. Hereafter cited in the text.

17. See the great outpouring of information in R. H. Tawney's introduction to Thomas Wilson, *A Discourse upon Usury* (London: Frank Cass, 1962); also Walter Cohen, *Drama of a Nation: Public Theater in Renaissance England and Spain* (Ithaca, N.Y.: Cornell Univ. Press, 1988), 195–232.

18. In the order quoted, Tilley, *Dictionary of Proverbs,* F697, F694, F725, F723.

19. According to Francis Meres, *Palladis Tamia* (London: P. Short, 1598), 323v, scriveners and notaries took oaths upon entering their professions never to draw up writs for usury. It may be an indication of how rarely such oaths were obeyed that Shylock is obviously familiar with the notary.

20. Douglas Cole, *Suffering and Evil in the Plays of Christopher Marlowe* (Princeton: Princeton Univ. Press, 1962), 132.

21. See Tawney's introduction to Wilson, *Discourse upon Usury,* on all these points; the credit financing of the aristocracy has been more recently studied by Lawrence Stone, *The Crisis of the Aristocracy* (Oxford: Oxford Univ. Press, 1967), 233–67. Thomas Moisan, "'Which is the merchant here? and which the Jew?': Subversion and Recuperation in *The Merchant of Venice*," in Jean Howard and Marion O'Connor, eds.,

Shakespeare Reproduced: The Text in History and Ideology (New York: Methuen, 1987), 193, observes that most of Shylock's character traits, when beheld against the background of the usury tracts, seem "merely a standard part of his job description."

22. *The Complete Plays of Christopher Marlowe* (New York: Odyssey Press, 1963), 205. Subsequent citations use this edition and appear in my text.

23. Marlow, *The Jew of Malta,* 2.3.17, 2.3.93; also used at 1.2.390 and 3.1.15. In the *OED* (*hard,* adv., 2c), the phrase is said to introduce a statement of what is almost sure to happen.

24. François Victor Hugo, as quoted in H. H. Furness, ed., *The Merchant of Venice* (Philadelphia: Lippincott, 1888), 128.

25. Seneca, *Thyestes,* 195–96, 1052–53. The first line is quoted by the ghost of a murdered father to instruct his son in John Marston's *Antonio's Revenge,* ed. G. K. Hunter (Lincoln: Univ. of Nebraska Press, 1965), 3.1.51. See my *Hamlet's Perfection* (Baltimore: Johns Hopkins Univ. Press, 1994), 137–39.

26. W. Kerrigan, *Hamlet's Perfection,* 13–15, 75–80.

27. W. H. Auden, "Brothers and Others," in *The Dyer's Hand* (New York: Random House, 1956), 235.

28. Cited from F. E. Halliday, *Shakespeare and His Critics* (New York: Schocken Books, 1963), 175.

29. On the possible relationship between Puritanism and the character of Shylock, see Paul N. Siegel's "Shylock, the Elizabethan Puritan and Our Own World" in *Shakespeare in His Time and Ours* (Notre Dame: Univ. of Notre Dame Press, 1968), 237–54.

30. Burckhardt, "*Merchant of Venice:* Gentle Bond," 246–47.

31. See Frederick Hawkins in Furness, ed., *Merchant of Venice,* 433; Harold C. Goddard, *The Meaning of Shakespeare* (Chicago: Univ. of Chicago Press, 1951), 96, 98–101; Burckhardt, "*Merchant of Venice:* Gentle Bond," 248.

32. This interpretation was suggested in the nineteenth century by J. Weiss, in Furness, ed., *Merchant of Venice,* 141. It is fiercely opposed by Danson, *Harmonies,* 117–18, among others.

33. The rhyme between "lead" and the rhyme words in the song was first suggested by A. H. Fox-Strangeways in 1923; see Mahood, ed., *Merchant of Venice,* 115, and S. F. Johnson, *Shakespeare's Universe* (New York: Scolar Press, 1996), 144–48.

34. Frank Kermode, "The Mature Comedies," in *Early Shakespeare,* Stratford-upon-Avon Studies 3 (London: Edward Arnold, 1961), 222.

35. Vannoccio Biringuccio contrasts gold and silver, targets of human avarice, with the utility of lead, without which the two bright metals could never be mined, in *Pirotechnia,* trans. Cyril Smith and Martha Gnudi (Cambridge: MIT Press, 1966), 54–55.

36. See Christopher Marlowe, 2 *Tam* 2.4.131.

37. Bassanio has, in fact, only his blood (3.2.176; 3.2.253–54)—a foreshadowing of what the flesh bond forgets.

38. The two best theological readings are Barbara K. Lewalski, "Biblical Allusion and Allegory in *The Merchant of Venice,*" *Shakespeare Quarterly* 13 (1962): 327–43; and John S. Coolidge, "Law and Love in *The Merhcant of Venice,*" ibid. 27 (1976): 243–63. See also G. K. Hunter, *Dramatic Identities and Cultural Tradition* (Liverpool: Liverpool Univ. Press, 1978), 60–102.

39. Kermode, "Mature Comedies," 223–24.

40. A possibility suggested by Cohen, *Drama of a Nation,* 209, among others.

41. I quote the lyric from J. William Hebel and Hoyt H. Hudson, eds., *Poetry of the English Renaissance 1509–1660* (New York: Appleton-Century-Crofts, 1957), 125–26.

42. John Milton, *Paradise Lost* 3.210, in Merritt Hughes, ed., *Complete Poems and Major Prose* (New York: Odyssey, 1957), 263.

43. An exception in this respect is Frances Shirley, who does emphasize Shylock's vow in *Swearing and Perjury in Shakespeare's Plays* (London: George Allen & Unwin, 1979), 31–36. She correctly insists that the oath "becomes the excuse for his intransigence when Portia mixes the request for mercy with the temptation of a triple repayment" (32), but his eventual forswearing is not intended, in my view, to lessen Shylock by "making him less single-minded than a tragic revenger" (33). The implicit punishment for his broken oath is not a vague diminishment in dramatic esteem but rather the specific loss of the faith on which his vow rested.

44. On *Merchant* as "problem play," see Leo Salingar, *Shakespeare and the Traditions of Comedy* (Cambridge: Cambridge Univ. Press, 1974), 298–317.

45. E.A.J. Honigmann is interesting on bed-tricks and Shakespeare's love for the "mixture principle" in *Myriad-Minded Shakespeare* (New York: St. Martin's Press, 1989), 147–68.

46. Of course the general rule that bonds will be enforced remains in sway. The tension of the scene depends on everyone believing that. But as Richard Hooker noted, in legal matters "general rules, till their limits be known . . . are, by reason of the manifold secret exceptions which lie hidden in them, no other to the eye of man's understanding than cloudy mists cast before the eye of common sense." *The Works of Mr. Richard Hooker*, ed. John Keble, 3 vols. (Oxford: Oxford Univ. Press, 1836), 3:49.

47. Hazlitt's *A View of the English Stage* (1818) is cited from Jonathan Bate, ed., *The Romantics on Shakespeare* (London: Penguin, 1992), 460. For Hazlitt's view of Shylock in relation to his essay on "Emancipation of the Jews;" see David Bromwich, *Hazlitt: The Mind of a Critic* (Oxford: Oxford Univ. Press, 1983), 406–7.

48. I have trouble accepting the view of Parrott, *Shakespearean Comedy*, 143, that Shakespeare assumed the forced conversion to Christianity to be merciful simply because Shylock can now go to heaven. But I do think that the conversion punishment was possibly intended to include Shylock within the comic community. The conversion motif also appears in "The Play of the Sacrament" in Joseph Quincy Adams, ed., *Chief Pre-Shakespearean Dramas* (Boston: Houghton Mifflin, 1924), 243–62.

49. R. F. Hill wrongly claims that the breaking of faith by Bassanio and Gratiano was "merely technical" in "'The Merchant of Venice' and the Pattern of Romantic Comedy," in Wheeler, *Merchant*, 157.

50. Tilley, *Dictionary of Proverbs*, W347 and W382. The second proverb was made into doggerel verse by John Taylor in *All the Workes of John Taylor* (London, 1630); it is somewhat hard to find things in this volume, but if one locates the poem called "Taylors Motto," the passage on a wife's wedding and death days occurs on p. 50. The proverbial idea of the happy husband concealing his joy under solemnity at his wife's funeral worked its way into Descartes's *Passions of the Soul*, in *The Philosophical Writing of Descartes*, 2 vols., trans. John Cottingham, Robert Stoothoff, and Dugald Murdoch (Cambridge: Cambridge Univ. Press, 1985), 1:381.

51. As was suggested by Furness, ed., *Merchant of Venice*, 96.

52. The point is bluntly made in Emilia's cynical homily on husbands: "They are all but stomachs, and we all but food;/They eat us hungerly, and when they are full,/They belch us" (*Oth* 3.4.101–3). For the psychological background to this attitude, see my *Hamlet's Perfection*, 73–74, and "*Macbeth* and the History of Ambition" in John O'Neill, ed.,

Freud and the Passions (University Park: Pennsylvania State Univ. Press, 1996), 13–24.

53. John Dryden, *Marriage a-la-Mode,* in *Four Comedies,* ed. L. A. Beaurline and Fredson Bowers (Chicago: Univ. of Chicago Press, 1967), 285.

54. Richard Levin, *New Readings vs. Old Plays: Recent Trends in the Reinterpretation of English Renaissance Drama* (Chicago: Univ. of Chicago Press, 1979); and Richard Rorty, *Contingency, Irony, and Solidarity* (Cambridge: Cambridge Univ. Press, 1989), 3–22. It is a bit anachronistic for Levin to fault "thematic criticism" for turning plays into ideas, statements, arguments, treatises, and the like, when as Majorie Donker observes in *Shakespeare's Proverbial Themes* (Westport, Conn.: Greenwood Press, 1992), xii, the rhetorical culture that trained the dramatist understood literature in precisely this way.

55. *Ring* means pudendum, as Eric Partridge notes in *Shakespeare's Bawdy* (New York: Dutton, 1960), 179.

Chapter 4. Ironic Vows

1. Stanley Cavell, *Disowning Knowledge in Six Plays of Shakespeare* (Cambridge: Cambridge Univ. Press, 1987), 132. Cavell's view of the play is criticized in Brian Vickers, *Appropriating Shakespeare: Contemporary Critical Quarrels* (New Haven: Yale Univ. Press, 1993), 308–20.

2. Geoffrey Bullough, *Narrative and Dramatic Sources of Shakespeare,* 8 vols. (New York: Columbia Univ. Press, 1961), 7:250–51.

3. For a close scrutiny of the little we know, see Lena Cowen Orlin, "Desdemona's Disposition," in Shirley Nelson Garner and Madelon Sprengnether, eds., *Shakespearean Tragedy and Gender* (Bloomington: Indiana Univ. Press, 1996), 171–92.

4. On the oddities of marriage law, consult Frederick Pollard and Frederic Maitland, *The History of English Law,* 2 vols. (rpt.; Washington, D.C.: Lawyers' Literary Club, 1959), 2:368–99; and Henry Swinburne, *A Treatise of Spousals, or Matrimonial Contracts* (London, 1686; rpt., New York: Garland, 1985). Ann Jennalie Cook's *Making a Match* (Princeton: Princeton Univ. Press, 1991) contains many useful details about the actual procedures and customs of courting and marrying in Shakespeare's day.

5. The word appears in *Cymbeline* 1.5.78. See the entry for *handfast* in John Foster, *A Shakespeare Word-Book* (London: Routledge, 1908), 288; and Cook, *Making a Match,* 154.

6. T.F.T. Dyer, *Folk-Lore of Shakespeare* (1884; rpt., Williamstown, Mass.: Corner House, 1978), 345 n. 1; J.H.P. Pafford, ed., *The Winter's Tale* (London: Methuen, 1963), 11, note on 1.2.104. Swinburne, *Treatise of Spousals*, maintains that a woman can fully consent to marriage by the giving of her hand (69, 70, 206).

7. For example, John Speed, *The Genealogies Recorded in the Sacred Scriptures* (London, 1620).

8. John Milton, *Paradise Lost* 9.997, in Merritt Huges, ed., *Complete Poems and Major Prose* (New York: Odyssey, 1957), 263.

9. T. McAlindon, *Shakespeare's Tragic Cosmos* (Cambridge: Cambridge Univ. Press, 1991), 153.

10. On the way Othello's self-describing metaphor at 3.3.460–65 unites elements from three passages in Pliny, see Kenneth Muir, *The Sources of Shakespeare's Plays* (New Haven: Yale Univ. Press, 1978), 188–90.

11. E.A.J. Honigmann, in his third-generation Arden edition of the play, compares the scene to a "comic 'cross-purposes' routine"; *Othello* (Walton-on-Thames: Thomas Nelson & Sons, 1997), 77.

12. For a defense of character criticism in general, and for interpreting *Othello* in particular, see E.A.J. Honigmann's *Myriad-Minded Shakespeare* (New York: St. Martin's Press, 1989), 60–72; also, on the history and value of character criticism, Brian Vickers, *Returning to Shakespeare* (London: Routledge, 1989), 197–211.

13. A. P. Rossiter, *Angel with Horns*, ed. Graham Storey (London: Longmans, 1961), 203, 206.

14. A. C. Bradley, *Shakespearean Tragedy*, 2d ed. (London: Macmillan, 1929), 179. F. R. Leavis's "Diabolic Intellect and the Noble Hero: A Note on *Othello*," *Scrutiny* 6 (1937): 259–83, with its famous criticisms of Bradley, is focused on the character of Othello.

15. As argued in W. Kerrigan and Gordon Braden, *The Idea of the Renaissance* (Baltimore: Johns Hopkins Univ. Press, 1989), 53–54.

16. As Ralegh observed, "honour is left to posterity for a mark and ensign of the virtue and understanding of their ancestors." Sir Walter Ralegh, *The History of the World*, ed. C. A. Patrides (Philadelphia: Temple Univ. Press, 1971), 195.

17. See Charles Knight's comment on her haplessness and her name in H. H. Furness, ed., *Othello* (Philadelphia: Lippincott, 1886), 300. "O ill-starr'd wench," Othello addresses her corpse (5.2.272).

18. At this point I may perform a small service by noting that a piece

of misinformation is circulating in recent *Othello* criticism. Michael Neill's "Unproper Beds: Race, Adultery, and the Hideous in *Othello*," *Shakespeare Quarterly* 40 (1989): 383–412, a much-cited essay reprinted in both David Young, ed., *Shakespeare's Middle Tragedies* (Englewood Cliffs, N.J.: Prentice-Hall, 1993), and Anthony Gerard Barthelemy, ed., *Critical Essays on Shakespeare's Othello* (New York: G. K. Hall, 1994), opens with Henry Jackson's supposed eyewitness account of an Oxford performance of *Othello* in 1610. As quoted by Neill, Jackson wrote that "Desdemona, slayn in our presence by her husband, though she pleaded her case very effectively throughout, yet moved us more after she was dead." He cites this from Julie Hankey, ed., *Othello* (Bristol: Bristol Classical Press, 1987), 18. Is it possible that anyone in the English Renaissance—that anyone, period—could say without courting illogic that Desdemona "pleaded her case very effectively"? She *was* murdered, after all. The document in question, in fact a transcription by someone else, probably made after Jackson's death in 1662, and perhaps from a Latin letter of 1610, was discovered by Geoffrey Tillotson and printed in his *Essays in Criticism and Research* (Cambridge: Cambridge Univ. Press, 1942), 41–42. Tillotson did not translate the Latin. Hankey's "though she pleaded her case very effectively throughout" is a misleading literal version of the original's "quanquam optimè semper causam egit." The subject of the passage is the actor who played Desdemona. The phrase, referring to the actor by reference to the character he played, means "though she always acted her part well." See E.A.J. Honigmann, *Shakespeare's Impact on His Contemporaries* (Totowa, N.J.: Barnes & Noble, 1982), 35, for a reliable translation of the entire passage. How the changeling "slayn," mimicking Renaissance English spelling, got into what has to be a modern English translation of a Renaissance Latin document, I'm not sure.

19. See the "long note" on 4.7.165–82 in Harold Jenkins, ed., *Hamlet* (London: Methuen, 1982), 544–45.

20. See, for example, Harley Granville-Barker, *Prefaces to Shakespeare*, 2 vols. (Princeton: Princeton Univ. Press, 1946–47), 2:69.

21. The full text of the ballad, from a manuscript in the Pepys Collection headed "A Lover's Complaint," was printed in Thomas Percy's *Reliques of Ancient English Poetry*, 3 vols. (London: Bickers & Son, 1876), 1:199–203. The stanzas directly relevant to Shakespeare's adaptation may be found in Furness's edition of the play, 277. I quote the text

from John H. Long, *Shakespeare's Use of Music: The Histories and Tragedies* (Gainesville: Univ. of Florida Press, 1971), 154–56.

22. John Heywood's version of the song, perhaps one of the oldest we have, shows exactly this ambivalence. "Alas! by what means may I make ye to know/The unkindness for kindness that to me doth grow," seems addressed to the song's audience; yet he only wants to present the lady with things "that may make her glad." The song is reprinted in Robert Bell, ed., *Songs from the Dramatists* (New York: White, Stokes, & Allen, 1885), 25–26. Many Petrarchan poems supply analogues for the song's hesitation between death-from-love as noble self-effacement or retaliatory indictment. See, for example, P. J. Croft, ed., *The Poems of Robert Sidney* (Oxford: Clarendon Press, 1984), Song 6, Sonnet 16, Sonnet 24, Song 24, and so on.

23. Editors usually prefer, at 5.2.94, Qq's "The noise was here" to F's "The noise was high." But Irving must have been right (Furness, ed. *Othello*, 308) to suppose that Othello refers to Emilia's knock. Though we have no stage direction about knocking, Emilia would not stand at the door and yell for Othello's attention without knocking. Was it like Shakespeare to invent for no end, no pattern, the knocking blast of wind that interrupts the "Willow Song"?

24. I am anticipated throughout this interpretation of the "Willow Song" by Carol Thomas Neely, "Women and Men in *Othello*," in Barthelemy, ed., *Critical Essays on Shakespeare's Othello*, 95–96.

25. Winifred M. T. Nowottny, "Justice and Love in *Othello*," in James Calderwood and Harold Toliver, eds., *Essays in Shakespearean Criticism* (Englewood Cliffs, N.J.: Prentice Hall, 1970), 469–70.

26. Bradley, *Shakespearean Tragedy*, note O, 438–39.

27. Ibid., 194.

28. In the Q2, Q3 stage direction, indeterminate "om [*omnes*, 'others']" enter with Iago.

29. McAlindon, *Shakespeare's Tragic Cosmos*, 143.

30. Bk. 3, chap. 3, of William Godwin, *Enquiry Concerning Political Justice*, ed. F.E.L. Priestley, 3 vols. (Toronto: Univ. of Toronto Press, 1946), 1:196. Godwin proceeds to develop the point made in my next sentence.

31. T. S. Eliot, *The Complete Poems and Plays, 1909–1950* (New York: Harcourt, Brace & World, 1962), 142.

32. On possible wordplays with the names of Othello, a "hell" inside

it, and Desdemona, a "demon" inside it, see Ann Barton, *The Names of Comedy* (Toronto: Univ. of Toronto Press, 1990), 121–30.

33. T. S. Eliot, *Selected Essays* (New York: Harcourt, Brace, 1960), 111.

34. Gordon Braden, *Renaissance Tragedy and the Senecan Tradition: Anger's Privilege* (New Haven: Yale Univ. Press, 1985), 168–69.

35. I agree with Graham Bradshaw, *Misrepresentations: Shakespeare and the Materialists* (Ithaca: Cornell Univ. Press, 1993), 29–30, 200–1, 245–57, that a too-sour view of Shakespeare's conception of Othello can in effect destroy the genre of the play, leaving in tragedy's place an Iago-like cynicism. E.A.J. Honigmann anticipated Bradshaw's argument by suggesting that Leavis had adopted Iago's view of an Othello "loving his own pride" (1.1.12) and full of "fantastical lies" (2.1.200) about his past; see his "Shakespeare's 'Bombast'," in Philip Edwards, Inga-Stina Ewbank, and G. K. Hunter, eds., *Shakespeare's Styles: Essays in Honour of Kenneth Muir* (Cambridge: Cambridge Univ. Press, 1980), 158–59. Yet Honigmann also maintained that Othello's language is "more dangerously inflated than that of any other Shakespearian tragic hero" (159).

36. Brian Vickers, ed., *Shakespeare: The Critical Heritage*, 6 vols. (London: Routledge, 1974), 6: 565. Steevens cited Zenocrate in *2 Tam* 2.4.70, "And let me die with kissing of my lord." See *The Plays of William Shakspeare*, ed. Isaac Reed, 21 vols., 2d ed. (London: J. Nichols, 1813), 19: 525.

Epilogue

1. William Godwin, *Enquiry Concerning Political Justice*, ed. F.E.L. Priestley, 3 vols. (Toronto: Univ. of Toronto Press, 1946), 1:203–4, 212–13.

2. Hugh Plat, *Floures of Philosophie* (London: Henrie Bynneman and Frauncis Coldocke, 1572), 57.

3. Nicholas Rowe, "Some Account of the Life . . . of Mr. William Shakespeare," in *The Works of Mr. William Shakespeare, in Six Volumes* (London: Jacob Tonson, 1709), 1: vi.

4. See O7.12 in R. W. Dent, *Proverbial Language in English Drama Exclusive of Shakespeare, 1495–1616: An Index* (Berkeley: Univ. of California Press, 1984), 562.

Index

Library of Congress Cataloging-in-Publication Data

Kerrigan, William, 1943–
    Shakespeare's promises / by William Kerrigan.
        p.   cm.
    Includes bibliographical references and index.
    ISBN 0-8018-6163-2 (alk. paper)
    1. Shakespeare, William, 1564–1616—Ethics.   2. Didactic drama,
English—History and criticism.   3. Promises—Religious aspects—
Christianity.   4. Promises in literature.   5. Swearing in literature.
6. Ethics in literature.   7. Oaths in literature.   8. Vows in literature.
I. Title.
PR3007.K47   1999   99-19683
822.3'3—dc21   CIP